Theatre Stories

THEATRE STORIES

EDWARD PAYSON CALL

Charleston, SC
www.PalmettoPublishing.com

Theatre Stories

First Edition

Hardcover: 979-8-8229-2711-7
Paperback: 979-8-8229-2712-4

PREFACE

Welcome to the creative genius of Ed Call. He wrote this book in the basement of his Seattle home, the same house he lived in till his passing, February 1, 2023. It is not a complete telling of his life in the theatre, but a telling of as much of his life, that he had the energy to tell. Pim, our editor and I have done our absolute best to honor Ed's intentions and desires as well as we could. This is it, to the best of our abilities. On his passing I had three instructions, 1. Do NOT do a big fancy funeral, 2. Publish my book and 3. Spread my ashes on Malibu Beach in Southern California. With this book I will complete task two,, task three is coming up in February of 24. Ed I miss your gravelly voice and unbounded curiosity terribly.

Peter Davis 10.9.23
Seattle WA

CONTENTS

INTRODUCTION

Theater stories. That's what this book is: a collection of short narratives from a life. That's just the way it came out, probably because I've never written anything longer than program notes, personal letters, and a few short articles for the subscriber magazine of a theater I once ran.

On the other hand, the book's episodic nature may reflect the fact that my life itself has been so episodic, lived for the most part in the two- or three-month increments it takes to put on a play. Another factor: At an early age I was utterly captivated by that brilliant, resolutely fragmentary look at America in a trilogy of novels called *U.S.A.* by John Dos Passos. There were parts of it I read over and over again. I loved its restless style.

So, here it is, my life in dribs and drabs, not always chronologically, and sometimes not my life at all but a vignette about a colleague or something that has nothing at all to do with me or theater—just something that I wrote because I happened to think of it at the time.

The later sketches here may also serve as a view through a window some 60 years back in time, offering a glimpse of the advent of the modern regional theater movement that has burgeoned in the United States. When I assisted in the birth of the Minnesota Theatre Company, I could name fewer than a dozen other professional resident theater companies. By 2005, more than 1,200 not-for-profit theaters were thriving, represented in every state.

In sum it's a hodgepodge, part memoir, part chronicle. But I hope you find it a nice hodgepodge, an amusing hodgepodge, at times even a moving hodgepodge. It's been a long time coming—more years than I care to remember.

The creation of this book turned me from a night person into a morning person, just as my career was winding down. Up most days at six o'clock (6:00 A.M., for God's sake!), I didn't even sit down. I ate an orange and a piece of toast, then went down to my study to scribble. Sometime around noon I came up for air, back upstairs to the living room, and sat down in one of two theater seats I stole from a playhouse I once worked in. The other seat was occupied by two stuffed bears, Emmet and Fred, and Grover, an odd blue creature, to whom I read the morning's output.

But now I've come to a stopping place. I need to get the reaction of some folks other than Emmet, Fred, and Grover. Now, *cher lecteur*, it's your turn.

What are theater stories?

Picaresque tales of the wild men of the acting profession, from Junius Brutus Booth to George C. Scott. Stories of boozy leading ladies in decline, their brains somewhat addled, but their whiskey contraltos still able to shake the rafters at the back of the second balcony. Stories of the saints of our profession, like Billie Burke at the end of her life: aged, infirm, but still able to be that joyous scatterbrained Billie Burke for two hours each night, soldiering on to pay off the debts of her late husband, Florenz Zeigfield.

The stories of mishaps: the moustaches that fell off, the doors that jammed. That English manor house set, with the fireplace and chimney flat up center that started to tilt ominously toward the stage and then broke loose. At the last moment, just before several actors were flattened, a hand from offstage shot through the fireplace opening, grabbed the mantel from behind, and pulled the whole unit upright. The actors went on with the Agatha Christie thriller. The hand, looking like some improvised heraldic device, stayed there till the curtain fell.

Teaching stories, passed from player to player, as when an old pro keeps a beginner spellbound, telling him what he learned one night long ago when he saw Laurette Taylor as Amanda Wingfield in *The Glass Menagerie* and, thunderstruck, walked the streets till dawn.

Stories of the thrilling beginnings of theaters when everything one dreamed of seemed possible. Stories of failure when success seemed assured and of success when all odds were against it.

Stories of magical inspiration: Anthony Zerbe on the opening night of *Richard III*, falling mortally wounded on Bosworth Field, unexpectedly takes off his crown and hurls it upward—up into a crowded fly loft jammed with pipes, lights, speakers, and set pieces. *There's no room!* It disappears from view for a few breathless seconds (miraculously touching nothing), reappears upright, spinning slowly, and comes to rest like an obedient falcon six inches from Zerbe's head. "I don't know," he says later when confronted by his distraught director. "I didn't want anyone else to get it."

Then there are the horror stories, the ones that usually elicit cries of outrage and dismay from theater folk—tales of troglodyte producers, cretinous critics, and Machiavellian agents.

From my father I heard about Johnston Forbes-Robertson's Hamlet and the sensational opening night of Barrymore's Richard III, but the stories I liked best were about him and my mother, about Broadway and their travels with productions on the road in the early decades of the twentieth century.

All these stories make up a chronicle of the painful joys and joyous travails of this proud profession of making plays. They are the currency of our trade. In these days of skin-of-our-teeth survival, when the ground beneath us seems far less solid than it once was, we need these theater tales to knit ourselves into the fabric of our profession, to bind groups of strangers into acting companies. Most importantly, they build a tradition, one that celebrates our achievements, laughs at our follies, and strengthens us for the daunting challenges that lie ahead.

Theater yarns will continue to unfold after future shows come down, when the theaters have emptied and all the stage doors are locked up tight, in bars from coast to coast amid shouts of laughter and slapping of tables and gasps of disbelief. And the bartender, smiling as he shakes his head, will pour another round and let the clock inch past closing time.

PART 1

The Genesis of a Theater Professional

My own theater origin story began in the fall of 1916, on West Forty-fourth Street in Manhattan, a pitted strip of asphalt that seems to hold some fateful significance for my family. All the big adventures begin there, and not just the theatrical adventures.

Imagine two men, father and son. One is a newspaperman, wonderfully engaging, possessed of great charm, beloved by most everyone he meets. He has a quick, energetic step—his silver-tipped walking stick swings in an easy arc before him with each stride. His name is Edward Payson Call; he is my grandfather. He has just left the New York Times Building where he works and is walking east on Forty-fourth Street to meet his son, my father, Donald Marshall Call, a recent graduate of the American Academy of Dramatic Arts, who is walking west on the same street from his actor's digs on Second Avenue.

My father, Donald Marshall Call.

They will meet at the City Club (55 West Forty-fourth) for lunch. They do this several times a month in the second decade of the last century. No dutiful father-son meetings these; they genuinely enjoy each other's company.

After amiable conversation over a civilized meal, son Donald walks on to the nearby Eltinge 42nd Street Theatre, where the first run-through of a road company is in progress. The producers are in the house. They do not seem happy. As the third act begins, they leave the theater noisily.

The producers who made the hasty exit were the Selwyn brothers, Edgar and Arch, who had been enjoying amazing good fortune both on Broadway and in the Los Angeles film world. They had recently produced Avery Hopwood's farce-comedy *Fair and Warmer*, the smash-hit comedy of the 1915 Broadway season. Considered deliciously risqué at the time, it told the story of Blanny (feather-brained but charming) and Billy (amiable but dull).

When these two young marrieds confide in each other the suspicion that the warmth they've observed between their rather glamorous spouses may have led to "something rash and indiscrete" (gasp!), they decide to try a little hanky-panky of their own. The second act deals with their attempts to carouse and be gay and ever so romantic, but their hearts aren't really in it. A comic tour de force for the right actors, it starts with their inept experiments at cocktail mixing (a newly fashionable pastime), about which they know absolutely nothing. It ends some hours later with them snoozing peacefully in a somewhat compromising position—a result of fatigue and too much gin rather than romantic ardor—in which position they are discovered by their utterly blameless and now scandalized spouses. Then inevitably, Act III sets everything to rights. Curtain.

The play was so successful that six road companies, all close copies of the Broadway original, were sent out to tour the country. Soon Avery Hopwood's comedy was delighting audiences from Baltimore to Bakersfield, as well as mightily swelling the Selwyn coffers back in New York City. Since the nation's appetite for *Fair and Warmer* seemed insatiable, the Selwyn brothers decided to add a seventh company to perform in some of the theaters the first six companies had missed.

But now Edgar and Arch were grumpy in extremis. It was that damned seventh company! Things had seemed to be going well enough until that fateful run-through, when they realized they had made a terrible casting mistake.

The principal female role called for a young, flirtatious ingénue, but the woman they had cast evoked a leading lady. More importantly, she had neither the technique nor the charm to carry off the role. She would have to be replaced. So when she arrived at the producer's offices on the arm of the assistant stage manager (my father), she was invited into the inner sanctum for a glass of champagne and, as genially as the circumstances would allow, given the boot. The Brothers started auditioning again, but after two days and thirty actresses they had found no one suitable.

They sat slumped in the empty theater, utterly dispirited. Neither spoke. Then Edgar sat upright; he had an idea. He turned to Arch and said: "You know, that little gal playin' the maid ain't half bad. I'll bet she could do it." At which point his brother cut him off: "Are you kiddin'? She's got no experience. This is her first job." After a pause he added, "But she's a looker, I'll grant you that—and that smile!" An ingénue was born in that moment.

This was the endeavor that introduced my parents to one another.

Backstory

My father, Donald Marshall Call, was born in Manhattan (1892) but did most of his growing up in Larchmont, New York. His father (the first Edward Payson Call) was a newspaperman, rising from a reporter with the *Boston Herald* to cap his career as business manager of the *New York Times*.

My father came to the theater by chance. The times conspired to reveal his true vocation.

Family Nomenclature
A note here, as we begin these tales, concerning some of the names you will encounter. Like all good WASPs of a certain period, everyone in my family had three names,

sometimes followed by a number. My full name is actually Edward Payson Call III.

My father's name is Donald Marshall Call, referred to in these pages as D.M.C. or occasionally as the Guvnor. This came about one day long, long ago when my older brother, Don, was toiling in our yard under my father's careful supervision. Don started calling him (no doubt with both derision and respect) "Guvnor." It was said with a slight Cockney accent, as a working-class type might address a toff. The name was so suitable, so descriptive of my father—from his easy charm and courtly manners to his sandy mustache and corncob pipe—that he became the Guvnor almost immediately within the family and to the world at large and so remains twenty-five years after his death.

My mother's maiden name was Catherine Lexow. She married the Guvnor and became Catherine Lexow Call (C.L.C.), a.k.a. Agnes courtesy of the family nicknamers.

From an early age my father showed keen interest in gardening. When as a youngster he heard the term "landscape architect," he decided that was what he was going to be. He studied drafting and surveying, worked for a florist, then in a nursery. Finally, after a three-year apprenticeship with an established landscape architect, he hung out his shingle.

However, few were interested in his services. The year was 1914, the war in Europe had begun, and in the United States the result was financial panic. Money for such luxuries as landscaping was going under the mattress. Not only did he lack clients, but he was now unable to find work of any kind in his chosen field. So he turned to the want ads, where one day he discovered the following:

"Wanted: Gents with tux. Apply 46th Street Theater."

He had a tux. He applied and as a result was cast as a walk-on in a play called *Just Herself* starring the eminent Russian ballerina Lydia Lopokova. It closed in a week and soon would have been a forgotten episode, save for one thing—my father had been badly bitten by that insidious insect, the theater bug.

He was an actor! Well, he aspired to be an actor; he just needed some training, that's all. Enter my great-aunt Annie Payson Call, ever a theater enthusiast and a lady of means. She underwrote two years of study for her nephew, at the American Academy of Dramatic Arts. After two years he began pounding the pavements and soon found the job that led to his rendezvous at the Chamberlain Brown Agency.

———

The ingénue, my mother, Catherine Lexow, grew up in comfortable circumstances in a big Victorian mansion on the shores of the Hudson River in Nyack, New York.

Caroline Lexow, in 1914, when she was serving as field secretary of the
Women's Political Union.

My mother, Caroline Lexow Call.

Her father, Clarence Lexow, was a lawyer and politician who
in 1894 as a New York State senator led the Lexow Committee
investigation into the Tammany Hall corruption in the New York
City Police Department. It may qualify as the first of the sensa-
tion-packed extravaganzas such as the presidential impeachment
trials, the Iran-Contra affair, and the O. J. Simpson murder trial
that have become our national pastime. The Tammany Hall inquiry
was filled with shocking testimony by dubious but colorful malefac-
tors, generating lurid headlines and scandalous reports of violence
and greed, of kickbacks, of payoffs, and of a long list of other abuses
by New York City's finest.

At the center of the Lexow Committee maelstrom was my grandfather—the Senator, he was always referred to in the family—a person of unquestioned probity. He was a trim, small man with a Van Dyke beard and penetrating blue eyes, eyes that more than once cowed the miscreants in his witness chair.

Those eyes had their effect on Catherine as well, who to the end of her life talked of their intimidating power. But it was a power she dared to challenge from an early age. She told me how, as a child, she would sometimes willfully provoke him.

It often happened at the breakfast table. She would walk into the dining room and go straight to her place, "forgetting" to give her father his good-morning kiss. She'd take the napkin out of its silver ring, tuck it in, and try to address the meal in front of her. But after a time, the paternal gaze of reprobation began to sear her cheeks. Not daring to look in his direction, she'd grit her teeth and try not to give way, but soon the tears would come and she'd flee.

But that was not the end of it. Before the week was out, Catherine would try the same stratagem again.

Despite such episodes, despite the family's stern German heritage and the unbending nineteenth-century rules by which they lived, my mother's growing up sounded at times positively idyllic in that storybook Victorian way. She was the youngest of the Senator's children, cherished by Mama (accent on the second syllable), fussed over by numerous servants, and doted on by her two much older siblings—and most of the time by Papa himself as well.

A Victorian Christmas

It was Papa, so I was told, who took the lead in that most extravagant of the family's festivities: Christmas. This was a production that involved several Lexows, several servants, and several days of preparation—most of it, if not all, for the delight of young Catherine. My grandfather brought a keen theatrical sense to these goings-on, marshalling his company, selecting props and set pieces, choosing the music, even rehearsing with great care the sound effects that were to be part of the production.

As the big Christmas Eve dinner neared its end the year Catherine was six, her brother Morton discreetly excused himself from the table and stole up to the highest tower in the house. Three maids took up their stations at various turnings of various stairways, to relay cues to Morton on Papa's signal.

The Senator called for silence. He thought he had heard something. "Listen!" he said. The table quickly became mute, expectant. "What was that commotion?" he asked. "Commotion" was the cue. With much waving of the maids' hands the signal was relayed aloft, and in a few moments, ever so faintly, *"jingle, jingle, jingle"* went sleigh bells on the rooftop. There was a collective intake of breath around the table. "Catherine, did you hear it?" the Senator whispered. My mother, breathless, nodded.

Then *"jingle, jingle, jingle"* again; this time even fainter. "Oh, no!" my mother gasped. "Do you think he's flown right over the house and forgotten us?" The Senator's blue eyes softened. He replied, "Or could it be that he stopped here at 401 Piermont Avenue and we didn't even hear him? I wonder."

At which point unseen hands slid open the big double doors and behold! The rather austere living room they had left an hour before had been transformed into

a child's dream of Christmas: a huge candlelit tree surrounded by a jumble of gaily decorated presents, tinsel,
mistletoe, and holly everywhere. In one corner a group
of servants began singing a carol, to which music the
family rose from the table and, led by a six-year-old tug-
ging her father along, walked into the enchantment of
it all.

The six-year-old grew into a spirited, athletic young girl with a
passion for the theater. She told me the first theater story I remember: On one of her first trips into New York City, she was taken to
see Maude Adams in *Peter Pan*. In those days, simple applause was
just not enough to revive the grievously ill fairy, Tinker Bell. When
Tinker Bell lay dying, Catherine stood up on her chair and at the
top of her lungs shrilled out: "I believe, Peter, I believe! I believe!"
until Tink's light glowed with life once more. (The last telling took
place when she was over eighty, but still those luminous ingénue
eyes glowed again as she said, "I believe, Peter, I believe! I believe!")
Her Victorian idyll came to an end in 1910, when she was eleven.
Her father died. Suddenly the family was in perilous circumstances,
and just surviving became the focus of their existence. Wishing to
be self-sufficient and no longer a burden, by age sixteen my mother
decided, without, so far as I know, a word of encouragement and
little if any experience, that she would go on the stage!

Where did this come from? Had her real desires been held in
check by her martinet father? Free from that intimidating glower
of reprobation, could she now do as she pleased? Or was she simply
desperate to help her family in any way she could?

I don't know. I only know she did it. Of a class and of a time
when such things were "just not done," she went ahead and got

dressed up, went down to the city, and started making the rounds. There were the inevitable chases around some tinhorn producer's desk. There were the ceaseless rejections. But she persisted, until one day she found herself in the inner sanctum of the Chamberlain Brown Agency being offered a bit part in a touring company while my father, in the next room, leafed idly through a copy of *Collier's* magazine.

———◆———

Scene: The reception room of Broadway agent Chamberlain Brown's office on Fourth Street, Manhattan. Spring, 1916. A door right, to the inner office, another up left, to the hall. On the walls, tastefully arranged, theatrical posters and photos of clients. Several armchairs against the walls, in one of which, down left, sits a lanky, rather nattily dressed young actor who is, at present, idly glancing through a recent issue of Collier's *magazine. The door right opens and a petite, delightfully flustered ingénue bursts into the room followed by the dapper, magisterially fey Mr. Brown. The ingénue is very excited, full of smiles and blushes. And why not? She is seventeen years old and has just landed her first acting job—playing the maid in the road company of the hit Broadway comedy* Fair and Warmer.

MR. BROWN (*standing in the doorway right, finishing his blessing*). ... but you'll be working for the Selwyn Brothers and that, my dear, is a very important first step.

INGÉNUE. Oh, I know, I know! And, Mr. Brown, I'll do my best to ...

MR. BROWN (*interrupting her, having seen the young ac-tor*). Ah, Catherine, here's someone you should meet.
(*Crosses a few steps into the room.*) Don, come here, my boy.
(*The young actor rises and crosses to center.*)
Miss Lexow, may I present Donald Call. I daresay you'll be seeing a lot of each other. Don will be an assistant stage manager on the tour; he's also playing that nasty boss of yours, Jack Wheeler.
Mr. Call, Miss Lexow.
YOUNG ACTOR (*stopping, looking her over playfully, arms akimbo*). Ah, so you're the little lady who'll be play-ing my maid, eh? What good taste I have in domes-tics. Ha, ha, ha!
INGÉNUE (*reddening, conscious of her size—just over 5 feet—and his condescension*). How do you do?
YOUNG ACTOR. How do you do? Sorry I'm going to be such a cad of a boss. Ha!
INGÉNUE (*quite innocently*). Oh, I'm sure you'll be a won-derful cad, Mr. Call.

Thus, so I was told, passed the first encounter of my parents.

Well, you can probably write the rest of the "You're-Going-Out-There-a-Chorus-Girl-But-Coming-Back-a-Star" dialogue yourself. You'll recall the Selwyn brothers' later casting dilemma for *Fair and Warmer*. Indeed it came to pass that my mother, C.L.C., wide-eyed and eager, irrepressibly buoyant, but with zero experi-ence, was plucked from her bit part of Tessie, the maid, and giv-en the role of Blanny Wheeler, the comic lead in the seventh road company of *Fair and Warmer*.

What a lucky break! What a challenge! What an opportunity to grow, to become a real actress. Was this "little gal" up to it? Indeed, she was.

———

So C.L.C. went to work, aided no doubt by an eager assistant stage manager, among others. When the touring show first opened, in the coal fields of Pennsylvania (my father always insisted that some of the miners actually came to the theater straight from the pits with blotchy faces and miner's caps), she was still struggling with the lines. If she succeeded in those initial performances, it was more on looks and charm than skill. But a month into the tour a real comedienne was beginning to emerge. The playwright took notice.

What an exciting time it must have been for D.M.C. and C.L.C.—playing all over the United States and Canada, discovering North America and each other; two young people falling in love, beginning to find their way in an exciting profession and nightly receiving the manna of prolonged applause.

They were also serving a rigorous apprenticeship. The year was 1916; there was no Actors' Equity Association to protect them from producers who could be chillingly indifferent to the creature comforts of their performers if no star were involved. The thirty-two-week tour included only three one-week stands; the rest were all one-nighters. They often had to contend with ill-heated theaters, bed-bug infested hotel rooms, or no hotel rooms at all when they had a long hop between shows and were forced to spend the night jouncing on a train ride through the heartland in a drafty coach car. They were young and resilient, but by the end of the tour they returned to New York exhausted.

They returned to New York at the end of the tour in the spring of 1917 to find a city in the grip of war fever. The conflict that had begun in Europe in 1914 had finally expanded into World War I and spread its contagion to the United States. Now General Pershing was getting ready to lead the Allied Expeditionary Force to France. President Wilson called one and all to the high duty of "making the world safe for democracy." Young men by the thousands signed up, eager to "do their bit."

My father was one of them. He sailed for France in a volunteer unit organized by the City Club of New York and spent three months driving a Model T ambulance, dodging shell holes and artillery fire, and evacuating wounded poilus (French infantry soldiers) from the front before enlisting. Later, not knowing what he was getting into, he signed up for service in an experimental unit called the U.S. Tank Corps under the command of an eccentric, squeaky-voiced colonel by the name of Patton.

Tanks, in those days, were clanking, untested, difficult to maneuver, inadequately armored death traps. The German artillery could pick them off with ease. Until he was wounded, Corporal Call took part in the early days of the Meuse–Argonne Offensive, which would end the war. He returned to the United States in February of 1919 with a lieutenant's commission, a fluent knowledge of the French language, a quarter-sized piece of shrapnel in his back (lodged too deep to remove) and the Congressional Medal of Honor, the citation of which reads:

> During an operation against enemy machine gun
> nests west of Varennes, Corporal Call was in a tank with

an officer when half of the turret was knocked off by a direct artillery hit. Choked by gas from the high-explosive shell, he left the tank and took cover in a shell hole 30 yards away. Seeing that the officer did not follow, and thinking that he might be alive, Corporal Call returned to the tank under intense machine-gun fire and shell fire and carried the officer over a mile under machine-gun and sniper fire to safety.

When I was a child, World War I came to me in many ways: in learning to sing "Over There" and stamping around the living room with soldierly zeal, in the dimple in my father's back where the shrapnel went in, and in his stories.

I heard D.M.C. tell of Carrier Sud, a rock quarry that served as a first-aid post in the Verdun salient; of how the wounded were loaded into his ambulance; and how on a signal from a French corporal who had an uncanny ability to time the departures so as to avoid the arrivs (incoming), he opened the throttle of that ridiculously fragile Model T and it scampered forward, bouncing over the shell-pocked landscape as the artillery boomed all around.

There was something else I absorbed: people died. It came to me as a seven-year-old looking into our stereopticon, that nineteenth-century 3-D viewer. The slides were mounted on gray cardboard as two identical photographs, side by side, that you put into a small rack six inches in front of the viewer. There was a set of slides that included some pictures of the war. One of them has stayed with me all my life. It is a photo of the French countryside. A stone bridge arches over a stream. Under the arch it is quite dark, but in the shadows you can make out the shapes of dead bodies. One of them lies on his back, arms splayed out, his right hand still locked around a rifle. You can't see the uniform well enough to tell which army he belongs to; what you can see is his face, or what's left of it—a battered white skull luminous among the shadowy heaps of dead. I stared and stared into those oversize binoculars, and the tiny broken doll's head stared back. Nightmare fears came; it took a long time to outgrow them.

My father the hero returned to America in a jam-packed troop ship in February of 1919 to find a radiant ingénue waiting on the pier, wearing a single red rose—the prearranged signal that she still loved him and wanted to get married. This was soon accomplished at my great-aunt Annie Payson Call's estate outside Waltham, Massachusetts.

———

Following the ceremony and a brief honeymoon, the newlyweds returned to their careers in the theater. Between 1919 and 1926 they added the following engagements to their résumés:

- A stint with the Henry Jewett Players, a first-rate stock company in Boston.
- *Martinique*, a big Broadway production at the Eltinge Theater by Lawrence Eyre in which D.M.C. played a small role. Hopes were high for its success, but it closed after a couple of months.
- *Don't Be Afraid* by Avery Hopwood of *Fair and Warmer* fame. C.L.C. played the lead opposite Ernest Truex. It was a talented farceur's attempt to write something serious; it closed in Brooklyn after four performances.
- *Irene*, the hit musical. It was D.M.C.'s big break; he played it for over a year. During the run my oldest brother, Don Jr., was born.

· A season with the erstwhile Kansas City Repertory Theatre. Much to my amazement, when I was going through some old scrapbooks I discovered that they took a flier in what we now call regional theater. It all came about when an actor friend, Erville Alderson, quit his job in Hollywood working for D. W. Griffith and traveled to Missouri, where he set about organizing a repertory company. My parents went out there to give him a hand. At first there were eloquent mission statements ringing with missionary zeal, high artistic ideals, and strong community support. Sadly, Alderson's highly eccentric management style doomed the enterprise. Productions opened without adequate rehearsal; sets and costumes were a disaster. One production had a peculiar feature: there was a character who seemed perpetually trapped behind the furniture. Despite the fact that she was on stage for a good deal of the time, she was always behind something—sofa, table, or chair. This was my mother, filling in because of an emergency, trying to hide the fact that she was six months pregnant with her second child, my brother Jack.

· A decent part for D.M.C. in a Louis K. Anspacher play titled *Dagmar*. It was a vehicle for Alla Nazimova, the first of the great Moscow Art Theater actresses to perform in New York. It turned out to be a bomb despite the presence of the star as well as magnificent sets by a promising young designer who at that time called himself plain Robert Jones (later Bobby Jones).

· *Zeno*, a mystery play by Joseph F. Rinn. C.L.C. replaced the ingénue and got to know a studious young actor by the name of Frederic Bickel, who later changed his name to Fredric March.

· A delightful summer tour on the Chautauqua circuit in a play by Langdon McCormick called *The Storm*. C.L.C. was the adorable French-Canadian lass Manette, who was trapped, because of the eponymous atmospheric disturbance, in a miner's cabin with an Indian guide and two white men—one fond and virtuous, the other (D.M.C.) foul and villainous. Our family was now a quartet: my two brothers (the new addition was Jack) had been stashed with their grandmother.

· Another western tour of *Fair and Warmer*, which my father coproduced.

Now a decade had passed. It was 1926. D.M.C.'s career had stalled. He had a growing family to support. So he decided to go back to his original vocation, landscape architecture. My mother was all for it.

At the same time, C.L.C. resolved to give up the grease paint and tinsel and become a full-time mother. I think she could have had a substantial career if she wanted it. As it was, she had several others. Friends and relatives I've talked to over the years always thought that my no-nonsense, *Our-Town*, Edward-don't-slouch-at-the-dinner-table mother was the real talent in the family. She was the one who could have made it in the theater in a substantial way—not, ironically enough, my charming, theatrical father. When she gave it up, she had several important professionals behind her, the playwright Mr. Hopwood included. She had also made a promising start in acting for the cameras out in Long Island City. But without, so far as I could gather, any regret, they both wrote finis to that part of their lives and moved to Old Greenwich, Connecticut, where a couple of years later their third son, Edward (myself), was born.

———

For the first ten years of my life, we lived in a charming shingle-roofed Cape Cod house with a big elm tree in the front yard, on a bumpy dirt lane called the Old Post Road.

Don Jr. was seven years older than I, and Jack was six years older. Don was handsome, easygoing, witty and irresistible to girls, loved literature and animals, dreamed of becoming a rancher. Jack was good-looking in an angular way, high-strung, a terrific golfer, never read much, dreamed of making a lot of money, which he ended up doing as a stockbroker.

Don died in a senseless automobile accident in Paris in 1962. Jack and I have not spoken to one another in twenty years. Yet their influence on my life continues unabated. What I am and always will be is a younger brother, forever trying to dominate or rival or please two formidable siblings.

The relationship with my brothers began with ridiculous, faltering attempts at domination. There is a family story of a Christmas morning when I was somewhere around four or five. Apparently I became annoyed when I thought my eldest brother was getting too much attention, so when the opportunity presented itself and he was sitting on the floor near the Christmas tree playing with a new toy, I picked up one of my gifts, a large red tin fire truck, hefted it over my head, and threw it at him.

Bad move. Retribution came swiftly. Suddenly I was flying across the room, hurled sofa-ward by my outraged father who then worked me over with a parental slipper.

Unable to dominate, unable to rival, I chose the easier path of younger brothers: I became a fan. Whatever they did, I wanted to do. That, of course, was impossible. I was too small, too young, too dumb. I was dismissed as "the dirty baby." They weren't cruel—indeed, for such a contentious family, we could be intensely affectionate—but the distance in years between us could be daunting.

When I was in kindergarten, Don was in sixth grade, Jack in fifth. When my brothers started wearing long pants, I still had years left of short pants (summer) and knickers (winter). I remember a day when they came home from school with ink stains all over their hands. My mother was annoyed, but to me those blotches were marks of sophistication and maturity. I was in the lower reaches of elementary school, laboriously printing with crayon or pencil, and here were these titans stained with the blood of literacy. They were using *pens*! I could only pray that somehow, some day, I would catch up.

Somewhere along the way I discovered an important fact about myself. I am a younger brother, not just chronologically but temperamentally as well. It informs a great deal of what I do. I have at times, attempted to escape it, at times I have used it to my advantage, but it persists as an unalterable part of my personality, burned into the bone.

———◆———

On the other side of the Old Post Road, over a crumbling drystone wall and beyond twenty yards of woods, was a palace in the Maxfield Parrish style, with geyser-like fountains and long curving stone benches, dewy lawns and brimming flower beds, and a winding pebbled path that led through a bower of wisteria to an imitation Greek temple.

The unlikely creator of this florid pastorale was Condé Nast, the short, dapper publisher of *Vogue* and *House and Garden* magazines. He wanted a printing plant constructed to look like an Ivy League campus, and no expense was spared in achieving that goal. My father's first project in his newly resumed career as a landscape architect was to supervise the making of the property's gardens. It was a monumental task: the site covered more than ten acres, and a significant portion of it had to be jackhammered out of solid rock. Several years later, when the work was done, he had no trouble finding another job at Condé Nast—head of the Pattern Department at *Vogue*.

These were palmy years in the Call household. My father had congenial work, the remuneration was generous, and there was always time for recreation—for hunting, for tennis and swimming, for sailing adventures and big parties fueled by bathtub gin. We joined the snooty Woodway Country Club, and soon plans were afoot to move from our modest Cape Codder into something that looked very much like a mansion.

The Depression was soon upon us, but my father didn't worry—he was head of the *Vogue* Pattern Department, which always prospered in bad times; women who could no longer afford that $100 dress at Sak's Fifth Avenue could afford D.M.C.'s kit containing the patterns that showed them how to make that same dress. We were sitting pretty. For a while.

No one was aware of the fact that the dapper, impeccably well-mannered Mr. Nast with his thirty-room Park Avenue penthouse and his Rolls Royce was in a real financial pickle; without a big infusion of cash, he wouldn't be able to survive. I don't know the details, but as it was told to me years later, some unsavory characters started to appear in the rustic purlieus of the Condé Nast plant in

Old Greenwich. They represented the faction that had rescued Mr. Nast from ruin, but now they were taking control. Since the Pattern Department was a real money-maker, they soon slithered in there and my father was forced to resign. Plans for the move to the big house were cancelled; servants were dismissed. My father started looking for a new job but was unsuccessful. Then he fell ill—strep throat.

Streptococcus sore throat in the age before antibiotics was a nasty, sometimes fatal disease. D.M.C. had to endure its torments for months before he recovered. When he did, he found that the heady F. Scott Fitzgerald champagne of his life had fizzled, and he was looking at some harsh Dickensian gruel: doctor's bills, kids to feed, and no job prospects. He looked around for the better part of a year, ready to turn his hand to anything that would put bread on the table. Nothing worked out.

Finally deliverance came in the form of a telegram from Washington, DC, asking if he would be interested in working for the government—in public housing. Indeed he would! He left promptly to live and labor in DC in the Housing Division of the Public Works Administration, one of the many enterprises that made up Franklin D. Roosevelt's New Deal. Eventually we all joined him there and settled into a row house on Cambridge Place in Georgetown.

———

In 1938, Georgetown was a far cry from the fashionable, overpriced, "olde worlde" neighborhood of today. Oh, it had the coach lights and cobbled streets, the tree-shaded lanes and jockey statuettes—all the props and set pieces of quaintitude—but it was also tough, really tough. For the police, it was Precinct Seven and had a reputation for lots of action and lots of crime. All the classes were represented there. Across the street from us lived a cab driver, down the block a senator; up on R Street were tenements, a few blocks further west, a poor black neighborhood.

Into this urban bouillabaisse wandered a dreamy ten-year-old with outsized buck teeth. He had some wising up to do. One of my first memories is of getting into a marble game with the locals. These kids were wily sharpshooters ("Knuckles down! No inchin!") who fired marbles with startling speed and precision; I was used to the Old Greenwich version of the game, which turned out to be rather wussy by comparison. They cleaned me out in half an hour. I went back home and robbed my brother's cache; they relieved me of that as well.

I was in a city now; it was a different existence. There were more kids my age around, so there could be pickup games of softball and football up in Montrose Park. I played with great passion and meager skill. Sometimes I was razzed, and I got in a few fistfights. And it was Washington, DC, a great place to explore. That I did on my own, to the Smithsonian and the Washington Monument; I may hold the record for ascents on foot.

Edward at age ten, arriving in our nation's capitol, might have received the following evaluation from Miss Waddey, his fifth-grade teacher: "A dreamy child, tall for his age, rail thin with a really remarkable set of buck teeth. (Several times I've had to have a serious talk with boys who insist on referring to him as 'Horse Teeth.') He has few friends. Doesn't contribute much in class. We should cast about for some sort of activity that brings him out of himself."

I finished fifth and sixth grades at Jackson Elementary School, just around the corner and up the hill, and went on to Gordon

Junior High, way over on the other side of Wisconsin Avenue (five blocks away). It was there I first stepped on a stage.

It turned out that my city life was only an episode. D.M.C. became a pioneer and built us a house way out beyond the borders of the District of Columbia, far from the reach of trolley or bus in the dark, mysterious forests of Maryland. Today its part of the suburban sprawl well inside the Beltway, but in early 1941 it was an experiment in rural living.

We often took trips into the wild to check the builder's progress. A series of photographs in a family album chronicles the whole project, from the excavation that exposed the heavy red Maryland clay to the final tasks of grading, sodding, and last touches to the interior.

One feature of the new house fascinated me. I discovered that the medicine cabinet in my parent's bathroom had a tiny opening at the back, like a miniature mail slot. What was it? For razor blades, I was told. The whole house was finished; lathe board, plaster, and paint covered every surface, every access to the skeleton of the house—yet here was this chink that gave onto a long dark shaft between two studs. My father would slide the used double-edged blades of his Gillette safety razor into that slot. Our world would change, war would come, there would be partings and reunions; there would be weddings and graduations, scenes of domestic strife, births, deaths; and all the while those incredibly thin blades would be drifting down the dark shaft onto the small heap below. How big a heap, I wondered, would make up a life?

We moved in. I soon had a paper route (*Washington Post*) and a dog (Irish setter) to keep me company. Life was looking up, not so much because of the move, but because the yearned-for time of tooth straightening had arrived. I felt blessed. All those metal wires, caps, and rubber bands were instruments of grace. Not tomorrow, but someday the offending incisors would be tamed, and my real life could begin.

My father's job for the government entailed a fair amount of travel—inspecting the landscape work in housing projects up and down the East Coast. In 1940, government policy held that all trips should be made by train. Air travel was out: too expensive, undependable, and probably unsafe. But my father was a nut about flying, and proved to his superiors that planes could be cheaper than trains, particularly over long distances. Thus, he often found himself happily zooming from Washington, DC, to Miami, from Miami to Buffalo, and then back home in a sleek new Eastern Air Lines DC-3.

Frustrated by the red tape and indifferent management of government work, he found that it was not to his liking; flying was a rare plus. Another benefit was the ability to send his sons to the superior DC schools, no matter where he was living. So when the time came, although the family was living in Maryland I went to Woodrow Wilson High School, a large urban high school in northwest DC.

I liked it about as much as D.M.C. liked his job, save for one thing—the theater. They put on plays at Wilson.

Passion Awakens

Some fascinating facts can come to light when you ask theater people about their very first appearance before an audience. "I was a radish in a vegetable pageant," a grave, serious leading man once told me. One of our most distinguished classical actresses began her career as a pancake.

I was a bridesmaid. I have no memory of the purpose of the entertainment, nor how I got into it, but one day I found myself prancing down the center aisle of the big auditorium at Gordon Junior High in DC, one of several bridesmaids in an all-boy wedding ceremony, after which I took my position off to the side of the stage.

As the preacher spoke his gibberish to the happy couple center stage, I became aware that the attention of some members of the audience was straying to me. I must have been quite a sigh: my skinny legs, my dress, my overbite. There were giggles, a whistle or two. Without thinking, I minced down to the footlights and did some hootchy-kootchy move that brought the house down. I hurried back to place and the show went on. I stood there, my heart pounding, thinking: "My, what an interesting sound!"

Two years later I was in Wilson High. I was looking more presentable, the orthodontist having worked his sorcery. So one day I braved tryouts and was cast as the lead's boyfriend, Ham Ellers, in *The Fighting Littles*, a domestic comedy by Booth Tarkington.

My parents came to see the opening. They were quite complimentary, or so I thought. It was not until years later that I wormed the awful truth out of them—what an absolute disaster the production had been, how execrable my acting and how divine was that George Grizzard who stole the show as my girlfriend's bratty brother. But that was years later. Bless them for not marring a memorable night.

I remember getting to school and the somewhat unreal quiet in the halls before the performance. I don't recall much about the performance itself. What remains vivid is what happened later—and of that, not so much where I was, or what I did, but how I felt.

You know how, very rarely, in moments of real joy, your heart can do some sort of crazy diastolic razzmatazz and you feel a throb that floods your whole being with happiness? Well, that night after the curtain came down on *The Fighting Littles* until well after the sun rose the next morning, that feeling, that throb was going off every twenty minutes.

Where did it come from? Well, the performance, of course: the thrill of being on stage, the relief that it was over without mischance, the applause, the praise. But there was something more important …

Look, here was this kid who had made a habit of deferring to others, of hiding in the shadow of his brothers or his parents, of covering his mouth so as to hide the buck teeth. Now those caps and wires that had reshaped his mouth were gone. "Hey, lookamee!" Now three hundred people had sat in the dark and approvingly (so he thought) watched his every move. Hadn't he found a way to race forward, to catch up with those two swift-footed rivals in the vanguard of his life?

"Hey, Don! Hey, Jack! Lookamee! Lookameee!"

———◆———

In 1944, thanks to the generosity of someone I called Uncle Arc (he was not a relative, but my father's best friend), I was delivered from the anonymity of a teeming big-city high school and sent to the graceful, elm-lined streets of Easthampton, Massachusetts, where I was to pass my junior and senior years in a crackerjack prep school called Williston Academy.

If I was uneasy at first, I soon realized that it was the perfect school for me. Williston was indeed a New England prep school, but it was a far cry from those oft-mocked citadels of the blazer-clad and lock-jawed scions of the wealthy, like Andover and Deerfield. No, the Williston student body had a far more egalitarian tone—made up of sons of liquor store owners, clothing salesmen, and farmers, as well as the more privileged.

Its classes were small, sometimes as few as a dozen students. There was a fine theater program. The faculty was first rate and, in some cases, lovably eccentric. Lincoln Depew Grannis offers one choice example:

> At about 10:00 P.M., there is a knock on the door. Neither my roommate Bob Werner (aka Ryeball) nor I rise from our beds to answer it. We don't have to, for soon, without any invitation, the door swings open and a sharp-featured, tweedy little man enters.
>
> "Tee hee," the tweedy little man says, "Tee hee! Little Call and little Werner all tucked up for the night, eh? Ready for Morpheus, are we?"
>
> Then by the dim light from the hallway, we see him trip about the room, croaking:
>
>> Double, double, toil and trouble,
>>
>> Fire burn, and cauldron bubble,
>>
>> Cool it with a baboon's blood!
>
> Ryeball and I whoop it up, egging him on. A dozen or so more of the witches' lines from *Macbeth* follow. Then suddenly he skitters out the door, closing it with a slam. Lincoln Depew Grannis, head of the classics department of Williston Academy and house master of North Hall, is making his nightly rounds.

Mr. Cook the math teacher, small and absent-minded, wore galoshes on overcast days and was known to get so excited about what he was writing on the blackboard that when he came to the edge of it, he'd just keep on going, scribbling indecipherably on the adjacent wall.

There were also the athletic activities, which were universal and compulsory. This last feature was the most important to me, for though I loved the studies and learned more at Williston than in all my years at college(s), it was the athletics, so unexpected, so leap-in-the-air exciting, that won me heart and soul. Previously athletic distinction was something I could only dream about, but damned if I didn't find myself, in my senior year, playing on *three* varsity teams—soccer, basketball, and tennis. I thus became, in that very small pond, a veritable BMOC, the three-letter man.

The sport at which I worked the hardest was basketball. I was the second-string center and got at most five minutes of playing time the entire season. But I didn't care, for just being on the team gave me a chance to play with and watch a truly great athlete by the name of Tony Lavelli.

Tony Lavelli, the Hero as Athlete

Tony was a tall, lanky kid from Somerville, Massachusetts. After a dynamite high school basketball career in his home town, he was wooed by most of the Ivy League scouts. He decided he wanted to go to Yale, but was counseled to wait a year, a year in which he could get his grades up and perfect his game. Williston was chosen for this interim year because of its challenging academics and its excellent basketball coach, Dale Lash. (Great name for a coach, isn't it? Dale Lash.)

So Tony came to Easthampton.

Tony was an attractive, somewhat enigmatic figure, as all good heroes should be. Hard to describe … an almost classical Italianate face; curly jet-black hair; height somewhere around six foot three, with a slender but strong big-boned physique; very clean (off the court he always looked as if he had just showered); shy, hard to get to know, but always friendly; the only man I ever saw who walked cat-like, on the balls of his feet; also a musician, with perfect pitch.

On the basketball court, he was as graceful a creature as God ever created. He did everything well, but his special contribution to the game was the hook shot. Many years later a wise sports writer put it this way: "Tony Lucetti invented the hook shot; Tony Lavelli perfected it."

This is a set shot: Stand facing a basketball hoop from fifteen feet away with a ball held at chest level between your hands. Everything is sensibly aligned—your eyes, your hands, the ball, the target. You see the hoop, you aim, you shoot.

A hook shot, on the other hand, seems to make no sense at all because it requires you to turn away from the basket and, contradicting that commonplace of all sports, demands that you keep your eye *off* the ball.

So, starting from the same position as the set shot above, turn sideways so you are in profile to the basket. Now extend the arm that is away from the basket out to the side, shoulder height, palm upward; put the basketball in that hand, look over your shoulder to aim, then with a sweeping motion launch the ball over your head toward the basket. What you have done is a hook shot, almost. The real shot is executed *on the run*.

The virtue of the hook shot is that it is almost impossible to block. The player guarding you wants to stay between you and the basket and never gets a good look at the ball (since it's being launched from the far side of your body) until it is arcing over his head, out of reach, on its way to the basket.

Why am I going on like this! What is the point of it all? Who's interested? Basketball fans know what a hook shot is, and those who aren't don't give a damn!

Well, it's the sports thing, I guess. I've spent most of my life putting on plays, but once, and only once, when I was young, I had an encounter with athletic greatness. I want to share it with you, that's all. Bear with me.

So, back to the hook shot. You rarely see it today. Oh, the announcers call them hook shots right enough, but the players cheat a little, turning to the basket as the ball is released or starting the shot already somewhat turned. And the shots are rarely made at any great distance from the basket.

I lack the skill to describe Tony in action. But consider this: A long time ago the world consisted of big, slow people and small, quick people. Then some time around the middle of the last century, Nature came up with a whole new concept: the big person who was also quick; think Mohammed Ali. In that new category was a miraculous subtype: the big, quick person who looks slow; think Alex Rodriguez.

Tony was in this latter group. While we all ran frantically down the court, and then ran frantically up the court, Tony was with us every step of the way—but he seemed to lope along in his own slow-motion movie.

Off to the right side of the court, he feints a move; his man is thrown off half a step. Tony ambles on, and when he is almost out of real estate (a few feet from the baseline) he launches one of those pure over-the-shoulder beauties, twenty feet away from the basket. Swish! Two more points. And our demoralized foes try to regroup.

We had an undefeated season. It wasn't all Tony, of course. The whole starting five, which included a quick-handed guard, my roomie the Ryeball, was first rate.

As for Tony, he did indeed move on to Yale and a storied and heroic career. From there it was a short trip to Boston and the Celtics. Now, finally, it was time for him to step out on the national stage. To many, it promised the beginning of a magnificent Hall of Fame career.

But as it turned out, that scenario didn't happen. An indifferent year in Boston with the Celtics was followed by an indifferent year with the Knicks, and then it was over.

When I think back to the years at Williston, I realize I might have seen where the trouble lay. On the practice court, as a second stringer, it was my job to guard Tony. I used to love the violence of the scrum that took place under the basket when the ball was loose—all that grabbing, shoving, elbows-flying chaos was exciting. Tony hated it. In the midst of the melee, I sometimes saw a look on his face of almost childish frustration—face red, teeth clenched, as if he were close to tears. That part of the game was repugnant to him. So as his professional career began and basketball at that level was becoming more and more of a contact sport, Tony found it harder and harder to play that graceful, heroic game of his.

Not for Tony Lavelli the hand-to-hand scuffles in the dark alleys, the chaotic tumult, the hail of blows. No, he was made for sunlight—a hoplite, a corsair who cruised the edges of the fray, launching his missiles over the heads of bewildered defenders into the very heart of the enemy's stronghold. Not to be able to play his game … what a loss for us, what a tragedy for him!

When I think of Tony, I also think of some of the actors and actresses I have known—artists of the very first rank, endowed with beauty and talent enough to fill us all with wonder, all deserving to be at the pinnacle of their profession.

But it doesn't happen. Something gets in the way. Sometimes it's the booze, sometimes drugs, but these demons can take all kinds of shapes. I once worked with an actress who I was convinced was our next Grace Kelly. She was easily as beautiful and far more talented, moreover by all outward signs she was afire with ambition. After we worked together, she moved to the West Coast, married a hot young agent, and soon everything seemed to be falling place for major film career. But then, after accepting some big offer, in the long wait between signing and the start of shooting, she got pregnant and had to withdraw. Hell, just one of those unlucky breaks, right? But then it happened a second time—a big offer, another pregnancy. At last report she has a growing family and no career. However admirable the family part, it was not quite what she had in mind. Bizarre.

Once on a break during a photo session for a show I was directing, I was chatting with the photographer. I complimented him on some work he had done in the past. He was pleased and told me he really hadn't had that much experience as a photographer (he was then in his late twenties) because what he had dreamed of being, what he had trained his whole life for, was a career as a dancer, a ballet dancer.

When he was younger, having begun classes at some ridiculously early age, he was soon on the fast track to realize his dream—in New York, studying at the School of American Ballet, under the watchful eye of Mr. Balanchine. Then, just after he had been invited to join the New York City Ballet, his body began to play him false. In the midst of a rehearsal his joints would suddenly lock in the most grotesque ways, sometimes requiring hospitalization. No physical cause for these seizures was ever found, but their effect, of course, was to end his career just as it was beginning. This, after those endless years of rigorous labor for what he thought he wanted.

Truly, the race is not always to the swift nor the battle to the strong, as the preacher saith, "for time and chance happeneth to them all."[1]

I was in heaven. It all ended too soon when I graduated from Williston in 1946.

———

There followed six desultory years of travel and higher education. I bummed coast to coast five different times and made numberless

---

1   Ecclesiastes 9:11

shorter jaunts. There was something deeply appealing to me about hitchhiking. I think it has some deep metaphorical significance in my life. On the other hand, it could have been my way of getting some attention when my brothers were busy fighting Adolph Hitler.

Route 26 in northwest Wyoming, outside Dubois. I stood on the bed of a rattly old stake truck, leaning on the cab as we whizzed through the pine forests and down into the valley of the Grand Tetons.

Route 66, "that winds from Chicago to LA," as the song says. One tough road. I remember Kingman, Arizona where U.S. air power was put to bed after World War II. Rank on rank of Flying Forts, hundreds of them, baking under the relentless southwestern sun. Beyond Kingman to the west, the Mojave Desert. At the side of the road, every twenty feet or so, a hitchhiker; maybe fifteen of us, trying to get to California. Few cars, fewer rides. Heat. My chances improved when three of our dusty fraternity gave up and made for the railroad tracks, hoping to catch a freight. But it didn't help. I was stuck in that desert for three days. Slept on the ground not far back from the road so as not to lose my place; then up with the sun and try again. By noon it was 120 degrees, so I stood there in the blistering heat, praying for a ride in a decent car, one that wouldn't break down or have a blowout on the way to Barstow. Finally deliverance! into a car and into the desert, all windows open, like riding in a blast furnace. Once in a while an oncoming car passed, making a mad dash in the opposite direction, canvas water bags hanging on the front bumper.

Route 101 on the Olympic Peninsula in Washington State. I awoke after sleeping in the forest and walked down the bright sunlit highway, not a car or truck in sight. On my right, the distant rumble of the Pacific, unseen, eighty feet below. To my left, towering Douglas firs, to which I bawled out Shakespeare at the top of my lungs, big noisy speeches to get their attention:

> What is it then to me if impious War,
> Arrayed in flames like to the prince of fiends,
> Do with his smirched complexion all fell feats
> Enlinked to waste and desolation?

My higher education ventures yielded, for the most part, a sorry record of nonachievement. When it came time to think of college, I looked with scorn at all the schools bulging with returning GIs. However, despite deciding to hit the road, I would pause from time to time to pursue my parents' insistence that I get a college education. But I was a lousy student, unless the theater was involved. I eventually did graduate; it took seven years.

First there was the local diploma factory—George Washington University in DC after my first cross-country trek. Classes of fifty, classes of 100. Its one bright spot for me was the chance to act in a historical pageant at the Carter Barron Amphitheater in nearby Rock Creek Park. *Faith of Our Fathers* was a symphonic dramatization of the life and times of George Washington. I played thirteen parts, ranging from the French sculptor, Jean-Antoine Houdon, to an oarsman in a tableau vivant of "Washington Crossing The Delaware."

However, aside from that venture I never opened a book. I endured GW for a year, then went back on the road.

After a time I wound up working at Paradise Valley on the slopes of Mount Rainier in the state of Washington. Through a contact there, I got into the University of Washington, which had a hot theater department. After eighteen months I ran out of money.

I hitched home and went to work teaching ballroom dancing at the Don Martini Studios (an Arthur Murray knockoff) in DC. A neon sign promised you could "Dance Your Cares Away."

I finally finished up at the University of Maryland in College Park. It had several virtues: both my brothers had gone there, tuition was cheap, and it wasn't far from home. As a student I was barely mediocre. I just didn't give a damn. I was more interested in having a good time. Every once in a while, a good teacher would ignite my interest, but that happened all too seldom, and I was too lazy and undisciplined to pursue knowledge on my own.

Thank goodness UMD had a theater department. Most of my focus was there, where I was getting good parts and praise. Even my folks said some nice things. Thanks to Rudy Pugliese, a dynamic teacher/director, I got to play one of my dream roles: Chris in Arthur Miller's *All My Sons*. I began to think I would give acting a try professionally, but somewhere inside I knew I lacked both the ego and the drive. I was simply floating.

A Grisly Scene

Scene: A history class at the University of Maryland circa 1952.

A trim, bow-tied professor stands behind a lectern mumbling his way through several decades of American history. Before him, slightly curved tiers rise to the back of the room. On those tiers, rows of wooden chairs, the right arms of which widen out into a small writing surface. Half the chairs are empty, the other half occupied by students in varying degrees of attentiveness—some doze, one foolish soul takes notes.

In what seems like an exercise out of the Theater of the Absurd, in a barely audible monotone the professor repeats exactly what is in the text (which he wrote); nothing is added, nothing omitted. Moreover, he seems oddly disconnected from the students before him—raised hands go unanswered, snoozing students unchallenged. Not even the odd clacking noise, making a jittery percussion to his soporific monotone, gets his attention.

This clacking is the sound of small metal knitting needles working busily in the nimble fingers of half a dozen adorable sorority girls who are engaged in that almost holy ritual of burgeoning campus love, fashioning argyle socks for their inamorati. These Tri-Delts, Kappa Girls, and Thetas, scattered like rose petals among the front rows, look as worshipfully at the professor as the management of their complex task will allow. Their pert little hands dance, clickety, clickety. The professor drones on. My thoughts wander aimlessly, and some important questions surface: "Why did I drink so much beer last night? Is Tippy still mad at me? Where will I spend the summer—Rehoboth with the folks or Virginia Beach? Who can I get to help me fix the cracked block on my A-Model Ford? Why doesn't the Guvnor buy a decent TV?"

———

I was soon to be awakened from my suburban slumbers; it happened this way, in 1952. One major assignment remained before I could get a diploma. For it, I could either write a long research paper or I could direct a play. Directing a play seemed the less arduous choice; also the more congenial. I set about making it as easy as possible for myself. I chose a play (Shaw's *Candida*) that I was familiar with, having acted a small part in it several years earlier at another university.

I cast a lot of friends and went to work in a loose, undisciplined way. I didn't do a lot of preparation. I let the blocking take care of itself and praised the actors, whatever the quality of their work. Rehearsals were fun but minimally productive. We cruised along amiably for a week or so. And then came that night when I decided to stay in a friend's spare bedroom near the campus rather than drive all the way home.

Act with Three Words
(a pantomime of self discovery)

Scene: A wall, in front of it a single bed, long side to the audience. A light bulb with cord hangs over the bed. Down left, a chair with books and papers. The student lies on his back, in bed, under the covers, head at stage left.

Student sits up in bed. Reflects. Pulls light cord, light on. Looks around. Gets out of bed. Crosses to chair DL. Finds script, opens it. Reads in mumbles. Stops, reflects. More mumbling.

Student closes script. Drops script into chair. Xes back to bed. Gets under covers. Pulls cord, light out. Lies back.

Long pause.

Explosive laugh. Sits up. Pulls cord, light on. Xes to chair. Picks up script. Finds place, writes in margin. Reflects. Explosive laugh.

Closes script. Drops script into chair. Xes to bed. Starts to get under covers, stops. Xes back to chair. Picks up script, Xes to bed. Puts script on floor by bed. Gets into bed. Pulls cord, light out. Lies back.

Silence.

Noises heard in dark, grunts as if student is wrestling with unseen assailant. Tossing about. Silence. Then humming is heard.

Sits up. Pulls cord, light on. Reaches for script. Sitting on bed, opens script. Finds place. Intense activity for five minutes in various positions. Sounds of arguing, gesticulations, muted cries. Whispers. Much scribbling in margin of script.

Puts script on floor. Pulls cord, light out. Lies back.

Repeat previous writing and blackout actions with variations for two hours. Then finally:

Sits up. Pulls cord, light on. Student swings his legs over, sits on edge of bed. Mouth slightly agape. Eyes facing front. Blinks. He's coming back from somewhere. Reflects. Reflects.

STUDENT *(after searching for a suitable utterance to celebrate this revelation, speaks slowly, softly with wonder).* Fuck a duck.

Smiles. Slowly gets under covers. Lies back. Hands under head. Eyes wide open. Long fade of lights to black.

And thus it was, dear reader, lying in a strange bed, at around 4:00 in the morning, that I found out what I wanted to do for the rest of my life. I don't remember many details of that night, what problems I was obsessing about, or what solutions I came up with. I only know that I got to a depth of concentration and focus that I had never reached before, certainly not as an actor. My whole being, every last molecule, was awash in the world of George Bernard Shaw. I had unintentionally fallen into a dream, and my life would never be the same.

———

A couple of years after graduation, a second historical production came my way, brought to life on an outdoor stage in west central Florida in 1955, I played the role of Chief Jumper, a Seminole Indian. *Florida Aflame* was the show; the Seminole uprising of 1835 was the subject.

This being the midcentury South, there were few real Seminoles in the company. In fact, when we opened there was only one, and he looked oddly out of place among all us phony painted Caucasians.

Because I am a paleface, I learned that to get the proper ruddy hue of the Native American, there is a must-have product; it is called Texas Dirt. I have no idea whether it really is dirt or whether it comes from Texas. I only know what a dismal occupation sponging it on and washing it off can be. And I only had to do my face and hands. Think of the poor dancers who wore only loin cloths, moccasins, and a few beads and feathers.

These painted Indian dancers, by the way, are crucial to the success of any given historical pageant. That's because they make possible indispensable numbers like "Iroquois on the War-path!" which are as important to a history epic as the South American number was to the '50s musical. I am convinced that *Faith of Our Fathers* (the G. Washington piece) went belly up after two indifferent seasons because there was no rock 'em, sock 'em Indian number—only effete Mount Vernon minuets. Failure was inevitable.

The real thing goes like this: Halfway through the first act, the tribal drums begin their familiar throb (BOOM, boom, boom, boom, BOOM, boom, boom, boom …). Then from stage right a line of fifteen bloodthirsty warriors emerges one by one. They face front, elbows and knees splayed sideways, crouching threateningly as they side-hop onto the playing area. First we see Chief Microbiology Grad Assistant, then that valiant brave, Second Year Accounting Major, followed by that scourge of the white man, Aspiring Systems Analyst. Others follow. The pulse of the drums quickens and reaches its crescendo. They all rush to surround their mighty shaman— Case Western Reserve Dance Major! He looks heavenward, eyes wild, and brandishes his medicine stick, or bow, or rifle, and emits a blood-curdling scream.

And we're off!

The drums begin again, louder and faster this time, and there's much twirling and leaping and shouting and colorful mock fights. Suddenly the audience sits up. After watching a half-dozen wooden re-enactments of significant scenes from American history, *the savages are loose!* Those Red Men may have lost the West, but, by damn, they just may save the show!

I'm getting a bit too Dave Barry here, I know. I really shouldn't knock it, because the historical pageant circuit is useful. It provides work for a lot of actors and gives tourists something to do at night. The scripts are the problem. It's a shame our best playwrights have never worked in the form. After all, it wasn't beneath the dignity of Will Shakespeare —that's how we got Hotspur and Falstaff.

Florida Aflame, the Seminole extravaganza, was performed in a newly constructed outdoor theater just north of a sleepy crossroads called Safety Harbor in west central Florida. The playing space was huge, something like 100 feet wide, with half a dozen distinct acting areas. As a result, the sets didn't move, the action did—a scene at the fort, stage left, in which a rebellious enlisted man was being disciplined, was followed by a scene on the hill, right center, where the Seminoles ambush a sentry. Next the action shifted to the large center area for the pow-wow, and so on.

My good friend Kelton Garwood brought his fiery dignity to the role of Osceola, the great Seminole chief. There was a nice panoramic sweep to the action, and however imperfectly we represented Indian life, a fascinating epoch in American history was on display. Soon the public began to show up in considerable numbers; *Florida Aflame* was in business.

We only performed at night, which left our days free for swimming, tennis, and other sunlit pleasures of Gulf Coast Florida. And "to one who has been long in city pent," it was a wonderful tonic. But after a few weeks of this sybaritic life, some of us were getting restless. So what do young theater people do when bored with sunshine and salt water? They put on a play, naturally. Or at least they talk about putting on a play.

We tossed some titles around, but soon realized they were plays that would get lost on our massive stage. Something of epic size was needed. I came up with Ibsen's *Peer Gynt*. We certainly had the actors; notably Karl Redcoff made a terrific Peer. And we had the scenery. By some happy coincidence every single one of the permanent sets made to chronicle a nineteenth-century Seminole uprising would fit the Ibsen play perfectly—we had a cabin for Peer's mother, a fort that could become the madhouse, virtually all scenic needs were taken care of, down to a big fat black pot (Osceola's campfire) where Ibsen's Button Molder could melt down errant souls.

Most of the company embraced the idea and didn't even object when I dubbed myself director. Within a week, twenty actors and almost as many volunteers were hard at it. Besides four or five hours of rehearsal each day and the performance at night, I found I had some producing duties, such as fundraising and publicity. My tan soon faded; I was overworked and short on sleep, but thoroughly content, or so I thought.

Late one night, on my way home after a performance of *Florida Aflame*, I had a strange experience, an odd sort of hallucination. I was walking slowly, my head full of *Peer Gynt*, when a thought swept through my mind like a breaking wave. I would almost swear I didn't think it, I heard it. The thought, or voice, spoke: "It must not be too good."

I froze.

Where did that come from? Was it my father's voice? my brothers'? Peer Gynt's? No, it was my own. I said that, or some part of me said it. Despite my profound absorption in the world of Peer Gynt, from some putrid depth this oily bubble of insecurity wiggled upward to the surface and broke. After years of irresolute drifting, I'd finally made a few tentative steps on the way to a career. Was I now to become an obstacle to my own success by distrusting my abilities?

Time stopped as I stood there on that hauntingly quiet, moonlit street for many minutes, then walked on, trying to get that voice out of my mind. It was not easy. The undertow lasted for several days.

It helped to realize that "being too good" was not truly a problem, given the inexperience of the director (me) and the pick-up nature of the enterprise. My Ibsen obsession returned in force and, that voice, I prayed, was silenced for good.

Peer Gynt was performed once, on a Monday night, the dark night of *Florida Aflame*. It turned out to be a worthwhile enterprise. It gave those bored actors an interesting challenge, it raised a fair amount of jack for the Pinellas County (the charity that the company decided should get the box office take), it provided a solid evening's entertainment to an almost full house and, most important (to me), it showed the director just what kind of director he wanted to be.

With *Peer Gynt* I had been working on an expansive canvas, and found I liked it mightily. At a time when membership in the Actors Studio was everyone's fondest dream (yes, even mine at one point), and Stanislavski's Method system was inspiring (or exasperating) everyone in the theater, when you couldn't walk from Sixth to Eighth Avenue in the streets of the mid-Forties without bumping into several Brando wannabes or James Dean impersonators, I realized that the theater of the inner life, explorations of plays that were wet and small and domestic, were not for me. I wanted to do theater that was big and noisy, rich in language and technically dazzling. Down with the Method and its constipated pusillanimity. Bring on the masterpieces!

I may have had a success with *Peer Gynt*, but Safety Harbor, Florida, was not what you would call a major theater center. I knew that if I was going to build a career, I'd better start working in New York City. The way things fell out, however, my next major gig was in another small town, a deceptively quiet village in southern Ohio called Yellow Springs.

Carving Out a Career

The path from realizing that I wanted to be a director to actually stating "1 am a director" with some conviction was long and circuitous and took a dozen years. It wasn't easy. Understandably.

It is not a measurable skill. You can't audition, as actors do, or show a portfolio of your work, like a designer. You can show pictures of productions, but the only thing photographs demonstrate is the skill of the photographer and the designers, not the director. Reviews carry some weight, but if your clippings come from small-town journals, as mine did (such as the *Safety Harbor Beacon* in Florida), they don't count for much.

Also youth is not necessarily an advantage, unless you're some mad young genius, in which case you make your own rules. No; by and large the mature discerning eye, the veteran showman's canniness, the rich life experience is what is needed. What the hell did I know? I was in my mid-twenties! I only knew that I wanted to direct, and none of the moustaches I grew could convince people that I was qualified.

So what was the solution? For me, stage management became the entrée to directing. I stumbled on it quite by accident, after several fledgling stints at acting and directing.

In my cold-water, sixth-floor walk-up on East Seventy-fourth Street, along with Clarence who worked in a big commercial laundry and numerous black-clad Hungarian widows, lived a few others like me, working on the fringe of the theater world. The Peltos, Matt and Dori, lived on the first floor on the left. Dorrie was doing the acting thing, and Matt was working as a stage carpenter.

One sunny autumn day in 1957—a noisy stickball game in progress in the street, kids playing on the stoops, women on upper floors leaning on window sills watching the action (all the long-gone East Seventy-fourth Street rituals)—I dropped in on the Peltos. Knowing I was out of work, Matt mentioned that the Jan Hus Playhouse, a nearby off-Broadway theater, was looking for a stage manager. I needed a job, but surely this was not for me. I didn't know, or have much interest in knowing, anything about stage management.

"Here, look at this," Matt said, handing me a small hardcover book as I stood there dithering. Newly published, it was titled *The Stage Manager's Handbook.* Bert Gruver, a veteran Broadway stage manager (SM), was the author. I looked it over; it seemed to be a down-to-earth how-to book written in crisply instructive prose, one that might, if I was inclined to join the SM ranks, be a perfect finagle.

Hmmm.

I decided I might as well give it a try. There were no other offers pending … and the fact of the matter was, I was broke. Had long since gone through my unemployment compensation after directing *Arms and the Man* that spring, had avoided complete catastrophe by hocking my Rolex. I had zero prospects. My gainful theater employment in New York totaled exactly three weeks!

A serious career in the theater? Who was I kidding?

I should have hugged Matt (shouting my eternal gratitude the while), grabbed Bert's Golden Book of Secrets, immediately dashed down to the Jan Hus Playhouse where *Pale Horse, Pale Rider* was in rehearsal, and insisted they hire me.

As it was, I condescended to appear at the theater some time the next day in the early afternoon, offered my services, and was hired on the spot. I didn't realize it at the time, but I had turned a major corner. I not only had a job, but incidentally I had also found a way upward into the ranks of working directors.

I started as SM, all the while following Bert Gruver's instructions slavishly as he took me chronologically through the production process, from the kind of binder I needed for my prompt script to how to keep curtain calls moving on opening night. "Buy this kind of notebook; use #2 pencils; this is what a call sheet should look like;" advice like that. It was organized chronologically:

> Part One: Prerehearsal Period
> Part Two: Rehearsals, First Weeks
> Part Three: Rehearsals, Final Weeks …

I read one part a week, and I turned out to be a fairly good SM. It sure beat pounding the pavement.

A stage manager is, above all, involved with the minutiae of performance:

- "Has the blotter that goes into the ashtray on the table by Buford's chair been moistened?" (so the cigarette that the colonel stubs out in it won't smolder).
- "Has wardrobe sewn up the hem of Emma's second-act dress?" (so she won't trip again tonight).
- "Was Olga reminded to sit after the line 'You're a philistine, Roderick' but not before?" (because that's the way the director wanted it).

Details, details, details—it's not everyone's cup of tea, but I found it much to my liking, organizing the gorgeous chaos. I particularly liked technical rehearsals, when light, sound, and music cues were integrated into the production. I was able to learn some crucial lessons about controlling the technical elements of theater. Most importantly, I was learning by watching other directors work.

Many years ago a producer told me he would not hire an SM who just wanted to stage manage; there had to be some other aspiration: director or producer. Nowadays, it turns out, that rarely seems to be the case; SMs are quite content in their invaluable niche, but it seems a shame to lose the job as a first rung on the ladder. Observerships or internships take up some of the slack, but they are usually on the outside looking in. SMs are at the very center of a production, learning how to handle mettlesome acting companies, learning invaluable tech lessons, and developing relationships with directors, actors, designers, and composers that can be built upon, later on. Observers, by comparison, are dilettantes.

One drawback: If you're good at stage managing, people want to keep you there. The only way out of that is to show them you're even better at directing. As soon as any production I was stage managing opened and the actors had some free time, I'd go chasing after them with a script I was burning to direct.

———◆———

Those rookie years began in College Park, Maryland, with my staging of Shaw's *Candida* performed for a small student audience in 1952. My Florida adventures provided a significant boost, and helped ready me for my next step: the Big Apple. In 1956, I made the move to New York, and first lived in a hovel on Twenty-third Street. Within a year, thanks to Eddy Barron, a mate from my U. of W. days, I went upscale and moved into that cold-water flat on East Seventy-fourth. As the name implies, the flat had no hot water—the bathtub was in the kitchen, the john (shared) was in the hall. Lap of luxury for the indigent; I was lucky. Throughout the mid-50s, those rookie gigs included:

- Handing out soap coupons door to door for Proctor and Gamble; typing; filing; working in the garment district; and proofreading airplane parts catalogues written in an infinitesimal type size.
- Spending a long winter season building scenery and acting bit parts at the Hilltop Theater, a former movie house in Baltimore, Maryland. Our resident company, called Star Stock, supported a new specimen of the breed: luminaries who arrived every week. All

these guest actors were movie types, but refreshingly, they turned out for the most part to be a fascinating, nontemperamental bunch of stage-savvy old pros— the likes of Basil Rathbone, Robert Preston, Edward Everett Horton, Gene Lockhart, Billie Burke, Jackie Cooper, Zazu Pitts, and on and on and on. The enterprise continued for over thirty weeks.

· Heading out of town for summer stints as an actor or director (sometimes both) at the Antioch Shakespeare Festival (Ohio), the Berkshire Playhouse (Massachusetts), and Barter Theatre (Virginia).

———

I did direct my first production in New York City: *Arms and the Man* (George Bernard Shaw) at Equity Library Theatre. My true apprenticeship, however, began at Circle in the Square. Thanks to the good words of director David Wheeler, a trusted friend of José Quintero's, I was hired in late 1958 to be the stage manager at Circle. I felt incredibly lucky, considering how little experience I'd gained by this point, to be working at one of the hottest show shops in New York. At first my duties consisted of overseeing the final performances of *Children at Night*, and during the day, running José's rehearsals of *The Quare Fellow*, Brendan Behan's drama about an execution in an Irish prison.

Children of Darkness was a breeze. The show had settled into a dependable routine as it neared the end of its run. I rarely had more to do than watch the fun and make sure the monstrous, ancient, thundering air-conditioning unit was turned on during intermissions.

Off-Broadway: Circle in the Square

Oh, there are still two theaters that bear that name—
one deep in the bowels of a high-rise office building
on Broadway at West Fiftieth Street, the other on
Bleecker Street in Greenwich Village, way east of Sixth
Avenue. But for those of us who worked there in the
1950s, Circle in the Square will always be that ratty old
nightclub-turned-theater on the south side of Sheridan
Square. It is now, sadly, gone with the wind, torn down
along with most of the block to make room for a bulging apartment house of more than usual vulgarity.

In truth, that original Circle was a difficult place in
which to put on a play: the stage was long and narrow,
there were three posts in a line down the center, there
was no offstage space, so most crossovers had to be made
in the street. The ceiling was too low, there was no SM's
booth, no green room, and no dressing rooms that deserved the name—only an inky pestiferous basement.
You froze in the winter and broiled in the summer. And
yet ... and yet in this game of chance called theater, it
turned out to be a particularly important player.

Brooks Atkinson, the highly respected drama critic of the *New York Times*, decided in May of 1952 to
venture off the beaten Broadway path (an unusual journey at that time). He wanted to have a look at a production playing in some dubious venue way downtown,
one that had been causing something of a stir in theater
circles. The play was one by Tennessee Williams that
had flopped several years earlier in its Broadway debut, but now seemed to be having some kind of rebirth

downtown. So he ventured south of Fourteenth Street to this unknown theater calling itself Circle in the Square and saw a production of *Summer and Smoke* performed by a company of passionate unknowns led by Geraldine Page and Lee Richardson and directed by a wild-eyed Panamanian named José Quintero. Mr. Atkinson was quite taken by these ardent young players and gave the production a rave review. Thus began the theater movement we now call off-Broadway, as well as the glory years of Circle in the Square.

Following the success of *Summer and Smoke*, director Quintero had another triumph with yet another play that had been coolly received by the critics when it first appeared on Broadway. This was *The Iceman Cometh*, Eugene O'Neill's examination of a motley group of deadbeat alcoholics living in the half-light of a squalid Bowery gin mill. To them enters Hickey, a hardware salesman who would be their tinhorn savior, but it turns out that Hickey is the greatest sinner of them all. His long, tortured monologue at the end of the play sent the critics searching for new superlatives, all of which were showered on an unknown actor by the name of Jason Robards Jr. The production ran for almost two years.

Next came *Children of Darkness* by Edwin Justus Mayer. This was an American playwright's attempt to write an eighteenth-century comedy/drama about London's criminal classes, a sort of *Beggar's Opera* without the music.

> *Scene: The Jailer's apartments at Newgate Prison. On hand: some bosomy trulls; an impecunious poet, Mr. Cartwright; the devious jailer Snap; his proud,*

beautiful (also bosomy) daughter Laetitia; and a
decadent aristocrat identified as Lord Wainwright.

With these latter—Laetitia and Wainwright—two more electrifying newcomers were introduced to the NY theater scene: George C. Scott and Colleen Dewhurst.

Children of Darkness is not a great play, but it was cast with such genius and was so well directed that it became succulent, dangerous, irresistible fun.

Mr. Scott as Lord Wainwright gave me one of the oddest experiences I have ever had in a theater, one of shivering with fear and hooting with laughter almost at the same time. This occurred shortly after his entrance when Cartwright the poet inquired what mischance had brought His Lordship to Newgate Prison? Elegantly attired in blue velvet and lace, Wainwright turned slowly to his interlocutor, favored him with one of those scary, vulpine George C. Scott smiles, and replied calmly: "I murdered my wife and a few of her intimate friends."

Gruver's book had taught me the basics of stage management, but I had learned nothing about overseeing a company during the course of a long run. How could I? The only show I had worked on prior to *Children of Darkness* had closed after a week. This educational lacuna was about to be filled during the seemingly endless months I was entrusted with the care and feeding of the twenty-strong, all-male cast of *The Quare Fellow*—one tough bunch of boyos. José had gone for authenticity in casting, and thus it was that at least half the company was made up of rough, charming, sometimes temperamental, often stubborn and irresponsible, classically dipsomaniacal, gen-u-ine Sons of Erin.

A week or so into rehearsal, sitting at the SM table, writing industriously, trying to keep up with José's blocking, subliminally aware of too much noise coming from the actors not involved in the scene, but resolutely pushing that static from my mind and continuing my stage managerial scribbling, I heard a voice at my ear, emphatic and deliberate, that whispered: "You'd ... better ... be ... good." I looked up; it was Paul Milikin, one of the native Irish company members who also happened to be the equity deputy for this production. He stared back evenly, then walked away.

The admonition was something I needed to hear. Mind you, I thought I was being a pretty fair SM—my prompt script was impeccably up to date. All Bert Gruver's checklists had been checked. What could be wrong?

What was wrong was that the SM was working awfully hard but neglecting one of his principal responsibilities: company discipline.

A couple of days later, back at the SM table, recording the proceedings unfolding before me, another whisperer approached. An elderly Celt decided that he had worked enough that day and should be dismissed. He poured his entreaty into my ear. "Wait 'til we have a break," I whispered back, "1 have to clear it with José." That was not good enough for him; he wanted to leave right away, so ... "No," I said, "you'll have to wait." But he wouldn't give up and bent down yet again, his whisper more insistent now, as if I were denying him some inalienable right. Suddenly the anger I had been holding down surged.

"1 am trying to run a rehearsal here, Pat, and I want you to *leave me the fuck alone!*"

The rehearsal stopped dead. Pat backed away. To hide my embarrassment, I busied myself with the prompt script. When the break finally came, I apologized to José. He didn't seem to know what I was talking about; the company was equally indifferent.

Yet I was uneasy. What I had done was out of character, not at all comfortable. I was the mild-tempered one, the peacemaker; it was part of my kid-brother DNA. Was this surliness really what was needed to keep my rowdy Irishmen in control? Couldn't I do it with charm and unassailable reason? No, I couldn't. It took time, but I finally got the message. This somewhat complacent canine had to bark as well as wag his tail.

Not long after we opened (to generally favorable reviews), numerous signs of trouble were appearing: The running time of the acts was disturbingly variable. Some performances were losing their polish. Late arrival for the half hour call was becoming a habit. Most disturbingly, the dressing room waste baskets were beginning to overflow with empty miniatures—cute bottles of Bushmills and Jameson's.

José Quintero had poured his heart into the show and had now moved on. He was not interested in coming back to have a look, give notes, bring everyone up to the mark, or for any other reason. Besides, at this point a director's insights were not needed. There was no mystery about what was wrong; it was all obvious. Well, keeping the show in shape is the SM's responsibility. So, fix it, Edward.

And so I did, or tried to do, with notes, with cajolery, with appeals to professional pride, and, yes, finally with barks, threats, any damn thing that would serve my turn. And, after a time, our tottering ship gradually began to right itself. But there was one actor over whom I had no control.

He was one of the principals, an elderly Irishman of irresistible puckish charm and great comedic skills—who showed off that puckish charm and those comedic skills only when he damn well pleased. He was that worst kind of actor to have in a long run: lazy. He would wander energyless through the performances in the early part of the week, then maybe turn it on come the weekend and the bigger crowds. Nothing I tried had any effect on his errant behavior.

Finally, I told Ted and José they had to chose between the lazy leading actor and me. They chose me. As a result the show became tighter and more disciplined, though our leading actor's replacement was a couple levels lower in the comedic department. I know I made the right decision; I only wish I could have found a way to make his predecessor shape up.

The only dubious activity I decided not to address was the accumulation of those cute little whiskey bottles. So long as I didn't see them, and the performances were not affected—and they weren't—I let it pass. The better part of valor prevailed. I didn't want to be waylaid in some Greenwich Village back alley by an outraged Hibernian deprived of his poteen.

Brooks Atkinson of the *Times* had given *The Quare Fellow* a generous review. For myself, whatever the difficulties with the company, I was immensely proud to be part of the enterprise and hugely admiring of the product. The authenticity of Behan's prison lingo was given authentic voice by my Irish charges, and despite its numerous drawbacks, the spare low-ceilinged Circle stage was able to suggest both cellblock and prison yard.

The tension in the play, often unspoken, is driven by an almost classical inevitability as the execution nears. (The "quare fellow," by the way, is prison slang for an inmate under sentence of death.) As the fatal time draws near, the "old lags" get more restless, the guards more twitchy, and the hammering clamor of the prison telegraph more insistent. Then, suddenly, unexpectedly, a quiet scene takes place, an utterly commonplace scene that always gave me the chills.

Night in the prison yard: a distant harmonica plays, two warders wait restlessly upstage, talking of someone they refer to as "Himself."

Then we hear whistling—a catchy Music Hall tune. The warders advance a pace or two, one holds up a lantern, and out of the darkness downstage appears a middle-aged figure possessed of a certain seedy panache suggestive of racetracks and betting parlors. He saunters across the yard followed by his short, vacant-faced assistant, and greets the senior warder with amiable chat, all the while, with a toothpick, artfully harvesting the last of his fish and chips. Then with the squinting mastery of a proud craftsman, he talks expansively of platform heights and body weights and the length of fall. "Himself," the hangman, has arrived.

Aunt Caroline

I had an aunt who was important in my growing up. Caroline Lexow Babcock was my mother's elder sister.

It was Aunt C. who, when I was a goofy, buck-toothed twelve-year-old, introduced me to Keats, Shelley, Buddhism, and Pierre-Auguste Renoir. I was spellbound by her love of the arts. She could talk about painting or poetry with an eloquence, a kind of aesthetic refinement, that entranced me. Her eyes would focus upward, a forefinger might lightly touch her cheek, and her pleasingly mellow voice would expand on the riches of Renoir's " Luncheon of the Boating Party." I listened enthralled, then dashed out the next day to the Phillips Collection in Washington, DC, so I could see the wonder myself.

When I knew her best, she was living with us in Georgetown, working for the National Women's Party, headed by Alice Paul. She was lobbying the Senate on behalf of the Equal Rights Amendment. This was in the

late '30s, mind. Its passage was to be the climax of a career spent fighting for women's causes.

When, over her objections, the amendment was
brought to the floor of the Senate too soon, it was
promptly killed. She realized that passage of such radical legislation would not take place her lifetime, and she
retreated to her ramshackle farmhouse on a mountain
in western New Jersey, where she lived for several more
decades, a lonely but still passionate pacifist, vegetarian, and proto-feminist visited from time to time by her
adoring relatives.

Shortly after *The Quare Fellow* opened, knowing she
was an ardent opponent of capital punishment, I wrote
to her about the production. A few weeks later, much to
my delight, she decided to make one of her infrequent
trips down the mountain and "put aside an afternoon
to see Mr. Behan's play." I arranged the matinee ticket
and was at curbside when her cab pulled up. She seemed
in good spirits as I escorted her to the best seat in the
house, then went about my stage managerial duties.

We met after the performance. She was oddly sub-
dued. I had been sure that our production of *The Quare
Fellow*—such an effective piece of theater, so consonant
with her political views—would elicit the old superlatives, but they were not forthcoming. It turned out
that what was bothering her was not the production,
which she admired, but the audience. She went on to
tell me about her theater-going as a young woman. She
had grown up in Nyack, New York, in a formidable
Victorian manse on the banks of the Hudson where my

grandfather, "the Senator" (he was a member of the NY State Legislature), a small, stern man with a crisp Van Dyke beard and penetrating blue eyes, held sway.

Because of her fine mind and unquenchable energy, as a teenager she was given a fair amount of latitude for that time. But when the Senator heard that she had gone down to New York City to see a play by that impious Irish blackguard, George Bernard Shaw, she got the full blue-eyed glower and was told that she would be disowned if he ever heard of such activities again. Being determined as well as rebellious, she went right on seeing such plays. She simply made sure Papa (accent on the second syllable) never found out.

How fascinating it was to hear that fifty years before I came to New York, my aunt was slipping into town to see the New Drama in some out-of-the-way playhouse, perhaps not unlike Circle in the Square.

"Oh, Angel," she said (Aunt Caroline gave her pet relatives hideously embarrassing nicknames, but since they were a mark of her favor, we never objected), "you just can't imagine how thrilling it was then. Just being in the midst of that audience, feeling the élan vital, was intoxicating. I don't think the productions were especially good, probably rather amateurish compared to what I saw this afternoon. But it made no difference whatsoever. We were all on fire with the messages in those plays. GBS, Ibsen, Strindberg—they were our gods. They talked to our souls. It was all fiercely exciting."

She looked around the empty theater. "All this is very nice, but you must forgive me, my dear … it seems a bit bland. The theater I remember was electrifying. Such a shame you haven't the same magic here."

She paused, reflecting, and then looked at me sadly. "We thought we could change the world, and that made all the difference."

Despite the high quality of the *Quare Fellow* production, despite the positive reviews, it soon became apparent that Brendan Behan's prison drama was not going to have a long run. Audiences were dwindling, so José began thinking about what to do next. He surprised (and alarmed) us by choosing that object of every stagestruck high school kid's fancy, that inoffensive low-cost epic, the renowned slice of "oh-gosh-gee-willikers Americana" *Our Town* by Thornton Wilder. Within three weeks, rehearsals started. Two weeks more, and our cynicism began to fade as we came to realize that our Panamanian magician was putting together a first-class revival of a great American classic.

Glowing reviews greeted the opening. The production ran for a year. (And I never had to raise my voice.)

Thornton Wilder reminded me of a favorite uncle, warm and chatty. Novelist, playwright, and one of the foremost intellectuals of his time, Mr. Wilder knew everything and everybody and yet seemed devoid of ego; he was as approachable and accommodating as your Uncle Fred.

In 1959, he was in his early 60s, stocky, tweedy, and fairly brimming over with captivating New England vigor—a real towering intellect in a deceptive package: folksy urbanity you might call it.

When I first encountered him, he was saying a few words to the cast of *Our Town*. He had been out of the country when we opened, but now a month later, back in the States, he came with his sister for a look-see, following which he asked to speak to the company.

If I was expecting a stumbling scholar's discourse, filled with long pauses as he attempted to decipher notes scribbled in the darkness, Mr. Wilder let me down. Suddenly, he was ranging back and forth in front of the company like a football coach at half time. There were noisy kudos for what the company had accomplished, praise for individual actors, and cheerleader-like exhortations to keep up the high level of play.

Then he stopped and changed course. He wanted to give us a little criticism—"just to show all the praise was sincere," he said with a wink. A friendly admonition followed about the tone of the third act—the one that takes place in the cemetery—that the folks who played the departed should resist any emotion, should keep the attack dry and remote. He didn't want to belabor it—just a reminder.

Next, a new subject: the stage. He wanted us to know that the playing space at Circle in the Square represented the future of theater architecture and the salvation of the theater as an art form.

How's that? If I had any thoughts about the stage at all, it was simply as the awkward, be-columned playing space we were stuck with, dictated no doubt by the size of the dance floor, the creation of the nightclub impresario who built the place.

No, Mr. Wilder said, we should think of our stage's shortcomings as strengths. No wings? Excellent. No flies? Hurrah!

I have an indelible memory of him, rubbing his palms together gleefully as he prophesied the mighty thunder that would sound when centuries-old, rot-encrusted proscenium arches came crashing down from coast to coast!

And what would replace them? Theaters like ours! That most ancient and best of all possible theater forms: the open stage!

The open stage. I may have heard the term earlier, but I thought of it as applying only to classical theaters like that one up in Canada where they were doing Shakespeare: Stratford, Ontario. Was this special pleading from the author of *Our Town,* with its bare-bones mise-en-scène, or could this peppery old sage be right? Was a big revolutionary change coming? If asked, I think most of us would have responded: "Not a chance."

But for now he was filling us with pride and delight. When he was finished, before we could crowd around him to hear more, he was gone. I heard he was staying in New York for a while and hoped I would get to see him again.

I don't think I realized until I began to write about this time in my life how important it was to me. At Circle in the Square I had to become an enforcer of discipline and so became more disciplined myself. And despite all the grief, I will always be grateful to those hard-drinking Irishmen for toughening me up for the road ahead. Finally, there was José, who showed this aspiring director, whose natural focus was on the externals of play-making, that there was a whole other way to go about the work, one that dealt more profoundly with the inner life of actor and character but without falling into the trap of dead-end Method self-indulgence. He was a beguiling and inspiring presence, which I'll underscore with one story about him and Circle in the Square, from the following year.

———

By 1959 the real estate moguls had decided that the south side of Sheridan Square would be better served by a Brobdingnagian apartment house, so a wrecking ball was waiting to reduce our poor old theater to so much kindling.

Not only did Circle need to find a new home, but also money had to be raised to finance the move. Eventually, a new theater was found way east on Bleecker Street. As for the funding, our producer, Ted Mann, decided on a time-honored theater means: the benefit performance! That's the one that takes place on the theater's dark night, for which actors contribute their services and well-to-do patrons shell out astronomical amounts of cash to get in the door.

This benefit—a one-time-only dazzling evening—was to consist of highlights of ten years at Circle in the Square. All those ex-Circle actors, now stars, coming back to do a scene from the play that was their launching pad! Then scenes from *Our Town*, with Mr. Wilder as the SM! And the capper: Jason Robards and the entire cast of *The Iceman Cometh* to enact the play's climactic scene!

A lot of the organizing fell to me. I was most uncertain about rounding up the *Iceman* cast, but once word spread about what was afoot, they were calling in, demanding to be part of the show.

Finally, there they all were, together again, back at Circle in the Square for one last rehearsal, all bright-eyed and Sunday School clean, that famous stinky bunch (fifteen strong) that had brought *The Iceman Cometh* to life, reunited with their erstwhile mentor, Hickey—Jason Robards.

I use the term "stinky" advisedly. When I started at Circle, I heard more than one salty anecdote about the conflicts that took place when stage managerial desire for at least a minimum standard of hygiene collided with actors' passion for realism that insisted that the clothing of the deadbeat alcoholic habitués of Harry Hope's bar had to remain filthy and malodorous, *or else*. Some nasty tugs of war resulted.

But now it was time for joyously reconnecting before the rehearsal began. First came twenty minutes of rowdy, backslapping "How-the-hell-are-ya? What-the-hell-ya-been-doing?" bonhomie. They were all on their feet—so many good buddies to hook up with. They didn't even notice when start time for the rehearsal had passed, and I was not about to tell them. No one knew where the hell José was.

Gradually the chatter thinned and they sat down, scattered around the theater. The talk continued for a time, then faded. It became quiet … dead quiet. The time was now 7:40 p.m.; rehearsal had been called for 7:00.

We hear a sound from downstairs: the outside door to the lobby closing. He's here.

Muffled footsteps as he climbs to the upper lobby. Now he is in sight. Some look away—others stare at him reproachfully. This is unforgivable.

He walks unhurriedly up the half flight to the theater, then onto the down right corner of the stage and stops. No one speaks; they are waiting for the apology. There will be none.

Robards is seated way up left. José walks slowly toward him, stops eight feet away, and holds out his arms. Jason rises with a wry shrug (you can almost hear his teeth grinding); he walks to José; they embrace. Then Jason starts to pull away, but José won't let him go completely; he holds him at arm's length. Their eyes lock. Then after several beats José lets him go, and watches as Jason walks back to his place and sits.

Not a word has been spoken—not by José, not by Jason or anyone else in the theater.

This silent ritual is repeated one by one with the entire company. Next José walks toward Addison Powell, who played Willie Oban. José stops, extends his arms, then Powell gets up and walks to José. Next the *abrazo*, then the holding at arm's length, the release, and on to another.

Never a word is spoken through the whole, endless ceremony. All these tough New Yorkers, all bound by invisible ligatures to their Panamanian *brujo*. Finally, it is done. The silence is broken, and they go quietly to work.

Sitting there, I wasn't quite sure what I'd seen—was it a performance? an improv? Or had I just witnessed some crazy eremite saint, down from his mountain cave, reconnecting with his acolytes? Or was it a foreigner who'd had a few too many and couldn't find the English words for an apology?

Whatever it was, it was unforgettable magic—Quintero-style. Potent stuff. Still alive in my memory sixty years on.

Myself in the Circle days.

Despite the rigor of my Circle apprenticeship, I did manage to slip in additional projects during those years, both personal and professional. First, I fell in with Rita Weinberg, bright, attractive, and terrifically witty. She was on the fast track of young producers at CBS. A successful two-year alliance went to hell after six months of matrimony. But it was Rita who, with numerous enticements and threats, argued this confirmed claustrophobe onto an airplane for the first time, thus making my continent-wide career possible, for which I'm forever in her debt.

I was given two more productions to direct at Equity Library Theatre in New York City: *The Torchbearers* by George Kelly and Shakespeare's *The Merry Wives of Windsor*. Run at that time by the shrewd and tasteful producer Lyle Dye, ELT is the union-sponsored Off-Broadway playhouse where many beginners like me got their start, a theater that managed to prosper on a shoe string—each show had less than a hundred bucks for sets, props, and costumes.

And, like everyone else in the New York theater world at that time, I acted in *The Fantasticks* at the Sullivan Street Playhouse. It was a brief stint replacing an actor who was getting married, but it was my New York debut and farewell performance all in one package. I played the ancient actor Henry Albertson: "Indians off left!"

The Antioch Shakespeare Festival

Great theaters begin with ideas: Stanislavski and Nemirovich-Danchenko talked through the night at the Slavansky Bazaar, and slowly ideas emerged that came to life as the Moscow Art Theater. John Houseman and Orson Welles, arguing noisily, hammered out the ideas and ideals that would take shape as the Mercury Theater. Great dreams, grand concepts, dazzling ideas that no doubt made readers of the first season's brochure gurgle with delight.

Ideas don't create theaters, however; people do—stubborn, dogged, often unmannerly people. Endless resources of energy are needed for the task. The savvy of a street fighter is a must, coupled at times with the brainless resolve of a charging rhinoceros.

Thinking of these qualifications, a real street fighter like Joseph Papp comes easily to mind. I remember him gutting it out with Robert Moses over that piece of real estate in Central Park. And all his other fights, with critics, with directors, and most anyone who got in his way.

But then, take a glamorous and erudite lady like Zelda Fichandler, cofounder of Arena Stage in Washington, DC—would she be up for that kind of conflict, mano a mano with the forces of darkness? You'd hardly think so, and yet … and yet …

I sat with her once as she told stories of the early times of her theater: how precarious it was, with utter ruin lurking around the corner for years on end. How between seasons the only evidence that Arena Stage existed was a shoebox. No money, no staff, no theater—just a shoebox where she kept the precious 3 × 5 file cards, each containing the name, address, and telephone number of a single subscriber. Season after season, starting all over again from nothing, from a shoebox! How many times did she have to prove herself?

When I asked her what aesthetic principles sustained her through those hard times, she exploded with laughter: "Aesthetic principles! Oh, no, Ed, it was nothing like that." (A pause—her eyes narrowed.) "1 was just determined not to let those bastards put me down." Suddenly, it was obvious that beneath the glamour and the erudition, the lady knew how to use her dukes.

I got to know one of those tough and relentless creators of theater many years ago. He came disguised as a college professor.

One look at Arthur and you knew exactly where he belonged. The tweed jacket, the glasses, the scholarly diffidence, the charmingly cluttered mind. Here was a man for the classroom, made to shine before adoring undergraduates and instill in them a love of Milton or ancient Greek or some other arcane corner of intellectual endeavor.

All wrong.

His entire life fired by unstoppable zeal, Arthur Lithgow created theaters, often out of nothing, in places where they never existed before. One day you'd be looking at a deserted foundry; ten days later you'd be lining up to see a production of *The Matchmaker* (Thornton Wilder). An art gallery got turned into a home for *The Trojan Women* (Euripides). If the playhouse he was running got shut down because of fire regulations, another would pop up nearby. And once, when a season he'd put together had a company and a staff but lacked a theater, he made up the deficiency by building one. And I don't mean that in the sense of "having one built," i.e., supervising architects and contractors. No, he built it himself with hammer and nails and a few passionate followers.

On a hot summer evening in southern Ohio, on the campus of Antioch College in 1952, the Antioch Shakespeare Festival had its modest beginning. On an outdoor platform built by A. Lithgow and friends with lumber salvaged from a burnt-out dormitory, peopled by a young semi-pro company, costumed on the cheap and illuminated by leko lights hung in the surrounding trees, an infinitesimal audience watched a production of one of the Bard's lesser-known chronicle plays, *The Life and Death of King John*.

Why in the world would you open a Shakespeare festival with such an obscure play? Well, Arthur had decided to do a season of the chronicle plays. *All* the chronicle plays. There are eight of them (actually ten, but his plan was to telescope the three parts of *Henry VI* into one evening), and simple logic dictated starting at the beginning of the story: in the thirteenth century with *King John*. Here is a list of the productions he hoped to produce that summer:

The Life and Death of King John
The Life and Death of King Richard II
The First Part of Henry IV
The Second Part of Henry IV
The Life of Henry V
Henry VI (Parts I–III)
The Tragedy of King Richard III
The Famous History of the Life of King Henry the VIII

His daring idea was to produce these monsters in summer-stock style, with a new play every week. Week One, *King John* plays in the evening, while *Richard II*, the next chapter of the chronicle, would rehearse during the day. Week Two, *Richard II* plays and *Henry IV, Part 1* rehearses, and so on, until all eight productions are mounted. At the end of the season there would be two weeks of "Grand Repertory": four centuries of English history unfolding night by night, production by production from the days of Eleanor of Aquitaine in the twelfth century to the birth of Elizabeth the First in 1533. At least that was the plan.

But the afternoon of the first performance, Arthur was somewhere beyond opening night nerves—this was almost suicidal anxiety. He had worked all the previous night until dawn (when the rising sun brings all outdoor techs to a screeching halt) trying to bring order to a ragged, ill-disciplined tech/dress rehearsal that ended with many problems still unsolved. Now he began to doubt the premise of the whole enterprise.

Getting a contemporary six-character comedy up in a week is one thing, but whipping a panoramic Shakespearean chronicle into shape in only forty hours of rehearsal? *Impossible*—as the ensuing performance would no doubt prove. The actors barely had their lines down, the lighting was a mess and production values nonexistent. For a play that cries for first-class spectacle, how much can you deliver when you have a pittance with which to mount each production? And then there were the clothes: a joke. To save money, a "unit costume" had been designed. The result? In their matching tabards and tights, with different colored sashes and jewelry to give them some individual identity, whether impersonating king or commoner, all the actors came off looking like a group of excessively vain pageboys.

Nothing could be done. Time had caught up with them. Now the audience was beginning to arrive. The debacle only awaited the setting of the sun.

Some things, however inescapable their crash and burning may seem, are not, let us rejoice, to achieve the expected result. Such was the case with the first performance of the Antioch Shakespeare Festival. Yes, the costumes were ridiculous, and the lights did not always come up where the actors were. Some of the actors were not even actors, so lines were dropped, entrances mistimed, and among several unwelcome surprises, late in the performance a stray dog decided to join the fun and bounded up on stage. And then there was the train …

But all this didn't really matter. The audience had decided the performance was going to be a success. The wild yowl of a train passing a few hundred yards from the theater (it was the 10:10 to

Xenia), which froze the players into inaction, only helped to make the occasion unique.

They were a small group, to be sure, but an enthusiastic one, made up of those bright folks you find in and around a college town. "It was almost," Arthur said years later, "as if they were willing the theater into existence." Shortcomings were overlooked, effective moments acclaimed, and the whole evening buoyed by their supportive spirits. Even the dog was not about to let the company down, for after a moment of disorientation in the lights, among the bizarrely clad actors, he moved slowly to the dying king and gave his hand a consoling lick.

There was a hunger loose that night, hunger for the kind of theater Arthur wanted to make. However imperfect this first presentation, nothing would be allowed to stand in the way of its success. And how that little group kicked up a mighty ruckus when it was time for curtain calls!

Succeeding audiences showed up with some of the same spirit. There was a problem, however: they also showed up in the same numbers. Opening followed opening, but they continued to play to small houses. By midseason, the company realized they were never going to make it financially; they were only digging themselves deeper into debt. The closing notice was posted.

Then, the miracle happened. Almost overnight, the crowds arrived. *Henry V* did it; no one is quite sure why. Was it the play itself? The popularity of the Olivier film that made the play familiar? David Hooks's performance as the king? Accumulating word of mouth? It's a mystery, but by the time they got to Grand Repertory, extra bleachers were added to take care of the overflow. Increasing crowds meant more money in the till. It allowed Arthur to hire a real costume designer; the awful tabards began to disappear. The great experiment could continue.

Quite unexpectedly, a hot spot was glowing on the bleak cultural map of the early '50s. First the curious came from the surrounding area, then from surrounding states and further afield. The press started showing up; even a stringer from the *New York Times* arrived. Reviewers had a few quibbles, but by and large they were charmed by the young company and the cheekiness of the enterprise.

———————

In future seasons, the company continued to work its way through the Shakespearean canon. The second summer (1953) featured the Greek and Roman plays, another group of eight. That season presented a greater challenge in many ways than the first year, containing theatrical godzillas like *Julius Caesar* and *Antony and Cleopatra*.

As the summers passed, the company learned how to cope with the feverish pace. Actors playing leads arrived in Yellow Springs with their roles well in hand. And even if shows wobbled a bit on opening night, they hit their stride within a few performances. The actors also learned to tune their voices and actions to the demands of a large outdoor theater—a good thing in the main, except when the comedy was allowed to get outsized and deplorably cornpone. I, myself, was responsible for a notable example of comic excess as the Second Gravedigger in *Hamlet*, who, incapable of getting a laugh, became even more excessive each night in the search for one.

On the other hand, sometimes the comedy could be glorious—which you well know, if you were lucky enough to see the young Pauline Flanagan play Rosalind or frightening, as when small, compact Jack Bittner with his mighty basso clawed his way onto stage as the brutal Thersites in *Troilus and Cressida*.

Each season the budget grew and with it, so did the sophistication of the physical productions. When I joined the company as an actor of small parts in 1956, there were no lekos in the trees; special lighting instruments had been designed for the long throws required by the outdoor theater. Arthur's jerrybuilt platform gave way to a sleek, many-leveled adaptation of the Elizabethan stage.

Henry Hewes, writing in the *Saturday Review*, was generous in his praise. He compared the Lear of a 26-year-old Carnegie Tech grad (Ellis Rabb) favorably with that of John Gielgud and found that "the overall standards of speech and movement compared favorably with those of the top Shakespearean repertory companies in England." He concluded by reminding us of an important milestone that we had completely lost sight of in the hurly-burly of production, for "on Wednesday night August 8, 1956, Arthur Lithgow became the first man ever to have produced all of Shakespeare's plays over five consecutive seasons."

The Antioch Shakespeare Festival took great pride in presenting all its Shakespeare uncut—every word Old Will ever put into an actor's mouth in all thirty-six plays, all learned, all said, all heard over five brief summers. Falstaff strutted, Iago skulked, deadly conspiracies were hatched, armies fought, and ghosts walked, as the great Shakespearean panorama unfolded on the Antioch stage.

We had been part of a feat that had never been done before and would probably never be done again. Add to that the favorable reviews, the overflow crowds, the scholars, political figures, and celebrities that were showing up—all these things combined to make it a triumphant summer. Truly, Arthur had come a far piece since whacking together that wobbly platform that supported *King John*. The tentative flickers that he had nursed to life in a little clearing in Ohio had now become a mighty bonfire, and those who had been part of it all, whether as watchers or doers, danced joyously in its light.

Then suddenly it was all over, period. Revels ended. Arthur's dream—pffft.

This is how it happened: All the while he had been mastermatinding the festival in the summer, come winter Arthur was a full-time professor in the Theater Department of Antioch College. What a lot of us in the company didn't know was that for years he'd been fighting a rear-guard action with his own department, which had quite different ideas about how the theater should be run than did Assistant Professor Lithgow. One of those hurtful conflicts between the profession and the academy ensued. As the years passed and the festival grew in every way—popularity, profitability, sophistication—so the tension between Arthur and his colleagues grew as well. By the end of the 1956 season, the situation was intolerable—old and dear friends had become sworn enemies. Finally the college began using its formidable muscle to oppose his plans. Arthur stayed on for one painful year of transition and then headed off to Toledo and Massachusetts for a short while.

Stan Hywet (pronounced "stan heewit") Hall is a large, graceful pseudo-Tudor manor house of some fifty rooms, built in 1920 by a rubber (not robber) baron named Seiberling on a generous plot of tree-shaded land in semi-suburban Akron, Ohio. The Seiberlings have long since departed, and the compound, now something of a tourist attraction, is run by a nonprofit board, along with a cadre of volunteers, some of whom (demon gardeners all), look after the grounds. In the spring of 1960, these guardians of Stan Hywet were in great distress. They had heard that a troupe of actors was coming to trample their delphiniums and deface their greensward with large wooden platforms and hundreds of folding chairs.

Arthur Lithgow, the American theater's Johnny Appleseed, was at it again. Having left Antioch and settled in Toledo for a spell (his final Antioch Shakespeare Festival was produced on a stage in the local zoo), he had moved twice again and was now leading his minions onto the back lawn of Stan Hywet in the very shadow of the manse.

I was among their number. After I had supervised an experimental workshop at Antioch, Arthur had given me my first professional directing jobs in the early 1950s—a one-act musical by Leonard Bernstein called *Trouble In Tahiti*, then later a full production, O'Neill's *Ah, Wilderness* (the one that was performed in that theater in the Toledo zoo). So when the producing duties at Stan Hywet demanded all his attention, Arthur turned the artistic leadership of the acting company over to me—more, l am convinced, from desperation than desire.

> *Scene: A cartridge snaps into a tape machine. The PLAY button is depressed.*
>
> DISEMBODIED VOICE. Good morning, Mr. Call. The job of artistic director of the Akron Shakespeare Festival, should you choose to accept it, will include casting a company of thirty actors, as well as directing the four plays of this season's repertory, which are:
> *The Life and Death of King Richard II*
> *The First Part of Henry IV*
> *The Second Part of Henry IV*
> *The Life of Henry V*
>
> They will, of course, be produced in accordance with the celebrated Lithgow Rules: a mere forty

hours of rehearsal per production—even such gigantic productions as these. The fact that you have never directed a Shakespeare play and that your knowledge of the Bard does not extend much beyond "But, soft, what light through yonder window breaks" and "Friends, Romans, countrymen" should not be looked on as a serious impediment since there are several months in which to school your native ignorance. The physical dangers of the enterprise are few. Wearing a weapon will be unnecessary. However, falling on your face is a real possibility.

Good luck, Ed.

Also, be on the lookout for indignant gardeners with trowels.

This tape will self-destruct in five seconds.

Arthur had given me an enormous challenge. Fortunately, he never bothered to ask me if I was up to it. Just as fortunately, I never asked myself; I just went to work. On-the-job training you might call it.

Overnight I became a scholar, something I had never managed in my desultory college years. I bought every modern edition of the four plays I could lay my hands on and set about exploring carefully, word by word, exactly what each text meant. Then I discovered those mighty compendiums of critical wind, the variorum (annotated) editions. With these I set about exploring carefully, word by word, what everyone since 1616 thought the texts meant. I was a happy man, alone with my books, dawdling over the niceties of interpretation. I even went so far as to start investigating the history of the real people who were the basis for Shakespeare's characters.

Meanwhile, the clock was ticking.

I finally realized I had to do something in the way of more practical preparation. So I put my books aside, unrolled a ground plan of our fleuricide stage, and began to address the first big blocking challenge: the court scene at the beginning of *Richard II*.

I didn't get far, because soon it was time to start casting. There was no money to rent space, so by default the apartment on Barrow Street in the Village where Rita and I lived became the casting office cum audition studio for Akron Shakespeare Festival's opening season. It was a basement apartment, a small, vermin-troubled basement apartment with the ceiling not much above head height. Needless to say, it was not the ideal place to audition for a vast outdoor theater. At times, the scene must have looked bizarre and Ionesco-like, with me sitting, courteously attentive, five feet from an actor I had just asked to reach northern New Jersey with his voice.

I had learned from Arthur that repertory was the ideal way to do theater—ideal for the actors, ideal for the audience. What he hadn't taught me was that putting it all together was a nightmare for the director.

What directing I had accomplished previously I'd done one play at a time: I made a list of the characters in the play, saw a lot of actors, found the right type for each role, then filled in the blanks opposite the appropriate character's name. Simple. But now I was looking at a list of 142 roles, to be performed by thirty actors, in four different plays.

A Brief Look into a Tortured Mind

Scene: Night in a basement apartment. Sitting at a card table, illuminated by the light of a single gooseneck lamp, the distraught Director pores over numerous lists, charts, jottings on shirt boards, etc. Papers and books strewn

about on the floor. Nearby the outline of his wife is seen,
slumbering on a pullout bed. The Director pulls at his
hair with quiet vehemence and then goes back to his lists.
We hear his thoughts.

DIRECTOR. Okay, let's try it this way: Fred will play Strood
   in *Richard II*, Lord Elgin in *Henry IV*, and Brillig in
   Henry V. No, wait a minute, he can't play Strood, I've
   already promised that to Ted. Maybe I could buy Ted
   off with Sir Walter Blunt—provided he could do the
   Midlothian accent and knows how to joust. And that
   would leave Ned with Surlington, Warthog, and Old
   Pizzle. That would work. No, no, dumbass! I'm forgetting the scene at Chipping Camden when Warthog
   and Old Pizzle bring a shrubbery to the Queen!
   They're on stage at the same time!

(Pulls at hair with quiet vehemence again, then goes back to
   his lists.)

Hmmmm. Let's see …

———◆———

Amazingly, despite the complications, after several weeks, the
company was taking shape. Only one major line of roles remained
unfilled, one of the best I had to offer, actually. It included John
of Gaunt in *Richard II*, Pistol in the *Henry IV* plays and Owen
Glendower for *Henry V*, but finding an actor capable of Pistol's extravagance, the prophetic dignity of Gaunt, and the posturings of
that warrior windbag Owen Glendower seemed impossible.

Time was running out. I was due to leave for Ohio the next day.
I had spent the morning on the phone, getting suggestions from

actor friends and the one agent who would talk to me. I set up auditions for the afternoon, but nothing came of it—a lot of no-shows and no one who was anywhere near right.

The day was ending. The sun was easing down into the slot between the buildings at the west end of Barrow Street. One more "suspect" to go. There was a knock.

I opened the door. The space was filled by a tall, gangly, bright-eyed young man. "Hi," he said perkily, "I'm your six o'clock." My spirits drooped; the voice was high and breathy. I turned away to allow myself one grind of my teeth for whomever had sent me this misfit. Having invited him in, I proceeded with a rather rote, end-of-day version of my spiel designed to warm the hearer to the idea of playing Shakespeare under the direction of a novice for marginal compensation on a sweltering lawn in the Midwest.

He was not deterred, however, and pipingly informed me that he wanted to read John of Gaunt. He rose and crossed the five feet to the center of the room, turned back with a serious mien and let fly. I had been hearing a piccolo—suddenly a great pipe organ spoke out:

> This royal throne of kings, this sceptered isle,
> This earth of majesty, this seat of Mars,
> This other Eden, demi-paradise,
> This fortress built by Nature for herself …

The novice director's jaw opened in wonder, his eyes glistened, the walls breathed outward, and all the rats of Barrow Street applauded wildly and called for an encore. He performed two encores, actually—one as Pistol, one as Glendower—and was hired on the spot.

The actor's name is Ken Ruta. By this time, his talent has been admired by millions, and that voice has mesmerized audiences all over the United States. I tell this theater story not only because it was the beginning of an important, if infrequent, collaboration for both of us, but also as evidence of the astonishingly good luck I had in casting the season.

Along with Ken, a cadre of terrific young actors joined at the beginning of their professional careers:

- Donald Moffat, newly arrived in the United States from the Old Vic, who would play Richard II and Chorus in *Henry V*.
- Robert Milli, recent grad of Catholic University in Washington, DC. Among the great Shakespearean leading roles, Henry Plantagenet is unique, appearing as a leading character in three plays: starting as the wastrel Prince Hal in the *Henry IV*s, he matures into the triumphant warrior king in *Henry V*. Bob was all charm and dashing good looks as Hal, then showed his serious classical chops in *Henry V*.
- McIntyre Dixon, a truly great comedian, hideously underused in small roles.
- Stanley Jay, the director's delight, a young actor who could impersonate great age convincingly. He played Hal's buddy, Poins, but also the aged Duke of York in *Richard II* and the doddering country Justice Shallow, in *Henry IV, Part 2*.
- John Carradine Jr., son of the famous actor. Quiet, a touch distant, but very hard working. Worshipped Olivier and, like Olivier, was obsessive about the nose

of any character he played. Kept a hot plate, a saucepan, and a gob of latex at a low boil near his dressing table, ever seeking the definitive schnoz. His principal role was Hotspur—a little light vocally, but an effective performer. Later changed his first name to David and became a kung fu master on TV.

· Two dynamite young character leads, Lee Henry and Ray Bieri.

· Also Arthur Lithgow's son, John, who recently reminded me that he did not just do walk-ons, as was my recollection, but had made his debut in *Henry V* as an actor, a real actor with lines. Two lines, actually:

Ambassadors from Harry, King of England
Do crave admittance to your Majesty.

Said, I am sure, with an authority beyond his fourteen years.

And a legion of others, among whom there must be mention of our invaluable costume designer, Oliver Olsen, who made magic out of nothing, and fast.

With the company set, I was off to Akron and the unavoidable crunch I had to face in attempting to direct Lithgow-style repertory.

———

Four Shakespeares in four weeks. The key in a situation like that is preparation, and I had not always been smart about how I spent my time. Too many hours luxuriating in subtle textual distinctions, not enough hours working out the moves. I should have had most of the blocking for all the shows in my head or on paper when I arrived in

Akron; that way, the productions would be on their feet quickly, and there would be time left for some real acting work. Remember too, that blocking, no matter how fast you do it, is still one important way of talking to actors. In giving a scene its physical shape, you are telling something about how it should be played. Avoid all those tedious time-wasting discussions about moves when the actors are still unsure of who they are and what they want. Let them do your moves two or three times, then talk.

So, here's how it turned out: I was overprepared for *Richard II*, underprepared for *Henry IV, Part 1* and completely unprepared when we got to *Henry IV, Part 2*. Fortunately, Arthur and his encyclopedic knowledge of Shakespeare came to my rescue, and he was able to start directing *Part 2* on a couple of days notice. That way I cadged some extra time to prep for *Henry V*.

Some memories: Introducing all thirty company members to the Akron supporters, knowing everyone's name and all the parts each played—this done without notes and deemed by those present to be an amazing feat of memory. If they had only known how many nights I spent ...

I remember pulling on a sweater against the dawn chill as the all-night lighting session for *Richard II* came to an end. With the stage lights out, we stopped and watched in the silence of a sort of sleep-deprived hypnosis as the soft glow from that hot red ball 93 million miles away crept slowly across the mullioned windows and ivy-clad crenellations of Stan Hywet—an excruciatingly long count, but a cue that put our lekos and vulgar strip lights to shame. We watched in wonder for a long while, then kicked into gear for another twenty-hour day.

I remember rehearsing in the broiling sun, watching game young performers working on the night scenes before the Battle of

Agincourt with much stamping of feet, rubbing of chilled hands, and shivering from the cold while the sweat poured into their eyes.

The rest of the experience passes as an amiable blur of maximum work and minimum sleep: the Month of the Scratchy Eyeballs. I had a wonderful, spirited company to work with and managed with Arthur's help to have each of the four plays in respectable shape by opening night. They were not the most profound interpretations of the pieces ever seen, but they were infused with youth and high spirits. That seemed to be enough for the critics and the audience, which latter grew through the brief season from a measly 150 to over 800 for the final performance of *Henry V*.

I returned to New York at the end of that summer in high spirits. Disappointed—that I would not be going into the *Guinness Book of World Records* as Fast Eddie, Conqueror of Four Shakespeares in Four Weeks—but feeling my apprenticeship as a director was going pretty well.

PART II:

The Genesis of an Early Regional Theater

The theater I found in New York City when I arrived back from Akron, Ohio, in the late summer of 1960 was not that different from what I found when I first arrived there in 1956. It was still a mecca of glamour and talent, still the wellspring of the best new plays and playwrights, and still the only destination if you were young, hungry, and seeking a career in the theater.

This was not altogether healthy. New York's dominance was so complete that it didn't leave room for much else. Everything theatrical seemed to emanate from there. Outside New York the road was active. There were lots of touring companies, but essentially they represented national circulation of the New York product. Summer stock flourished all over the country briefly each year but only with a fare of tested and approved Broadway plays.

As an example, if you lived in Kansas City in 1962 and were a serious playgoer—and by that, I mean someone interested in seeing great plays performed by first-rate actors in a setting of cultural significance—here is what you had to choose from: Touring shows, summer stock, music tents, and university and amateur productions.

In 1962 Kansas City had a population of 3 million. As in many fair-sized cities across the country, the generous citizens supported a first-rate opera company, a ballet ensemble, a major symphony orchestra, and a professional baseball team. How was it, some people began to ask, that the theater was left out of the cultural mix? We have tutus and tenors and trumpeters but no Hamlets, no Heddas, no Helens of Troy. If theater at its best can be the most popular and invigorating of the lively arts, why are we settling for only what New York decides to send us? Why not make our own theater?

Why not indeed?

It was the beginning of a national debate in which a new word entered the theatrical lexicon: decentralization. The American theater would enjoy a great new renaissance, the sages told us. Vibrant theater centers would spring up all over this great land of ours to slake our cultural thirst, if only a way could be found to "decentralize." The need was obvious, the logic irrefutable, and the prose lush and extravagant—sometimes foolish, sometimes inspiring from the likes of the *New York Times, Theatre Arts,* and others.

It represented the first stirring of an artistic idealism that would capture the imagination of several generations of young theater people and eventually lead to the creation of over 350 new professional theaters across the country.

A few intrepid pioneers were already out there, to be sure: Pasadena Playhouse, Arena Stage in Washington, DC, the Cleveland Play House, and Houston's Alley Theatre. They were a brave and enterprising vanguard, but they were too few in number to represent anything like a national movement.

Meanwhile, back in Manhattan, schemes were being devised to fill the national void. One of them was promulgated with much fanfare by the American National Theatre and Academy (ANTA), which at the time was neither a theater nor an academy, but a hothouse seething with High Ideals and Far-Reaching Visions. ANTA's solution was called the Forty Theatre Circuit Plan. In it, every city with a population over 750,000 (there were about forty at the time) would have a member theater. By some feat of cosmic entrepreneurial genius, forty different productions would open in these forty theaters on the same date. After a two-week run, they would all play continental musical chairs, and the production of, say, *Dear Brutus* starring Brian Aherne, would move from Milwaukie, Wisconsin, to Portland, Oregon, while *Macbeth* with Basil Rathbone would move from Portland to San Francisco, and *On Borrowed Time* featuring Gene Lockhart would move … and so on. The idea never got beyond the drawing board. There were others equally impractical, equally doomed.

———

In the midst of all this national head-scratching, three experienced theater men, one Irish and two American, hit the road with the idea of making something happen, and fast. They pulled up in cities from coast to coast, collected as many of the local movers and shakers together as they could, and then pitched the concept to them. In vivid and mouth-watering terms, they described the theater of artistic distinction and international prominence that they were determined to build in some city right here in the good old U.S. of A.

These cheeky junketeers were top Broadway SM Peter Zeisler, producer Oliver Rea, and director Tyrone Guthrie, the star of the group. The "glamorous troika," as I thought of them. At that time, Guthrie was the most famous, the most distinguished theater director in (as the press liked to state it) "the English-speaking world." He had risen to prominence as the leader of The Old Vic in London during its pre–World War II heyday, where he nurtured the careers of such promising young British actors as Laurence Olivier, Ralph Richardson, and Edith Evans. By 1962 he seemed to be everywhere: on the West End in London, on Broadway, and at the Metropolitan Opera House. His autobiography, *A Life in the Theatre*, had become a bestseller; he was also the founder and guiding genius of the Stratford Shakespeare Festival[2] in Ontario, Canada. Recently added to Guthrie's distinguished resumé was the Order of the Garter. He was now a knight, Sir Tyrone Guthrie, a genuine transatlantic theater colossus. When he talked about decentralization, people listened.

His message was quite simple: "Just as you have a symphony orchestra to play the great musical works and an art gallery for the masterpieces of painting, then, if this great city of (fill in the blank) is to be a true cosmopolitan center, it must have a theater in which the great works of dramatic literature can be brought to life."

What he proposed was the establishment of a *major, professional, resident repertory theater*. Here, for some, a definition of terms might be useful:

Major: Many successful theaters started small and then grew as they gained acceptance; Arena Stage in DC and Alley Theatre in Texas are two notable examples. This would not be the case with the theater Guthrie was proposing. It would be a large, first-class operation from the outset, with the best acting talent, the finest designers, the most innovative artisans and technicians, as well as state-of-the-art equipment for them to work with. He warned his listeners that it would not be cheap; Guthrie-style theater never was.

Professional: The company would be made up of professional performers—members of Actors' Equity Association—but it was

---

2   The current name is the Stratford Festival.

a far more exclusive club Guthrie intended to tap: simply the Best, top-rank stage actors from both sides of the Atlantic. Only someone as prestigious as Guthrie could attract such performers to such a remote outpost.

Resident: The nature of the theater would require that actors with a wide range of skills be sought: actors who could play a variety of roles in a variety of styles, who would be as comfortable in the plays of Tennessee Williams or Arthur Miller as they were in those of Shakespeare or Shaw. Fencing and dancing skills would be important, and for the relentlessly musical Guthrie, an ability to sing and read music was taken for granted. These actors would not be hired for a single production but for an entire season, preferably for a series of seasons. Along with the artisans, technicians, designers, and directors, they would not be briefly sojourning glamorous guests, but true residents of the city that was selected, involved not only in its artistic but also its civic life.

Repertory: A repertory company is, or course, a company with a repertoire, in this case a repertoire of theatrical productions, all of which are ready to be performed. It has two principal virtues: it avoids the deadening effect (to actors) of the endless repetition of the same role night after night, and it makes it possible for the audience to see a great deal of the theater's work in a short period of time. So when Mr. and Mrs. Watkins drive 200 miles to see what this new theater is all about, they don't just see a single show and go home. They see *Hamlet* on Friday evening, catch the matinee of *The Miser* on Saturday, and watch *Death of a Salesman* Saturday night.

Theater: At Stratford, Ontario, in 1956, along with the inauguration of a big new theatrical institution, Guthrie and designer Tanya Moiseiwitsch had launched what was identified as a new form of theater. Actually, a modern adaptation of classic and renaissance stages, it nevertheless seemed to the proscenium-sodden eyes of many as new, radical, and liberating. It is and has been historically known, much to the Stratford Festival creators' chagrin, as the thrust stage. The term they preferred (and the term used throughout these pages) is the open stage. Basically, it consists of a platform with the audience on three sides, a scenic back wall, and two or more tunnel entrances like those in a sports stadium that allow actors to enter through the audience, usually at the two front corners of the platform. The theater in Canada had been built almost exclusively for Shakespeare productions, and for that an open stage worked miraculously well. For Guthrie and Moiseiwitsch, the next step in the experiment was to create a theater of the same type that would be suitable for contemporary/realistic productions as well as classical ones, one that would serve Odets as well as it served Shakespeare. Thus, this new institution was to include a major experiment in stage architecture. Exciting to contemplate; also expensive.

And how were these proposals received? Guthrie's magnetism, his energy, his title, his eloquence, and the clarity of his vision, even his sprightly vulgarity, all combined to carry the day. Initially, he no doubt profited by the cultural deference Americans usually grant the British, but finally it was a quintessential American virtue that won them: thinking big.

The civic leaders smiled, swallowed hard, and then went about trying to get him what he wanted. Several cities became major contenders. Eventually it was narrowed to two: Detroit and Minneapolis. Both had made generous offers, but Minneapolis ("Old Minn" as Guthrie liked to call it) got the nod. He had been quite impressed by the youth and energy of the exploratory committee; they were all under forty. But the clincher was location. Detroit seemed to him part of the great Eastern megalopolis. He wanted to be out there in the middle of the continent—in the American heartland.

My destiny was to join him there for seven amazing years.

Early Days at Guthrie Theater

In the spring of 1962, it's my turn to face the peashooters of the Fates on West Forty-fourth Street, as my father had done before me. Just now I am full of myself. The long drought may be over. Directing work is starting to come my way. After doing two shows at a classy summer-stock theater, the Berkshire Playhouse, I have just been approached about directing a great Spanish classic at a burgeoning hot spot in the early years of the regional movement: the McCarter Theatre in Princeton, New Jersey. So, lubricated with self-regard, I'm whipping along Forty-fourth Street when I see a familiar face. It is Peter Zeisler, king of Broadway SMs, now set to be one of the leaders of a new theater in Minneapolis. He is standing in front of The Lambs Club, the actors' social club, hunched and glowering. He is dark, with penetrating blue eyes. He has a cigarette in his hand; he has a voracious way of smoking, as if each puff were the last before flicking away the butt and facing the firing squad.

We greet. I know him socially. His wife, Helen, played Mrs. Gibbs in José Quintero's production of *Our Town*, which I stage-managed at Circle in the Square; we met a couple of times at theater parties. "What's going on?" I ask. Interviews for the stage-management staff in Minneapolis, he tells me. Not going well. He seems too prickly to spend much time with. I move on.

A block further down Forty-fourth Street my pace slows. To work with Guthrie! Now that might be something to go for. I stop and retrace my steps, and as I do, Calderón de la Barca is losing his grip on my imagination.

"Listen, Peter, you know, I'd really like to see that old bastard direct a play."

I am ushered into the paneled quiet of The Lambs, and my journey to Minneapolis begins. A week later I'm signed on as an assistant stage manager (ASM)—one of two—and start packing.

Guthrie Nomenclature

I was hired to work *at* the Tyrone Guthrie Theatre, but that was only the name of a building. I signed a contract with, and my loyalties were to, the Minnesota Theatre Company. That name was dropped many years ago as an unnecessary confusion. Why, the cool managerial types inquired, have two different names, one for the theatre, another for the company? It only confuses the audience. So nowadays, if you perform in the Guthrie Theater, you work for the Guthrie Theater Company. It makes sense, I suppose, but I have an almost tribal attachment to the former label. Because I'm writing about those original days of the Great Guthrie Pleasure Palace, I'll stick with the names as I knew them then.

Tyrone Guthrie did not come to the heartland to create "Old Vic USA" or some oasis for ex-pat Brits. No, he wanted to make a specifically American theater, and what better way to announce that intention than by giving it an American name? Hence the Minnesota Theatre Company.

The fact that the name of the building swallowed the name of the company was entirely unexpected. After all, we know and celebrate the Group Theatre and the Moscow Art Theatre, but do we know the names of the buildings they played in?

Further, Guthrie made it plain he wasn't going to be around long. As he was a self-professed "mover on," it was his oft-stated intention to give up the reins of leadership after three years, adding genially, "then you Americans can fuck it up."

One more note, about the name of our leader. He had been granted a knighthood, so the proper form of address was Sir Tyrone, a moniker he did not encourage. For those who didn't feel they knew him well enough to call him "Tony," as most did, then "Dr. Guthrie" was the way to go. This was made possible by an honorary degree he had received from somewhere. However hard I tried, "Tony" was an impossibility for me. I settled on "Dr. Guthrie," later shortened to "Dr. G."

In 1962, Minneapolis had:

- A population of 510,000.
- The Foshay Tower, one of the highest buildings west of the Mississippi River, at 22 stories.
- A professional baseball team, the Minnesota Twins.
- A fashionable restaurant, Charlie's, often relied on for entertaining visiting big-wigs. Prime rib was the specialty. Appetizers were served on an immense lazy Susan, smack in the middle of the table: raw carrots, broccoli, cheese dip, and such. Classy.
- Lots of Scandinavians.

- A big state university with an active theater department led by Frank "Doc" Whiting, who was a pivotal figure in getting Guthrie's theatre company to Minneapolis.
- The Mississippi River, which meandered unnoticed on the eastern flank of the city.
- Numerous lakes, some quite large, close to downtown.
- Months of gray, forbidding, bone-chilling cold each year.

I cannot say that what I learned about Minneapolis in the seven years I was there would significantly enlarge the above compendium. The world I lived in was a miniscule circle, maybe half a mile in diameter, the center of which (when I first saw it) was an undistinguished-looking building in the last stages of construction behind the Walker Art Center on Hennepin Avenue, just south of downtown Minneapolis.

I was not disappointed by the sight, just puzzled. Two stories of glass wall brought to mind not theater but supermarkets or automobile showrooms. Later, large open screens sprayed with some kind of pebbly aggregate were anchored into place several feet in front of the glass. Standing on Vineland Place, one saw through big open rectangles in the screens to the theater beyond. From looking ordinary, the Tyrone Guthrie Theater went to looking different in a mildly arresting way. But why quibble about the exterior? Inside was a miracle.

I remember the smell of fresh-cut lumber and the sight of a wooden promontory, bordered on three sides by rising tiers for seats. A far cry from the theater Guthrie had made in Stratford, Ontario, with its classical pedigree and restful symmetrical grandeur—this place was all angles and juts. The platform defied description; there were no parallels, no comforting proportions. The damned thing wouldn't stay still.

I first saw it absolutely bare, looking jagged and impatient, floored with raw, almost white timber. The term "thrust stage" must have been inspired by the first sight of that wooden fist crashing into the center of the auditorium.

The seating was also irregular. On one flank (house right), a long sweep of seats rose from the edge of the stage to the top of the building at a daringly steep angle, while the rest of the arc surrounding the playing area had an easier slope with a shallow balcony overhead.

Even the seats themselves were resisting uniformity. Instead of the usual sea of red velvet or royal blue, each chair had its own color and not subtle pastels but noisy reds, blues, and greens. "Confetti seats," *New York Times* theater critic Walter Kerr aptly named them.

Despite the fact that I had worked on a similar stage at Antioch College, his platform seemed utterly unique. It had a spell, like Madison Square Garden set up for a prize fight, a spell that drew us. Meetings that could have taken place anywhere were held in the upper rows of the theater. It was weird, but we just liked being there. No one spoke of the ulterior motive, but the meeting over, we stayed on, shooting the breeze, always aware of that presence below us: the jagged platform, sizzling with possibility. What spectacles would there be? What theatrical magic awaited?

But all that was a way off. First there were practical considerations to be taken care of. Where was I going to live? Who were my coworkers? What exactly would my duties be?

The search for living quarters sent me trudging through the snow. After having seen and rejected several unpromising prospects, I arrived in front of a comfortable-looking old house on Summit Avenue on a hill behind the theater. I knocked. No answer. I knocked again, louder. Finally the door opened, and I was confronted by a beefy redhead, looking out of sorts—a large bear awakened in mid-hibernation. "Yes," it said in a somewhat theatrical baritone.

I explained my mission. I was told the lady of the house was out; he was one of the "lodgers." I asked if I might get a look at the room that was available? He allowed me to pass.

The interior was large, slightly rundown, and wonderfully inviting. The third floor, which had a private entrance, was occupied by several students from a local trade school. The first floor was the province of Mrs. Van Horne, the landlady. It was to the second floor, now being taken over by the theater folk, of which my surly redheaded guide seemed to be one, that I was now escorted. I was shown a big sunny front room filled with heavy old mahogany furniture; private bath (with marble shower yet); kitchen to share. Perfect! I told the bear I'd take it, and then I fled.

Back at the theater I checked into the SM's office. Rex Partington, the production SM, was genial and easygoing, the kind of boss you immediately wanted to please. Partington identified my landlady's housing guide: he was Guthrie's second in command, associate artistic director Douglas Campbell. Not a promising first encounter with the top brass.

The other ASM was Gordon Smith. We eyed each other uneasily. Both about the same age and though we were not noisy about it, both extremely ambitious. It looked as if there might be turf wars. As it turned out, we made a good team. Zeisler had chosen us shrewdly. We were both good SMs, but with contrasting strengths. My focus was all on directing, while Gordon had immense technical expertise. We came to each other's rescue more than once.

My first official task for the Minnesota Theatre Company was to go to the airport and pick up two company VIPs who were arriving together from London. Annette Garceau was to head the new costume shop, and Tanya Moiseiwitsch, the famous costume and set designer as well as Guthrie's longtime collaborator, was the architect of both the Stratford and Minneapolis stages. I was given a van with our newly created logo (a long red pennant in the shape of a G) freshly painted on the side, equipped with a map and directions, and coached on the correct pronunciation of Tanya's name: "moy-SAY-a-vich."

Nobody had told me what the ladies looked like, nor did I think to ask. Lodged in the back of my mind were a few grandiose assumptions, however.

I got lost, so was late arriving at the airport, and I dashed to the gate just as the passengers were descending the rolling stairs. In the lead was a formidably beautiful, foreign-looking lady enveloped in black fur. "Miss Moy-SAY-a-vich!" I gasped as I arrived at the foot of the stairs. Suddenly I was pushed aside by an annoyed associate. The beautiful lady swept past, the beautiful lady who I later learned was opera singer Anna Moffo, come to the Twin Cities to concertize.

But where could my quarry be? The plan was almost empty; the lounge was filled with the happy clamor of the newly reunited. Then I spotted her. She and her companion were just now coming down the stairs. She was striking—turned out just the way I expected a costume designer to be: bracelets, earrings, pins, some leather, a bit of fur. After heaving a mountainous sigh of relief, I began: "Miss Moy-SAY-a-vich, welcome, it's so ..." The lady raised an objecting hand and directed it toward her rather plain companion. "This is Miss Moiseiwitsch," she said.

I was now looking at a tired, unglamorous lady. She had what the British would call a homely face, not in the American sense of "unattractive," but evocative of home and mother—a mom face, endearing, but for one feature: the eyes. Black, Russian eyes, heavy brows. Those eyes could only belong to a Moiseiwitsch.

> ME: Ah, how do you do? And how was your trip?
> MOISEIWITSCH: (*dryly*) Long.

The luggage rituals followed with few words exchanged. Finally, with the van packed and the ladies seated behind me, we started off for town. Few words were exchanged, save when they awoke from their jet-lagged torpor to denounce my careless driving. ("Watch the road, you fool!") I didn't seem to be making a real hit with the Upper Echelon.

Two days later most of the company had arrived. Actors and staff were invited to a kick-off reception the evening before the first rehearsal of *Hamlet*.

Guthrie wanted to produce a wide range of plays on his new platform. For the inaugural season he had chosen:

Hamlet
The Miser
Three Sisters
Death of a Salesman

He had cast an appropriately diverse group of actors to people this mix of classics. They collectively embodied most of the recent history of theater, film, and television in the United States and the United Kingdom. Whether they could be melded into a powerful collective called a company was yet to be seen. What was immediately apparent by their participation was that a new level of talent and glamour was being brought to theater *outside* New York.

Here below is a list of some of the gang at that reception, as well as their principal roles.

Our leading actors (the word "star" was a no-no) were Hume Cronyn (Harpagon in *The Miser*, Willy Loman in *Salesman*) and his wife Jessica Tandy (Gertrude in *Hamlet*, Olga in *Three Sisters*, Linda Loman in *Salesman*). They had recently become a formidable acting couple, ready to rival Lunt and Fontanne. Tandy, justly acclaimed on these shores as the original Blanche DuBois in *A Streetcar Named Desire*, also had a solid background in British repertory. Cronyn, on the other hand, was more a product of Hollywood, including the films *Lifeboat* and *The Postman Always Rings Twice*.

Lee Richardson (Claudius in *Hamlet*, Biff Loman in *Salesman*) was a creature of the downtown theater in New York. He and Geraldine Page had played the leads in the production that began the off-Broadway movement—*Summer and Smoke*, directed by José Quintero in the converted nightclub where I had learned to be a stage manager.

Rita Gam (Elise in *Miser*, Masha in *Three Sisters*) was our drop-dead beautiful glamour puss. She had a modest film and TV resumé but was best known to most of us as the ex-wife of film director Sidney Lumet. Gam surprised everyone by being a talented, down-to-earth, and thoroughly committed member of the company.

John Cromwell (Player King in *Hamlet*, Uncle Ben in *Salesman*) was an old-line director. He had started in the theater (my father remembered auditioning for him), then gone west in the 1930s and lived most of the early history of Hollywood. Now, having run afoul of the Hollywood blacklist, he was returning to his theater roots. Ruth Nelson, Cromwell's wife (Player Queen in *Hamlet*, Afisa in *Three Sisters*), was also a Hollywood transplant. Her background was in the theater as well, but theater of quite a different sort. She had been a founding member of that wellspring of Method acting and Hollywood stars, the Group Theatre.

One of the most exciting leading men in the business was Robert Pastene (Polonius in *Hamlet*, Vershinin in *Three Sisters*). He had wonderful broad-jawed good looks that also radiated great intelligence. Out of the business for some time as the result of a disastrous Broadway experience, he had been lured back by Guthrie and Zeisler.

Fortunately for me, there were also a couple of familiar faces, two old friends. George Grizzard (the Prince in *Hamlet*, Solyony in *Three Sisters*) was an old amigo with whom I attended Wilson High School in DC and who, in our debut there, acted me off the stage in the part of my girlfriend's bratty brother. The other was Ken Ruta (Ghost in *Hamlet*, Bernard in *Salesman*), veteran of the Stan Hywet Hall days.

Also, surprisingly, the most boisterous and demonstrative member of an already noisy gathering, a major actor at The Old Vic and Stratford, Ontario, veteran of many a Guthrie adventure, my dour redheaded housing guide, Douglas Campbell. And finally, there he was, the master of the revels, the reason I was in Minnesota: Sir Tyrone Guthrie.

After all these years, it is difficult not to confuse the man with the legendary figure, subject of numberless anecdotes that are cherished and repeated endlessly in theatrical circles. Many of them are only marginally true, but they serve to celebrate this outsized and colorful man who changed the course of so many of our lives.

However, I will try to stick to the facts as I remember them.

He and his wife, Judith Bretherton, were meeting the company in reception-line style. Introductions, where necessary, were being supplied by Zeisler or Oliver Rea.

I got on the end of the line. I began to notice something odd. My right hand had turned to ice, really frozen; the left one was room temperature and utterly complacent, but the right, in spite of furtive attempts to warm it, remained arcticly incapacitated. The line inched forward.

At the head of the line stood an extremely tall man. He had a great hawk-like nose over a nondescript moustache. He towered over his interlocutors like a benign seabird; not much excess weight save for an odd pot belly which, along with the schnozz, made him look like a British version of Charles de Gaulle.

And there we were, face to face. He seized my hand and, pumping it energetically, gave me a hearty welcome—the same energetic pump and hearty welcome he had been giving to everyone else. Then I was opposite Lady Guthrie, only slightly shorter than her husband, with a rich, husky cigarette contralto. We greeted one another and I moved on.

> *Scene: The small, impossibly cluttered office of a cigar-smoking literary agent. Mountains of manuscripts on every available flat surface, including the floor.*
>
> AGENT (*smoking cigar*). Look, Eddie, let me level with you here. We need a stronger meeting. You understand what I'm saying? It's a natural. Bumbling ASM meets British knight. Punch it up. It's got real possibilities. He jumps when you hand him that cold fish. You spill punch on him. Something like that. Think of *Pride of the Yankees*—Lou Gehrig meets Babe Ruth for the first time, trips on a bunch of bats, falls on his ass. Like that.

ME. But nothing much happened. I shook his hand, then I shook hers. That was it.

AGENT. Did you say anything to him?

ME. I don't remember.

AGENT. There, you see? You don't remember. Look, it's been more than forty years, for Chrissakes! Who's to remember? He's dead. Write something with some *zetz*!

Next morning we went to work.

Work Begins

I remember it all starting in brightness—blue sky and sunlight, savoring crunchy snow and soda-pop cold air as I made my way to the church meeting room that was to serve as our rehearsal space until the theater was ready.

Inside, the clack and whirr of metal tape measures being reeled and unreeled, with lots of head scratching and grave discussions about the best way to lay out the jagged shape of the stage on the floor in quarter-inch masking tape. Then Gordon Smith took over and had it all organized before we could blink.

Later, witnessed through a big picture window, the company arriving—much stamping of feet and spirited voices echoing in the vestibule. Finally, we all sat quietly in a big semicircle, scripts open before us, all reborn and bright-eyed, many of us delivered from cockroach-infested rooms, crowded subways, and stupid jobs in the indifferent metropolis. Now here we were, at the center of the country, the center of our profession—the center of the world!—eyes wide, dazzled by the brightness, the snow, the white paper, the wonder of it all.

And so we began. No ceremonies, no fanfares, no ribbon cutting to mark the beginning of this great adventure. No press, no cameras, no embarrassing speeches by over-emotional producers. ("Oh, God! It is so great to see you all here today! And what a privilege to work with this Great Man, I feel ...") No, none of that. We began to read *Hamlet*. Guthrie, uncharacteristically, as I soon learned, sat most of the time. We read a bit, a few initial scenes were blocked, some admonitions were given about the proper way to move about on this three-sided stage. And that was it. Our beginning was, you may say, *pianissimo*.

As rehearsals progressed, Partington was assigning me a lot of tasks that took me outside the rehearsal room. I may have been missing the action (Guthrie was soon on his feet, and the fingers were snapping), but I now had time to poke around our new theater as it neared completion. In the process, I began to understand the scope of what we were up to. I felt at times like the hillbilly moonshiner who was hired at the Jack Daniel's plant. ("My God, Jethro, just look at the size of them vats!") It's not that I hadn't handled all this before, but I'd never experienced it on such a scale, with such class.

Here was the costume department—not three young girls dizzy with fatigue, two cranky old sewing machines, and a dented coffee pot, but a host of eager new employees, a lot of them from England or Canada, with job titles I had never heard before, like cutter, draper, first hand, finisher. They were all presided over with sage, feline grace by Annette Garceau, the lady I had mistaken for Tanya Moiseiwitsch. In the sunny room that was now their home were rank on rank of new sewing machines and numerous spotless cutting tables, some of them piled high with the mouth-watering materials with which the costumers would practice their alchemy.

And there were other wonders: a backstage elevator, a SM's booth that was not some airless cubbyhole but a vast glass-fronted room at the back of the center balcony with a panoramic view of the stage. I was told that each production was to have an original score played live. Further, there would be a quartet of musicians, dressed in dark blue blazers, each with our new logo (now christened "the Flying G") embroidered on the breast pocket. They would take their places in the lobby and, with a roll of drums and a mighty blast from those long-belled herald's trumpets, summon the audience into the theater. For someone like me, who had typed sides for actors because the budget only afforded one script, who had scrubbed flats and straightened nails for reuse and scrounged props with earnest beseeching and the promise of program credit, the outlook was downright utopian.

I did find one odd anomaly. Our new rehearsal space looked somewhat cramped for such a big company. How could that be? Well, the theater's founding fathers were determined that the Tyrone Guthrie Theater and its company would not begin life burdened with debt. To that end, all the money to build the theater was raised in advance of construction. Then came the predestined miscalculations and cost overruns that the contingency budget could not cover. Instead of going back to the public, those self-same fathers decided to shorten the building by however much was needed to stay out of the red. Zeisler described the process to me as rather like slicing off the end of a loaf of bread. The building cost so much per square foot, so it must be measured down until the books balanced. That slice was twenty feet thick. Unfortunately, our rehearsal space was on the wrong end of the loaf.

But this was a minor flaw in a palace of wonders. The scale of it all, the talent of the people involved, the daring of the stage architecture, all filled me with a sense of infinite possibility. After years of false starts and irresolute wandering, I was where I was meant to be. I had hit the ground running in Minneapolis in 1963. Oh, deeply fortunate me!

As the days passed, I spent more time in the rehearsal room, mostly to record blocking. I soon began to realize I was watching a subtle tug-of-war between the director and actor George Grizzard, who was feeling his way into the role of *Hamlet*.

First of all, why *Hamlet*? A year earlier, when it had been announced, you heard a collective groan from the theatrical community. Not only *Hamlet*, but *Hamlet* uncut, all four and a half hours. It seems such an odd choice.

Shouldn't the opening of a new theater be something of a celebration? If it's necessary to set a classical tone with Shakespeare, then why not something lighter? *Much Ado About Nothing*? Zoe Caldwell as Beatrice, Moiseiwitsch's finery—music, wit, and a happy ending. But an uncut *Hamlet*?

Yes, it was an odd choice, but not an ill-considered one. He wanted to challenge the audience and, I am convinced, make a strong statement about American actors doing Shakespeare.

Then there was the choice of Grizzard to play *Hamlet*. What *did* Guthrie have in mind?

Until his untimely death in 2007, Grizzard was a highly respected character actor. In 1963 Grizzard was a fascinating, edgy young leading man. If you were trying to find a film actor today who resembled him, you might think of someone like Michael J. Fox in his prime, before the onset of his Parkinson's symptoms. Fox's career was lightweight compared to Grizzard's at the same age. Grizzard left playing the role of Nick in the original production of *Who's Afraid of Virginia Woolf?* to come to Minneapolis and he was a much more dangerous actor than Fox, but they shared a quick-witted, bad-boy charm. You would not, however, think of either of them as strong candidates for the Melancholy Dane. Grizzard had scant, if any, experience with Shakespeare, nor was he possessed of great vocal power. This seemed to bother Guthrie not at all.

Almost a year had elapsed between the time Guthrie cast Grizzard as Hamlet and the first rehearsal in Minneapolis. You can only guess what happened in that time. Did Grizzard spend long hours talking to dames and sirs who filled his head with tales of the noble, delicate Prince of Romantic tradition? Did Guthrie not take time to discuss his radical ideas for Hamlet and Grizzard? Was it simply that Grizzard, who was always playing 5'8" now had a chance to play 6'2" and went for it? Who knows?

In any case, when they met again in Minneapolis, it became obvious they were not on the same page.

We are now in the recently completed, cramped rehearsal room of the Tyrone Guthrie Theater. The work is going well. Hamlet's first encounter with the Ghost is being rehearsed.

Actors know their lines. Guthrie has been working carefully with Ken Ruta as the Ghost, whose acting and whose rumbly bass/baritone obviously delight him. They communicate easily. Most of the talk today is about dynamics: "A little brisker here;" "No pause before 'O horrible'"—things like that. Then Ken rumbles his last "Remember me!" and moves off to the side. Now it's George's turn. He lies face down at center. He rises slowly.

GRIZZARD (*stirred by growing passion*).
    O all you host of heaven! O earth! What else?
    And shall I couple hell? O fie, hold, hold my heart
    And you my sinews …

GUTHRIE (*A loud clap.*) No, no, dear boy. Not all that acting. Just speak it. (*In a bad midwestern accent.*) "Oh, all ya host of hevvin, oh earrrth!" Do all those Method things you do.

GRIZZARD (*stirred by growing passion*).

O all you host of heaven! O earth...[et cetera]

"Do all those Method things you do." An amazing piece of direction. But that was Guthrie's style. Always the ironist, so out comes this exhortation mixed with a faint condescension. And it was exactly what he meant. He did not want the exciting young actor he saw in *Virginia Woolf* to get lost in classical attitudinizing. I think he had in mind a gritty, not particularly well-spoken Hamlet who would scandalize the pedants and thrill the young and defiant—a sort of divine brat, more like a tormented rock star than the Hamlet of Richard Burton, say. Guthrie wanted a Prince who would kick over some hoary old traditions, who would mutter, bawl, or screech but never intone.

There were a few more incidents like the one recounted above, with no great change in Grizzard's approach and a lessening of Guthrie's insistence. Guthrie was stepping back; this was also true to form.

It is instructive to focus on this. Given his reputation for directorial arrogance, I was surprised to find how considerate he could be with leading actors. However high-handed he was with what he called (rather high-handedly) "the lower orders," he could be downright deferential with his leading players. In the case of Hamlet most particularly, he felt strongly that the relationship between actor and director was not one of leader–follower but of two collaborators.

Perhaps Guthrie's admonitions did serve to temper some of Grizzard's more Victorian impulses, but they never resulted, I am convinced, in the performance Guthrie had in mind. The Hamlet that Grizzard eventually showed us in performance was a sensitive and tormented young Prince, but it was recognizably in the tradition. To his credit, he had risen to a gargantuan challenge and brought it off with honor. But how I would have loved to see that other Prince, the wild Kurt Cobain one. Grizzard could have realized that vision superbly, but Guthrie was not about to inflict on him an interpretation of the character that he would find uncongenial.

As the weeks sped by, Dr. Guthrie, as I came to know him, began to seem like some outlandish combination of Dionysus and a British public-school headmaster. The latter figure, a character encountered in British films of the period, was a wry, scholarly old duffer usually played by an actor named Wildred Hyde-White. A lot of Dr. G's utterances had a headmasterly ring:

Of the first day's rehearsal: "Simple tasks, simple tasks—bead-stringing for the new boys, then send 'em home."

After someone had made a mistake: "Ah, blotted your copybook, did you, old boy?"

And many others I can't remember. I only know that on encountering that figure of imposing height and eagle gaze on any given morning before rehearsal, it would seem natural to say, standing rigid in my blazer with the school crest, "Call, sir, fourth form, very nice to see you today, sir."

Dionysus, god of wine and theater, appeared later in rehearsals. He was a far cry from the sedentary gent of the early *Hamlet* sessions.

Then, there was the wardrobe. Guthrie didn't give a damn what he wore—any old relic from his limited supply would do. As the weather warmed, however, his favorite attire appeared: worn white tennies, no socks, nondescript slacks that were often slipping down and had to be hiked up. Above the slacks a loose-fitting (also non-descript) short-sleeved sport shirt, worn tails out, which, in the whirlwind of his passion, flapped around exposing a fair-sized zone of knightly belly.

The man himself is rarely at rest. He paces from side to side before the actors. His sharp eyes take in every nuance of what is transpiring before him and not a little behind as well.

When he wants to stop the action, he snaps his fingers. Guthrie's finger snaps, like most everything about him, were distinctive. Those big pianist's hands could make a sound that was more like a detonation than a snap. It was capable (once the actors learned the signal) of freezing the noisy court of Denmark or the army of Fortinbras into sudden silence and immobility. It was usually *Snap!* (right hand), *Snap!* (left hand), then a single *Clap!* (right fingers into left palm). Like a musical theme, it had many markings. Just now it is *piano*.

> PAUL BALLANTYNE (*playing Marcellus, on the battlements*).
> ...Peace, break thee off. Look where it comes again.
> GUTHRIE (*snap, snap, clap*). Paul, dear boy, it's not your dear
> old Uncle Herbert back for a visit, it's the ghost of the
> dead king. Where's the terror? Where's the fear?
> PAUL BALLANTYNE. But, Tony, I...
> GUTHRIE. You can do it. Right! On!

And off we go, swept along, trying our best to keep up with this irresistible Pied Piper, arms flailing, fingers snapping, elated with himself, with America, with Shakespeare, and with the giddy glory of making theater on such a large scale.

For actors working for Tyrone Guthrie, they soon became aware of some basic rules. The four Guthrie Rules, one might call them.

Guthrie was a man of huge impatience and would rather swallow hemlock than get involved in tiresome chats about character, motivation, adjustments, intentions, and so on. Did he not care about such things? Was he insensitive to all that? Not at all. He simply thought of it as the actor's private turf, not to be pawed over by nosy directors. He would supply the What. The Why and the How were up to you.

Nicolas Coster found out about Rule Number One as he was rehearsing Laertes. He stopped one day after running through his long scene with Claudius in Act IV, in which Claudius furtively takes away Laertes's weapon (a pistol, not a sword, in this modern-dress version). Coster strolls in silence to the front edge of the stage.

> COSTER (*perplexed, searching for words*). I just don't...I can't find a way...how can I let the king take my pistol?
> GUTHRIE. Well, it's in the script, dear boy. You'd better find a way, hadn't you?

It looks cruel on the page, but Guthrie said it genially, without passion—just a simple statement of fact. It was also one of half a dozen air-clearing remarks with which Guthrie revealed his modus operandi. It was early in rehearsals. I think he sensed in Coster a highly skilled performer, but one who, given the chance, would relish a lengthy discussion of motivations and adjustments. That simply would not happen.

This incident was noised around. "You can't talk to him," frustrated actors would complain. No, you couldn't, not about acting, at least not directly. But there was another way to communicate with him on the subject. And that gets us to:

Ed Flanders was playing Fluellen, the voluble Welsh captain in *Henry V* during our second season. At rehearsal one day, Flanders had a new idea. He didn't tell anyone about it; he just implemented it. It was radically different from what Guthrie had asked for. Everyone waited for the tongue-lashing to begin. It didn't happen. Guthrie saw immediately that Flanders's choice was much more interesting than his own. He seized on it and restructured the whole scene to make it work. There were fifteen people on stage; it would require a lot of reblocking. No matter: this was the kind of challenge Guthrie relished; he went quickly to work. I would have fled back to the model and fiddled with my coins or model men for hours to re-work the blocking. Guthrie snapped his fingers a few times, quickly changed a dozen or so moves, and it was all solved. For good.

Guthrie had a storied reputation for working quickly. Peter Zeisler told me some tales about the Leonard Bernstein–Lillian Hellman musical of *Candide* (which Zeisler stage-managed and Dr. G directed) that sounded hardly credible. There was one beast of a scene—quite long, 25 people on stage throughout, three musical numbers and a staggering number of props and set pieces. Guthrie kept putting off working on it. Finally, in frustration, Zeisler just put it in the schedule. Knowing what he did about the average director's speed, he calculated it would take at least two days of blocking and review. Guthrie put it all together in half a day and never touched it again. He never had to, it worked so well.

If Guthrie was an electric presence in the rehearsal space, he was positively radioactive when we moved into the new theater.

"7:00 Act III, scene ii – Full company plus extras," the call board had said. Three-two, the Play scene in *Hamlet*. "The play's the thing /

Wherein I'll catch the conscience of the King," Hamlet had said, and this is the scene in which he does just that—invites King, Queen, and court to see a play in which a fictional version of his father's murder is re-enacted, a big scene with big effects and lots of people. One that starts decorously and ends in chaos. The principals had already been blocked; at this rehearsal, the extras were called for the first time.

Seeing how Dr. G handled a big ensemble scene was one of the reasons I was in Minneapolis. I felt I did them adequately, but never well. Sometimes the outcome was acceptable, but the process was a mess. I just couldn't find a way to keep everyone engaged. If I concentrated on one group for any length of time, everyone else developed those blank stares that indicated more interest in the next break than in the profound tapestry of Edward Payson Call's production of whatever it was. At times I felt like an overworked border collie, darting hither and yon, nipping at my lethargic charges, trying to move them all in the same direction.

Watching Guthrie work on a big scene was an almost scary revelation. Something happened to him when large numbers of people showed up for rehearsal—the after-burners kicked in, new juices started flowing. The spirit of Dionysus ruled. He was on fire with making theater.

We would all try to keep up with mad Ahab at the helm but were always several boat lengths behind. "Could we do that again?" some brave soul occasionally ventured. "No," was invariably the answer. Everyone had to move at his pace; if not: "No, Frank! Not here—there!" And one of our extras, Franklin Peters, a retired undertaker of advanced age and somewhat stiffened joints, was hurled across the stage into a clump of his surprised fellow Danes.

So we crowded on sail, picked up speed, and went bashing through the waves. He drove us on relentlessly, creatively, wittily, and all the while a huge amount of work was being accomplished. No one tuned out. We were all a-quiver with fear and excitement.

Recording this creative rampage was my job. Keeping track of the principals was hard enough. Now, sitting at the SM table halfway back in the auditorium, I was trying to put on paper (8.5″ × 11″ diagrams of the stage) exactly what the fifteen or so newcomers were up to. I was having a terrible time keeping up.

Meanwhile, I was beginning to apprehend something about the Guthrie celerity and how to keep thirty or more people engaged when only a few of them had lines. A rule Guthrie had for himself read: Never Sit Back and Watch Big Crowd Scenes. In other words, don't fall into the routine of running a scene and taking notes, then stopping and giving notes, then running the scene again and taking notes. ... If something is wrong, get up and fix it *now*, while it's going on.

The first time Guthrie tried to do this was in *Hamlet* rehearsals.

The principals stop speaking as soon as his foot hits the stage. "No, no, don't mind me. On you go." Then as the text is heard again, Guthrie moves swiftly among the courtiers. Not much talk at first. He seems to be concerned with making the groupings more interesting. Someone's hand is placed on another's shoulder. A young woman, Mary, who is facing flat toward the small stage where the play within a play is taking place is moved to an angle. Now she has to watch over her shoulder; it looks more interesting that way, and later when the time comes for a big reaction, she will have a strong move to make: she can swing around to face the action.

Then he begins to give out business in an excited whisper, very quickly, insistently:

GUTHRIE (*having dragged a surprised extra halfway across the stage, now bent over, whispering in her ear*). Mary dear, you're such a shrimpy little thing compared to these giants in front of you.

(*Guthrie indicates two burly extras playing guards.*)

Blocking your view, don't you see? Jump up and down a few times to see what you're missing (*the 6′5″ Guthrie demonstrates*), then push your way between them and sit on that poof.

MARY (*uncertainly*). Now?

GUTHRIE. Now!

(*Next we see the top of Mary's small head bobbing up a few times behind the massive bodyguards, then she slithers between them and sits.*)

GUTHRIE. No, no—not so fucking ladylike. Kick Pat in the shins; *make* him give way.

(*Mary has been a secretary for six years; now she's in the court of Elsinore; her palms are sweating, and she's afraid she's going to pass out, but she wants to please this odd, crazy person.*)

MARY. Now?

GUTHRIE. Now!

(*Mary rears back and fires. Pat clenches his teeth to suppress a yelp. Mary flounces through and sits. Guthrie chortles to himself and moves on.*)

All this while the principals are struggling to keep focused and get their lines out. Suddenly giggles are heard in the back ranks. Guthrie has just given one of the ladies-in-waiting a fierce tickle. It seems to be getting out of hand, until you realize that what he is creating is not unlike the spirit of a group of rather coarse aristocrats who've had a few too many and are gathering for a light theatrical diversion.

As the scene darkens, so do the directions. Some panicked scurryings are encouraged.

> GUTHRIE. Sssst! Patrick, work your way through the
> crowd toward Michael. (*Patrick starts off.*) Move
> quickly. Careful! Try not to attract attention. That's
> it. When you're next to Mike, whisper something in
> his ear. (*Patrick cups his hand and whispers*). No, no!
> Fiercer! It's not a proposition. You've discovered what
> Hamlet's up to. (*Patrick tries again*). Yasss. Jolly good.
> GUTHRIE. (*As the scene nears its climax, he waves a hand
> to get all the extras' attention.*) Listen all! Weight over
> the balls of your feet. Lean into the action. Your fu-
> ture is at stake. Blood may be spilt.
> (*Now Hamlet is about to interrupt the players and attack
> Claudius.*)
> GUTHRIE. Everyone! A big intake of breath after
> Hamlet says, "he murders him in the garden for his
> estate." Ready?

"God, what a cornball effect," I'm thinking, as I scribble frantically on. Then Grizzard says the line. They all gasp on cue. It's
electrifying.

Now they are all into it. The principals catch fire from the extras,
the extras from the principals. It really starts to cook. Guthrie backs
off and watches.

Finally, it's over. We've been at it for two hours. Those with a
chair or any kind of sittable surface nearby slump down a bit dizzily.
"Where have we been?" they seem to ask.

GUTHRIE *(crosses to center, positively chipper; he looks around at his somewhat glassy-eyed coworkers)*. Well done. That comes nicely. *(Turns and ever so jauntily exits up left.)*

Sitting at the SM table, I collapsed (only half facetiously) head down onto a pile of indecipherable blocking diagrams. It was a decent interval before I spoke. My gaping jaw finally closed around the word "un-be-lievable!"

My education had begun.

Oh, I had an education, to be sure, but, as recounted above, it was on the sketchy side. I had been a college bum, jumping from university to university, and the fact that I was not a diligent student did not help matters. Eventually I got a diploma from the University of Maryland, much to my parents' relief, but in Minneapolis in 1963, I had once more to face the fact that I just didn't know enough.

I remember walking into the back of the theater one day looking for Dr. G. He was there in the front row; Douglas Campbell was sitting next to him. They were poring intently over a slim coffee-table-sized book, laughing from time to time. Must be a book of cartoons, I thought, as I approached Dr. G with my errand. My business quickly carried out, I looked down at the book. What they were so delighted with was not *The Thurber Carnival* but an orchestral score! I walked back up the aisle and watched unseen. From time to time I would hear tum-ta-tums as they traced the tiny black dots across the page. Suddenly they stop. "What in the world?" Campbell said. "No, no, look," said Guthrie, "it's in the bassoons!" Delighted laughter. More tum-ta-tums.

Skills like that, knowledge like theirs, made a lot of us want to be better, made us undertake projects of self-improvement. For myself, I was soon to be found late at night seated at the old upright backstage, trying to reconstruct the two Chopin preludes I used to play as a teenager; then I brought some sheet music...

On my rounds, after a performance, I would bump into other furtive self-improvers. In the basement I came upon one of the less physically adept actors, working on his fencing skills, repeatedly thrusting an épée into a cinderblock wall. From a dressing room, long since deserted (the show was over and it was now near midnight), I heard the sounds of an actor trying to fulfill one of Guthrie's more extravagant pronouncements, to the effect that anyone who couldn't speak seven lines of blank verse without taking a breath had no business in the theater. Age and decades of smoking were making it an uphill battle, but he was not about to give up.

Beginnings are always exciting, always bring out the best in us. I have been in on a few, but there was a kind of excitement around the Minnesota Theatre Company in those early years that I can only describe as invigorating anarchy. Anything could happen. Here was this huge institution being created in the blink of an eye, and no one, but no one, had any relevant previous experience. The usual image for rising in any profession is a ladder, but we weren't thinking about ladders—the earth was flat, the entire horizon was clear in every direction, every point on the compass was open and contained a different destiny. You simply had to decide which was yours and set out in that direction.

So I strolled northeast toward Peter Zeisler:

"Say, Peter, after all these shows are open, what's the chance of doing some workshops?"

"Possible. You got something in mind?"

"Yeah. I got a script. I'll bring it by tomorrow." (I did just that.)

When we got about two thirds of the way through our scheduled rehearsals, Guthrie decided we were progressing well enough to take a few extra days off. I was glad to be able to catch my breath and pretty up my production book, but the break made me uneasy. I wanted to get back to work.

After a shaky start, things had changed for the better. If not yet on friendly terms, I had been accepted as a coworker by Moiseiwitsch and Campbell. Also, I had been given the responsibility of recording all the blocking for the first two productions. Next, Zeisler told me that I would also be running both *Hamlet* and *The Miser* from the spacious SM's booth. It was a big challenge. I had run shows before, but that was in tiny off-Broadway theaters with primitive technical resources. I knew nothing about running big shows in big theaters. Time to learn. Another reason I wanted to get back to work.

Entr'acte: Some Thoughts on Deracination

Working in the theater, as any fool knows, demands a decent amount of vagabond blood. Given the daunting size of the American landmass, the native practitioner sometimes needs multiple dwellings. The '60s saw the birth of the "bicoastal actor" who, with digs on both sides of the country, could settle down on short notice in Los Angeles or New York—wherever the work was.

The beginnings of the regional theater gave rise to a lot of creative ferment and fulfillment but also a lot of domestic deracination as well. An actor might, in the course of a season, put up in half a dozen separate cities. For the young and single, it was part of the adventure; for the young and married, it could be difficult; for the young and married with kids, it could be a nightmare.

Charles Keating and his family knew a lot about the rootless life. They had spent years moving around as Charles pursued his acting career. But now he was living and working in Cleveland and doing quite well. After several seasons, he had become a popular actor at the Cleveland Play House. His family—wife Mary and two young sons had settled in. The boys liked the schools and made troops of friends; Mary had taken to the semi-suburban life of Shaker Heights with a will. After three years, Cleveland was becoming home.

But then Charles got an offer from the Minnesota Theatre Company, one he felt he could not turn down, and so he uprooted his family once more. Very soon all four Keatings found themselves staying in a musty old hotel for transients not far from the theater, passing days inside the drafty Keating station wagon, rattling around frigid Minneapolis in a so far fruitless search for living quarters. Understandably, after a few days of this, tensions were rising. In the back seat, The squirming boys were getting cranky and disputatious. Charles was concentrating on the dual tasks of driving and map reading, trying to find his way around this new city. Mary, in the passenger seat, was fretting. She didn't mind the move herself but felt guilty about uprooting the kids. They had been so happy in Cleveland, enjoying something like a normal growing up. Now this.

Noise from the back seat; the brothers were starting to fight. This was quelled by a few stern Irish father-type admonitions from Charles. Then silence.

After a few minutes, the younger boy started blubbering. Soon blubbering gave way to a wail.

"I want to go home!" he cried.

The way he wrapped his mouth around the word "home," with such yearning, such heartbreaking need, left Charles and Mary quite undone. Charles looked at his wife; their eyes were brimming with tears. How could they have done it? How could they have been so selfish as to abandon the nurturing environment of Cleveland, that would have provided their children with such an ideal boyhood and thrown it all away to indulge Charles's ambition to play Mark fucking Antony?

Charles drove on blindly, accompanied by his son's sobs. Mary bit on a handkerchief to control her whimpers. Suddenly Charles was struck by an idea. He swerved off the road, stopped the car, and turned around to look at his inconsolable son. When he spoke, it was crisply, logically. "Son, where's home?"

The youngster gathered force for a major emotional outburst. "Back at the hotel," he wailed.

When the day finally came to go back to work, things proceeded on schedule and fairly painlessly. Oh, there were hitches, to be sure. Some elements on the open stage just take longer; lighting is one. The audience is on three sides of the playing space, and we sometimes had to deal with the fact that what looked terrific from the front looked a lot less terrific from the sides and had to be adjusted. There was also the problem of bounce: lights mounted high on one side of the auditorium could hit the stage and practically blind people sitting on the other side. Part of this was Guthrie's fault. He had an aversion to colored light, so there were to be no gels. "Don't color the light, color the lady" was his motto. Since white light reflects so effectively, finding a stain for the stage floor that would cut down the glare was a major challenge. It was a process that went on right up to opening.

And we did hear of disputes at a higher level, mostly between the artistic leadership and the architect, but we were not affected at all. The troika (though primarily Peter Zeisler) had done an extraordinary job of making a schedule that avoided last-minute hysterics.

Finally, there I was, running technical rehearsals for Tyrone Guthrie's production of *Hamlet*. Not even Christopher Craft, talking astronauts into orbit after a flawless lift-off on a crisp Florida morning, ever felt such exhilaration as I did in late April of 1963, perched almost weightless over the playing area in that Olympian SM's booth. The trumpets did not sound, nor the actors enter, nor the lights transform the space, without my leave: a whispered "Go" into that lopsided halo of omnipotence, my headset.

"Stage management is boring," you say? All those tedious tasks, endlessly repeated? Watching all the other people do what you want to do? No, wrong, all wrong. I sang in my catbird seat, my eagle's nest in the sky.

I was ready for the openings. Yes, openings in the plural, because after all we were a repertory company. The first two productions, *Hamlet* and *The Miser*, had been rehearsing in tandem and would open on successive nights. *Three Sisters* and *Death of a Salesman* would be added, together, later in the season.

If everything was peachy in Elsinore, there was a somewhat different atmosphere *chez* Harpagon. Douglas Campbell seemed to be putting together what some regarded as a slightly overwrought production of Molière's great comedy. "Is he going too far? Will it really be funny?" someone asked. I had no idea. That's not what SMs get paid for.

If there were some doubts about the work in general, there were no doubts about the new addition to our company, the young

Australian Zoe Caldwell. She was going to be terrific as Frosine, the matchmaker in *The Miser*.

She arrived late in Minneapolis. There had been some sort of "dust-up" with Actors' Equity that had delayed her.

What a surprise she was, to those who thought they knew Guthrie well! She was simply not his type. Didn't he always hire those long-stemmed, finely bred ladies with the upper-class airs and brittle voices? That wasn't Zoe Caldwell—not at all. She was a mutt, a working-class Aussie and proud of it.

She was at that time in her mid-twenties, a brunette, not tall and certainly not beautiful in any conventional sense. But there was a spirit that shone from those brown eyes that could light up a room (or a stage) in seconds.

She was perfect for repertory, with a truly protean talent, who could show you a tough Russian peasant one night and an elegant, self-absorbed eighteenth-century aristocrat the next—both performed with stunning authority and irresistible appeal. She had a distinctive voice that was both strong and mellow. Part of that dazzling group of young actors, led by Albert Finney and Peter O'Toole, that was just being heard from in England, she brought not only her talent and experience (seasons at Stratford-on-Avon and Stratford, Ontario) but also a consuming enthusiasm for the work, both on stage and off, that in short order made her to many of us the spiritual center of the company.

I fell in love with Zoe. (Hell, the entire Minnesota Theatre Company fell in love with her.) And in a few days, a sizable portion of the Twin Cities would be similarly smitten, when, as Frosine the matchmaker, decked out in Moiseiwitsch's dowdy finery, her face set off by cascades of henna curls surmounted by a ridiculous black straw hat, she would sashay out of the right tunnel, stride onto the stage, and turn Cronyn's tough old walnut of a Harpagon into so much watery jelly. "Monsieurrrrrr," she would say (her voice emanating from some delicious sub-woofer level), "Bless me, how well you look! Never have I seen you looking more rosy, more hearty."

Miss Zoe Caldwell, Sydney's gift to the Upper Midwest, was about to show them how it's done.

So we fretted about the color of the stage floor for the last time, solved the problems of opening and closing the grave trap, cleaned up some light cues, and saw to it that every item on Zeisler's to-do list (now oddly bound to his right wrist with a red rubber band) had been checked off. Then after one free preview performance of *Hamlet* for the guys who had built the theater, plus taxi drivers and assorted friends, it was time to show the world what we had been up to.

Opening Nights

At 7:30 in the evening on May 8, 1963, our inaugural opening-night audience began to arrive. It was a distinguished bunch, and some yellowing newspapers tell us it included:

- Robertson Davies, Canadian novelist and a great friend of Dr. G's
- McNeil Lowry, then head of the arts program at the Ford Foundation, which under his guidance became America's largest private arts patron
- Rose Muckley of St. Paul, who wore a formal dress and a special green eyeshade, for what purpose we are not told
- Arthur Naftalin, the charming mayor of Minneapolis, and his wife Frances Healy Naftalin
- Mrs. James Otis, in her cornflower blue chiffon

- Tom Prideaux, theater critic and senior editor of Life magazine
- Vincent Sardi, the New York restaurateur (he was the vanguard of numerous curious New Yorkers who would make the trip during that first season)

And ever so many newspaper critics and reporters and well-wishers and scholars and poets and any number of Pillsburys and Cowles and other heavy hitters of the Twin Cities elite.

But I was indifferent to the gala atmosphere or the historical significance of it all. I was in the SM's booth with Chuck Wallen, our genial electrician, waiting impatiently for all these spiffily decked out folks to settle into their seats so we could start the goddamned show. The fanfares, glorious, galvanic, and rafter-rattling, were not having the desired effect.

The minutes plodded by. Then, finally, the last joking comment about the multicolored seats had been made ("My dear, I can't sit in that one. It's green! Ha, ha ha!"), and they began to settle down.

Then a strange, oddly arresting sound was heard. It was only produced at 725 Vineland Place in Minneapolis, Minnesota. It became just as familiar to the theater's regular patrons as all that thumping is to the French. An usher stood in each of the twelve entrances to the auditorium. On a given signal they released the stops that held the doors open. Each made an odd, hollow thunk. Then a dozen doors edged softly shut, closing the audience in for the alchemy to come.

In the half-light of the SM's booth, I called the first cues:

"Warn house out, warn Lights One, Two, and Two-A. Warn Music One, One-A, and One-B."

Then I flicked a switch on the top of my console in the booth. It turned on a red cue light backstage for the actors (on for warn, off for go).

I waited until I heard "Ready" from Chuck and Herb Pilhofer, our music director, who with his dozen musicians was perched in the orchestra loft high above offstage left. Then I said:

"House out—go."

The house lights slid downward. Just before blackout I snapped off the cue light and said:

"Music One—go."

In the darkness a single muted trumpet was heard.

I called "Go, Lights One." In the soft glow that followed, a single caped figure could be seen moving slowly across the stage. He wore a helmet and carried a pike over his shoulder.

Suddenly he froze, swung around, and leveled the pike toward downstage left.

BERNARDO. Who goes there?

FRANCISCO. Nay, answer me! Stand and unfold yourself...

The Tyrone Guthrie Theater was in business.

And I was there. I was there when it all began. I take great pride in that. Whatever else I've accomplished; whatever honors, pleasures, rewards have come my way; I was there on the bridge of the Great Guthrie Pleasure Palace when it let out its first resounding hoot, one of those resonant ocean-liner blasts that rattle the windows for miles around. Then the great ship eased slowly away from the pier and moved off into the deep and mysterious stream that is the history of the arts in our sad and exuberant land.

We are accustomed now to seeing Shakespearean plays set in every conceivable period save the one in which they were written. Space-age *Tempests* and flapper *Twelfth Nights* abound. In 1963, however, smoking cigarettes and sipping martinis while speaking blank verse still had a certain cachet. Guthrie's *Hamlet* was early twentieth-century Graustarkian, elegant and aristocratic. Forty-some years onward it still comes back to me in faded images:

- Hamlet and the Ghost. No smoke, no mirrors, no Guthrie *coups de théâtre*, but a father-son scene. Ken Ruta as the Ghost looking like a warrior painted by Rembrandt. Hamlet kneels inches away from him, sometimes circling.
- Ruth Nelson as the Player Queen bringing an archaic acting style to life. "Protesting" her innocence and declaring her undying love, she smiles sweetly and twines her fingers beneath her chin—the oldest ingénue cliché suddenly becomes chilling and Machiavellian.
- Hamlet after the play within the play, wild as a dervish, madly beating on a drum while Rosencrantz and Guildenstern shout to get his attention—then all ice as he hands one of them the recorder. "Will you play upon this pipe?"
- Ellen Geer as the mad Ophelia, gently, insistently making the courtiers gather around an imaginary grave, then shrieking, fists flailing at her belly trying to end the life within her, before she dashes out to end her own.
- Jessica Tandy, regal, spent, that haunting voice intoning "There is a willow lies aslant a brook…"

All these moments and a thousand others indelibly shaped by our resident Irish magus, all building to the wizardry of his arrangement of the final court scene with its high melodrama and proliferating corpses.

And it all looked different, more original, newer somehow because it was not trapped inside a gilded frame but swirled about on an open platform in amongst the audience. It had a sculptural excitement unlike any staging I had ever seen.

So there it was: the first production of the Minnesota Theatre Company. It had the sublime language of Shakespeare spoken by a terrific new acting company molded by a world-class showman on a brand-new stage. I didn't have to be sold. I had found the place where I wanted to work (in whatever capacity) as long as they would let me.

On the outside, the lobby side of those doors that were swinging shut on opening night with that nice premonitory whisper, were the people who had made it happen. After four years of planning and eight weeks of unremitting labor, they suddenly had nothing to do. Zeisler walked over to Guthrie, arms outstretched for a congratulatory embrace, but Guthrie walked away unseeing. A disturbing thought had just seized him: "I was wrong!"

What had he been thinking of? These people hadn't come to see *Hamlet*; they'd come to celebrate an amazing civic milestone, one that would put Minneapolis, Minnesota, home to grain merchants and stolid Scandinavian farmers, on the cultural map in a big way. What they needed was something light and joyous (and short) in keeping with the occasion, then send 'em on their way. And here he had just closed the doors and sentenced those good people to four and a half hours of an uncut *Hamlet*!

He need not have worried. The Twin Cities can turn out avid theater-goers, and they were in the house that night in goodly numbers. The response was warm and generous, culminating in a standing ovation.

If there were those who thirsted for something lighter, they had only to return the next night. Everyone took to Campbell's production of *The Miser* with relief and delight. Caldwell was at her best, and Cronyn was definitive in the title role. It became a great popular success and was revived two years later.

Director's Notes

Directing plays is a highly organized, disciplined activity. It is also deeply mysterious. In common with psychiatrists and fortune-tellers, directors do their work in secret, behind closed doors, which leads to endless fascination by the uninitiated; they always want to watch rehearsals.

"Please, please, please!" Just a peek?"

"Not just now. We're at a very sensitive stage."

or, "Oh, impossible. You'd be bored to death."

or, "Sorry, the director never allows it."

That curiosity is not confined to outsiders. Mike Nichols wrote an amusing piece for the *New York Times Magazine* years ago in which he asserted that the humid confines of the rehearsal space, and the intimate activities that sometimes take place there, were in many ways analogous to the sex act. And he confessed that when he supervises these emotional disrobings, he often finds himself wondering, "Are we doing this right? Are we doing it the way the people next door do it? What do they do, anyway?"

No one knows how it's done, really, this thing of directing. Not even the people who call themselves directors are especially trustworthy on the subject. Books are written about it, but usually by people who aren't particularly good at it. No one has any idea how to judge it—not the critics, nor the public, and certainly not the people who are closest to the whole process: the actors. Their livelihoods, egos, and careers are at stake, all in the superheated, claustrophobic confines of a rehearsal space. They are the least likely to be objective.

During rehearsals for one of the most successful productions I ever directed, the producer was cornered several times by delegations from the company, trying to get me fired. It had become obvious to them that I was incompetent. Fortunately, the producer stood his ground.

There may be as many ways to direct plays as there are directors. At one end of the scale, sitting jauntily, was Sir Tyrone Guthrie, high-handed, autocratic, flashy, abundantly entertaining to watch. He was demanding but not cruel (well, rarely). His method was: He is the director; he will direct. You are the actor; you will act. And there will be no dawdling over imponderables. "Right," he would say impatiently, "On!"

At the opposite end of the scale was José Quintero, probably one of the most beloved practitioners of the craft ever. In his very Latin way, he adored actors and had a deep respect for (what is called nowadays) their process. He refused to deal in externals and would sooner denounce Eugene O'Neill before he'd say things like: "Faster!" or "Pick up your cues!" or "I want more emotion here, people!"

A talented young performer, playing the lead in one of his productions, was once so excited to be working with him, so eager to please him, that she began overacting. To solve the problem, José sent the company away and worked with her alone. They went through the entire role, beat by beat, and as they did José would suggest a softer, less intense motivation than the one she'd been using. Then they'd get on their feet and try it, José and his SM filling in the other roles. Two days later, when the company reassembled, a performance that critics would praise had begun to take shape.

Confronted with a similar dilemma, Guthrie would snap his fingers, clap his hands, and say, "Jolly good, but overdone, dear. Turn down the heat a bit next time. Right. On!"

Guthrie's distance could be useful, but then José's affection could be reassuring to insecure performers (read most performers). Under certain circumstances, however, Guthrie's fireworks could be intimidating and José's quiet empathy, stifling. So what kind of director do you want to be? Like Guthrie or Quintero? Or somewhere in between? When you start out, there is a lot of floundering to do. Young directors tend to simply be themselves as directors and often find out being themselves does not get the results they want. It is helpful to keep in mind just where on the Guthrie–Quintero continuum you want to end up.

Don't get me wrong. I'm not saying that directing is a performance, and you get to choose your directorial persona. Yet there is a sense in which that is exactly what I'm saying.

—◆—

With the first two openings under our belts, with the audiences beginning to fill the houses nightly (we played to something like 90 percent capacity that first season), during the days we turned our attention elsewhere. It was time for Chekhov.

Chekhov to be directed by Tyrone Guthrie? To many it seemed an unlikely pairing. Given his obsession with externals, his overbearing ways that can stifle the actor's creativity—with all that glossy panache, they asked, what could Guthrie possibly bring to a play like *Three Sisters*?

As it happens, quite a lot.

I sometimes think we mistake British style (of which reticence is an important part) for shallowness. How long did we dismiss Noel Coward as trivial and diverting? He made it easy for us, with his ever so gay, bon-vivant persona, so it took us a while to catch on to the profound comic genius he really was.

So with Guthrie. All that flash and flamboyance seemed to come from a wonderfully nimble but superficial intelligence. Not for him the thoughtful probing, the careful exploration of the wellsprings of behavior, the evocation of a Deeper Reality, and so on.

Oh, Lord, no. "But," he asked, "is that what Chekhov really needs?"

Mind you, this was a time when Chekhov was being taken *verrrry* seriously in this country. The "Methodists" had claimed him as their own and told us that the only way to approach his plays was by immersing ourselves in the system of that other Russian, Konstantin Stanislavski. If we were beginning to think that maybe it was true, Guthrie's views came as a bracing antidote. That acute critical intelligence he sometimes seemed at pains to conceal, I encountered in his writings. This is from his preface to his own translation of *Three Sisters*:

There was something else: his home address. It was Annaghmakerrig, Doohat P.O., County Monaghan, Ireland. He was a pedigreed Anglo-Irish toff, the lord of a large, slightly seed manor house, dominating a small town, of which he was the most distinguished citizen, just as his forebears had been for generations. As his biographer points out, if you searched the Earth for the English-speaking equivalent of a late nineteenth-century Russian dacha, you just might wind up at Annaghmakerrig with its rambling, slightly down-at-heels grandeur, where eccentric relatives were to be found in odd corners and new guests turned up daily, and where boozy Irish workmen—ever so charming to the guests with their quaint locutions—were ever so exasperating to their employers with their careless, larcenous ways.

We went to work on *Three Sisters*. After opening a theater, after performing in two difficult classics that had tested their mettle and stretched their talents, the Minnesota Theatre Company considered working on *Three Sisters* a wonderful reward.

Did Guthrie's change his style in any way to suit the different material? Not a jot. The same breathtaking speed, the same authority, the same impatience with chat.

Rita Gam, our glamorous Hollywood lady, had turned out to be a valuable and talented member of the company. She was now at work on her plum role of the season: Masha in *Three Sisters*. In rehearsal one day, she was trying to please Guthrie but not succeeding. After a third failed attempt at the same speech, she burst into tears. At the SM table, heads were bowed in embarrassment and sympathy. Suddenly we heard the fingers snap, then the crisp British voice intoned, "Sorry. Won't do. Won't do at all. You were hired to play the part. Either play the part or get off the stage."

A pause. Eyes wide, Rita swallowed hard and went back to work. Rule number four: tears don't work either.

At a time when the settings for Chekhov's plays get more and more bizarre—mirrored walls, steam curtains, abandoned ferry boats, you name it—dwelling at any length on what in 1963 was Guthrie's "radical experiment" of performing *Three Sisters* on an open stage, seems foolish indeed. But it was odd to see that chaste and pristine platform cluttered with furniture, lots of furniture. The original floor plan was so dense with chairs, tables, footstools, sofas, credenzas, and so on that you had to move crabwise from place to place. He took one look and began thinning it out. If still crowded, it began to look plausible.

What soon became apparent, however, was that a certain kind of production was going to be impossible—the languid Chekhovian twilight, beloved of lighting and set designers, where low sunlight streaked the faded wallpaper, and the delicate tracery of birches (why is it always birches?) was etched against the sky. This production would be yanked out of that sentimental cocoon and placed on the palm of a huge hand that thrust toward us, and the message was "Here! Look!" Clarity was the result.

I worked "the deck," as we called it, which meant that I was working backstage, concerned with sets, props, costumes, and performers. It was something of a comedown after the eagle's nest, but it gave me a chance to be around the company more, which I relished.

Guthrie approached the piece with his usual sure-handed brio; the production was swiftly given an indelible shape: the flow of the movement, the dynamics of the scenes, the parameters of character were precisely communicated.

There are fourteen parts in *Three Sisters*. They are all quirky, human, obsessive, and lost, each stunningly unique. It is not an easy show to cast, but it fit terribly well on this group, from the sisters to the servants, from Rita Gam's haunting beauty as Masha to Ruth Nelson's doddering, lovable nanny, Anfisa.

It was also a superb illustration of what the repertory system is all about. So where was Lee Richardson, whom you saw last night as Claudius in *Hamlet*? Playing, with touching charm, a walk-on, one of the soldiers, Fedotik. And where was Prince Hamlet himself? All steely-eyed and murderous as Solyony. And Hume Cronyn, whom you saw two nights ago as Harpagon the miser is now Chebutykin the old doctor, fond and foolish, full of love and rage and feigned indifference.

If the nature of the platform gave the play a new kind of clarity, Guthrie's work reinforced that clarity. It was honest, uncluttered (save for the furniture), witty, unsentimental. It let the actors shine.

It was, Zoe said, the play that made us a company.

It was received with great warmth by the audience, and no one seemed to miss the birches.

Zoe was playing Natasha, the social-climbing schemer who makes life hell for the Prozorova girls. Dr. G took her aside somewhat conspiratorially at one rehearsal and suggested that Natasha should sound like Dolly G——. Zoe's jaw dropped. Dolly G—— was one of our most loyal and hard-working volunteers. Moreover, she was popular with the company. (It was also true that she had a distinctively shrieky midwestern voice...)

ZOE (*very distressed*). Oh, Tony, I couldn't!

GUTHRIE (*with a mad gleam*). Let's be cheeky!

And so they were. Act III takes place on the night there is a fire in the town and the Prozorov household, much to Natasha's chagrin, becomes a sort of aid station. I have a vivid memory of Zoe as Natasha, waddling about switching a cane noisily back and forth under the beds to be sure no refugees have strayed into the upper rooms, all the while haranguing Olga ("Ole-ger") in a flat, irritating voice about her unfortunate habit of treating the servants far too indulgently. It made a memorable impression, but nobody seemed offended.

It could be that there was more Aussie in Zoe's voice than Akron, but whatever the reasons, I got the feeling that Guthrie was disappointed. I had learned something else about him: he loved, as the English might put it, to be naughty.

———

In social situations when the going got particularly stodgy and people were getting slightly too self-important, Guthrie was wont to fall back on a certain Anglo-Saxon directness.

In 1963 using the word "fuck" could set off alarum bells of outrage much more effectively than it does nowadays. They were bells that Guthrie loved to ring. The more rigid the audience, the more outrageous he could become. Audiences made up in part or wholly of nuns were a favorite target. At one such gathering— some sort of theater roundtable that took place in an auditorium liberally sprinkled with black habits—after half an hour of learned observations by the experts, one of them turned to Guthrie, who had yet to say a word, and asked why such and such a Broadway production had failed. Guthrie replied blandly, "Well, it wasn't much fucking good, was it?" First there was a short, charged silence; then shrieks, gasps, and blushes followed. He sat there, arms and legs crossed, a genial grin on his face, one foot dancing wickedly. Then he started to speak. Within minutes they would have renounced their vows for him.

Sometimes, it was more than a simple desire to scandalize. It was more serious than that. He had a profound aversion to hypocrisy and emotional posturing of any kind and was not loath to vent his displeasure.

Pat Slingsby was one of the extras in *Hamlet*. He was a big, robust, likable kid who played one of the palace guards. Unknown to us, he had a serious heart condition, one that if he heeded his doctor's advice would prevent him from doing any kind of strenuous physical activity. Slingsby loved to waterski, and he refused to give it up. A week after *Hamlet* opened, he went water skiing and died.

We got the news in midafternoon. A rehearsal was scheduled in advance of the evening performance. Since we had no time to cast a replacement, it was a question of finding actors who could take over Slingsby's tasks in addition to their own. Because I had the blocking notes, I was the one who knew (or thought I knew) exactly what Slingsby did.

Later in the theater, most of the company having arrived, we set rather sadly to work. Guthrie wandered in. He had no interest in running the rehearsal; he was just checking to see how things were going. This was, after all, our first real company crisis. It all went smoothly enough, accompanied by heartfelt sighs of sympathy and loss, until we got to the fencing scene in Act V. The way it was blocked, Nic Coster (Laertes), after he was stabbed by Hamlet with the poisoned sword, struggled toward the front edge of the stage, then pitched forward to be caught by...whom?

There was some discussion. Was it Slingsby, or Slingsby plus several others? I interrupted to intone a shade portentously, "According to what I have here" (in the book), "Pat Slingsby caught the full weight of Nick when he fell."

A helpful Anglo-Irish voice to my right offered brightly: "Hmmm, perhaps that's why he's not here tonight." Like everyone else, I swung around to look at him, disbelieving. He was looking right at me. The eyes were wide—mad and defiant. There was a pause, then he giggled. Not laughed, giggled. I was appalled. How could he be so unfeeling? It was his way of telling us to stop the b.s., carrying on so solemnly about someone we hardly knew. So he struck, and what a zinger. It is hard to forget those mischievous eyes.

———

Starting to work on *Death of a Salesman* was like a homecoming. Finally, this predominantly American company would get to work on an American play. An irony, perhaps, in the fact that the Lomans, Willy and Linda, would be played by a Canadian (Cronyn) and a Brit (Tandy) respectively, but the general feeling of the reach being very much within the grasp was palpable.

It was Guthrie's stated purpose to produce not only "classic" plays but plays of a more recent vintage that might achieve that exalted status with the passage of time. In this regard, the standing of *Salesman* in 1963 was in doubt. Though it was clearly an important play in its time (it was first produced in 1949), the jury was still out on its staying power. It was high time for a second look.

There was also an interesting sidebar. Arthur Miller had one reservation about Lee J. Cobb, the original Willy. It was one that Cobb couldn't do much about. The author thought the actor was the wrong type physically. Cobb was a bear; Miller wanted a weasel. Willy, he thought, should be small, intense, and wiry.

You want small, intense, and wiry? We've got small, intense, and wiry. His name was Hume Cronyn. We also have Jessica Tandy, long-suffering and poignant (Linda); Lee Richardson, strong but sensitive (Biff); Nic Coster, flashy and shallow (Happy); and more—a really terrific cast. We knew we were on the way to a major re-examination of a great play.

But it didn't work—just never came off.

I don't really know why. Maybe it was the chemistry between director Campbell and Cronyn. Maybe it was the treasury which seemed to have been seriously depleted by the first three productions and left *Salesman* looking makeshift and forlorn. Maybe we were all just too tired from being in rehearsal almost continuously for so many months. Maybe it was all of the above. Whatever. But *Death of a Salesman* was nothing to be ashamed of. It was a good, solid production, was praised and well attended, but it never came close to fulfilling our (perhaps excessively) high hopes.

At Dr. G's show shop back in 1963, all four plays of the first season's repertoire were up and running. It was time for me to start chasing actors again.

Two days after *Death of a Salesman* opened, I posted a notice in the green room. All in caps, in prose that I had evolved with excruciating care, it outlined the project I had in mind and asked for volunteers. "Please sign up below if you are interested." I put it up just before the half-hour call, then fled to the booth. I was not optimistic. Everyone was just too tired after the long ordeal of opening a theater and four big productions to undertake something that would eat up all their free time. I thought that, with luck, I would get a few of the junior members of the company. I'd have to use my powers of persuasion to find the rest.

I stayed in the booth long after the performance of *Hamlet* was over. For some reason I wanted to be alone when I saw the results of my flyer. I walked to the green room. Everyone had left. The theater was locked up tight. Only a few nightlights were burning. One of them threw a dull glow on the call board. In the half-light I could see my signup sheet. It was filled with names—twenty-five at least—and at the top, Hume Cronyn and Jessica Tandy. I was on my way.

The program I wanted to do consisted of two one-act plays and a long poem. They were *The Hour-Glass* by William Butler Yeats, in which an atheist teacher is visited by an angel; Robert Frost's *Masque of Reason*, subtitled "The Forty-Third Book of Job," that took place in the hereafter when Job and Mrs. Job finally get a chance to ask God "Why?"; and what I thought of as the main event, my staging of T. S. Eliot's masterpiece *The Waste Land*.

They were three pieces by poets in which God or some manifestation of a deity appears, and I had combined them with stunning alliterative erudition (or so I thought) under the title *The Poet as Prophet*.

This was the script I had given to Peter Zeisler earlier. It had been approved, and I set about casting. I did not have anything attractive enough for Cronyn or Tanner, unfortunately, but I did wind up with a splendid company led by Zoe—and Ken Ruta, predictably as God.

I soon discovered that the whole program was more than I had bargained for. It was a serious production. It had to be produced. It needed set pieces, costumes, props, music, sound. I would need a lot of help. Moreover, in rehearsal, I realized that the works I had chosen were not what you might call surefire material. The title might have a nifty ring to it, and it was nice to be able to toss around the names of Yeats, Frost, and Eliot, but I had a real piece of work cut out for me.

One day after a rehearsal, the results of which you might call ambiguous, Zoe made a remark not overly imbued with affectionate concern. "This," she said, "better be good, mate." She was right—it *had* to be. I had made up my mind that this was where I wanted to work. If my future was to entail anything more than stage managing, this project was my ticket upward. Most importantly, Guthrie was still around. All the shows had opened, but he had not yet departed for Ireland. I was told he would see *The Poet as Prophet*. I bore down with a will.

I had always felt that T. S. Eliot was a lousy playwright. *Murder in the Cathedral*: heroic and bland. *The Cocktail Party, The Confidential Clerk*: bloodless. For some reason, his talent as a playwright shone in his poetry. To me there was more real theater in something like the seduction of the typist in *The Waste Land* than in any of his plays. My understanding of the poem was not particularly deep, but I understood it as theater, as a work teeming with characters and dramatic situations. I thought if I could give it shape on a stage, I might clear up some of the obscurity. It would also give me a chance to try my hand at staging of epic size on that unique platform.

One night, only a week before we were to perform, Herb Pilhofer, the theater's music director (as well as jazz pianist, serious composer, and entrepreneur) came into the theater with a half-dozen musicians in tow to record the score he had written for *The Waste Land*.

I had felt music could be valuable for the piece and had approached Herb about writing a score. He agreed. Great! I outlined what was needed. Now several weeks later it was time to hear what he had been up to. I was particularly excited because for the first time I was going to have a score composed specifically for a piece I was directing. No more tedious searches, listening to piles of recordings, trying to find something *like* what was needed, and endless hours patching together a tape.

The musicians set up, mikes were placed about and tested. We were ready for the down beat. One problem. There was no music. No tiny dots on the lined paper.

Herb!

Pilhofer was sorry, but he had been too busy. There was simply no time.

I was clenching my teeth, exhaling through my nose. How could this happen? And what was the sense of bringing in all these musicians? What could we do?

Well, what we could do, Pilhofer suggested with annoying insouciance, was something called "instant music." "Just describe what you want, and we'll make it up as we go along," he said. The whole idea seemed futile and amateurish. But what choice did I have?

I started out somewhat resentfully. I felt I was being shortchanged. Happily, that did not last long.

I would describe a scene: "The bank of a river, late fall, getting chilly, wet leaves, broken bottles…" Pilhofer would think a bit, and then it was: "Clarinet, try this…(suggesting a theme while making those extraordinary sounds only musicians can make when imitating a musical instrument), and flute, try this…" Then he'd sit down at the piano and away they'd go.

> PILHOFER (*still playing*). Something like this?
> Me: Almost.
> PILHOFER. What's wrong?

ME. The piano: too many notes.
(Piano music is thinned out.)
PILHOFER. Okay?
ME. Better. Maybe a slower tempo?
Tempo slows.
PILHOFER. That do it?
ME. Great.

Then we'd record.

It became a wonderful, creative jam session. By the end of it, when I felt a certain cue didn't sound right, Pilhofer simply said, "Hum it." "What?" "Hum what you hear." I wasn't a musician. I didn't hear a damn thing. But I managed "La, la, la" for a couple of bars, and we went on from there.

I can't remember how long the session lasted; I only know that it was an exhilarating ride. I also learned an important lesson—that expertise was not mandatory. I could get along without knowing how to read music fluently, or without a mastery of period costuming. They would be wonderful skills to have, but I don't think the former would have changed the outcome of the recording session. What I learned that night has stayed with me the rest of my career: in the face of all sorts of intimidating expertise, the only thing a director has to know is what he wants. The more knowledgeable you are, the better, but finally it comes down to knowing what you want. That and, importantly, the ability to communicate same.

It was time for the single performance of *The Poet as Prophet.* That Sunday evening attracted a decent-sized crowd, maybe a hundred or so, and there in the audience—the Good Knight. Let's go!

First came the Yeats play. I had directed it broadly, as a folk farce. I wanted it to warm up the audience, get them reacting. It did not quite have the desired effect. Hmm. Maybe they were too spread out in the big 1,400-seat house?

A short intermission, then Frost's biblical piece. The poet's stage directions were brief: "A fair oasis in the purest desert." I had made it a celestial beach with God (Ken Ruta) a superannuated lifeguard in one of those high chairs, and Job (Bill Pogue) and Mrs. Job (Kate Emery) just coming back from a dip. The Devil came in later, played by Jimmy Lineberger, who at the time was a hot young playwright. He had put his writing aside to join the apprentice ranks under the Flying G. He had a wonderful bad-boy face. We put him in knickers and a sport shirt plus one of those beanie hats like the type Spanky wore in the *Our Gang* comedies. The only thing that gave him away was a bright red tail. It went well. The audience responded warmly.

Then another pause. When they came back, it was time for the chef d'oeuvre, *The Waste Land*. This would be my passport out of the stage managerial ranks—the piece that would make Messrs. Guthrie, Zeisler, and Rea sit up and take notice.

It went well. Pilhofer's music was splendid, the actors were at their best, the staging sizzled with panache (or so I thought), and the big choral stuff that we had labored long and hard over in the last section of the poem ("What the Thunder Said") brought it all to a terrific close.

No one stood up; no one yelled "Bravo;" but there was enthusiastic applause and heartening compliments after we finished. "Of course, I didn't understand it, but—."

Zoe had set up a small party in the basement of Mrs. Van Horne's house after the show. Cast, crew, and some of the audience came, Dr. G among them. As I was finishing my first drink and the tempo was picking up, he tapped me on the shoulder. "I suppose you want to know what I thought?" I answered in the affirmative. We repaired to a window seat.

> GUTHRIE. Never could write for the theater, could he?
>
> ME. Who's that?
>
> GUTHRIE. Eliot. Always trying, poor thing, but nothing worked.
>
> ME. But don't you think the poetry is …
>
> GUTHRIE. Now, the Frost. Very original. Loved it. Nicely staged. Wasn't Jimmy a treat! (*Guffaws—Jimmy was a favorite.*)
>
> *(Pause.)*
>
> GUTHRIE. Yeats.
>
> ME. Yes.
>
> GUTHRIE. Don't know fuck-all about the Irish theater do you, dear boy? It was really appalling. How in the world…

And then he went on at some length, rather heatedly. When there was a gap, I jumped in. I reminded him of a passage from his own book, *A Life in the Theatre*, in which he tossed off the following dictum casually, as an acknowledged truth that hardly needed restating. It read, "The first task of the director is to make up his mind what the play means to him."

Did you get that? **The first task of the director is to make up his mind what the play means to him.**

Now back to Mrs. Van Horne's and Dr. Guthrie.

> ME. To him? To *him*! I couldn't believe it. Wasn't the most important person the playwright? Shouldn't

the director be trying to find out what the play-wright had in mind? The ideal performance *he* envi-sioned? I really wrestled with these thoughts; it took a long time, but finally the truth began to sink in; it was dangerous and liberating and a little scary, but it gave me the guts to do *The Hour-Glass* the way I did.

Oddly, my memory fails here, a short power outage. Our discussion ended amicably enough, but I can't remember the details. I recall it as sort of a draw. I do remember that he left soon thereafter, and the party didn't last much longer – not because he left, but because Zoe had hidden the liquor bottles. I was ready to go all night, but Mrs. Van Horne, who was after all our landlady, had given us a curfew.

It was quite true, what I said. Those words in *A Life in the Theatre* gave me the courage to do *The Hour-Glass* the way I did, the way *I* understood it. Yes, it was brash, tasteless, and an insult to any literate Irishman. Thank God I had textual backup when one of them confronted me.

In his writings Guthrie enlarges upon this point. The best play-wrights, he says, working instinctively, can sometimes be quite in-nocent about what they had written. He uses the example of the Scottish playwright James Bridie, who, when Guthrie approached him about elucidating some piece of text, said, "I don't know, old boy, you'll have to figure it out. I just wrote the thing."

There's that story of O'Neill delivering the newly completed manuscript of *Ah, Wilderness* to the Theatre Guild saying, "I don't know what this is. It's a dream I had." And we shouldn't forget Mr. Browning's line to the inquiring Elizabeth Barrett: "There was a time, Miss Barrett, when the meaning of that line was known only to God and Robert Browning. Now, I'm afraid only God knows."

Even if there were a pure, ideal author's production, would it make any sense fifty years after the play was written, when social context, political climate, and even acting styles may have changed radically?

The clincher for me was an appreciation of the process of directing a play. That long, soul-consuming journey can't be ignited by a weak flame of earnest brainwork. A play has to vibrate at a deeper level than the intellectual concept of an ideal production. It must rattle the guts and assault the brain like a fever. It must shake the director. How else can he be sustained over the long and debilitating course that is a production's genesis? A director must inspire actors; what he communicates must be fired by passion, not intellectual rectitude.

It is also true that directorial egoism of this kind can lead to all sorts of tasteless excess. Certainly, this present age of Deconstruction and Re-Examination has produced more than its share of mangled classics. Directorial solipsism must be tempered by a wide knowledge of literature, art, and the taste it engenders; if not, the result is liable to be superficial and flashy—great technical mastery informed by an aesthetic that is commonplace and vulgar. Speaking for myself, in Minneapolis in the '60s I was making up lost ground and learning a lot very quickly. But, alas, for all the best efforts of my mentors, they could not save me from leaving a few mangled corpses along the way: here, with a stage brace through his heart, *Julius Caesar*; there, headless in the dust, *Cymbeline*.

———

It was now the late summer of 1963, before the Vietnam War ruined everything, at a time when the cognoscenti were beginning to write about a "cultural renaissance" abroad in the land, when the Minnesota Twins were only a game and a half out of first place, and the Tyrone Guthrie Theater, in the midst of its first season, was hosting near-capacity houses. Being a member of the Minnesota Theatre Company was as sweet and enviable a position as could be found on the face of this Earth.

Aside from the heady atmosphere at work—side by side with the best in the world—we were discovering, now that we finally had some free time, that there was an entire community out there waiting to spoil us rotten. There were so many parties, excursions, picnics, and day trips that soon the whole company began to reel from overindulgence.

Sally Irvine, a spirited and witty lady who was also a generous patron of the arts, opened her house on White Bear Lake to the entire Minnesota Theatre Company for the first of the yearly Lucullan extravaganzas that came to be known as "The Irvine Do." It was an entire day of tennis, boating, golf, swimming, or what you will, followed by a night of revels and dancing till dawn.

Evy Nordley opened her house to the Minnesota Theatre Company *and* the Minnesota Twins. It was an unforgettable night. There I was, chatting with Don Zimmer, while across the room Billy Martin was trying to teach Bob Pastene how to give signals like a third-base coach. In a quiet corner, John Cromwell was deep in baseball theory with catcher Earl Battey.

And then there were trips down the Mississippi and picnics by the lake (choose one). And Mrs. John Getz gave that wonderful dinner with succulent lamb roast.

Along with this giddy social whirl, there was some learning going on. Zoe, particularly, was showing us what this thing of being a resident artist in a community was all about. I had never given it much thought. Summer stock and off-Broadway were, after all, transient institutions; such concerns never surfaced. But now, as members of this very visible institution, we had a new kind of work. People, even if they were not attending the productions, were hugely curious. They wanted to know what we were all about.

"Why aren't you supposed to be making any money?" "Why can't I see Hamlet on Thursday?" "Why is the stage that odd shape?"

We would try to explain what nonprofit theater was, how a repertory works, and the thinking behind the open stage. Everything was so new. It was going to take a lot of time to get the message across. The Tyrone Guthrie Theater, as the eponymous knight had told us, was to be their theater. It wasn't yet. Part of our responsibility was to encourage that sense of ownership.

Even before the first opening, some of us were being sent on goodwill missions to other theaters in the Twin Cities. I did my best to charm them and, per instructions, to reassure them that the opening of the Tyrone Guthrie Theater was not a threat to their honored place in the community. We produced quite different work, after all. Moreover, far from having a depressive effect on Minneapolis theaters in general and siphoning off audiences that might rightfully be theirs, the opening of this big new theater would have a positive effect, leading to a reawakening of interest in theater in general that would, if anything, *increase* their attendance. Several years hence we could anticipate a time when new theaters would be springing up all over town.

I didn't quite believe it myself but, by God, I was right. Or rather, the folks who had prepped me were right. Our opening did lead to a keener interest in theater, all kinds of theater. And before long new theaters *were* springing up, in great enough numbers to start Minneapolis on the road to being a real theater hub. Show shops as varied as Mixed Blood, the Old Log, the Minneapolis Children's Theatre Company, and many others currently flourish along with the Guthrie.

———

By the end of August 1963, the first season of the Minnesota Theatre Company came to a close. Zoe and I went traveling. She showed me Stratford, Ontario, where I got a chance to see that magnificent theater (the Mother Church, really) up close. And I showed her New York City. We spent a couple of weeks there at Christmas fitting in everything: galleries, shops, hockey games, opera, and plays, plays, and more plays. Also the founding storefront of famed fast-food restaurant Nedick's, the Staten Island Ferry, the Cloisters, Central Park, and Times Square on New Year's Eve.

After an initial rush, the playgoing became oddly unsatisfying. We were seeing these hit productions, but somehow we weren't being fed. There was Zero Mostel being ever so funny in *A Funny Thing Happened on the Way to the Forum,* and lots more, but we left unmoved or unamused or un-*something.* We were getting desperate for some other kind of creative fix.

Then we found it. Shortly before leaving New York, we went down to Circle in the Square Theatre and saw a matinee. We walked in with grim resignation and walked out a few hours later, ten feet tall, born again, all doubts vanished! We had just seen Michael Cacoyannis's spare, deeply moving production of *The Trojan Women.* Stunning chorus work, brilliant acting by the principals, dominated by Mildred Dunnock, who brought to the role of Hecuba a desiccated grandeur that I shall never forget.

After New York we got in a car and started south. I was taking Zoe to Washington, DC. But there was an important stop to make on the way, at a ramshackle farmhouse in western New Jersey, the mountain redoubt of my Aunt Caroline. These two formidable ladies, Caroline Lexow Babcock and Zoe Ana Caldwell, took to each other with a will. The Aussie free spirit met the aged Shavian New Woman, and the sparks flew—sparks of delight and discovery. A two-day conversation covered everything from cooking on a wood stove to the poetry of Dylan Thomas. A grand time was had by all, or so it seemed.

When we drove away, a light rain was falling. Inside the car, I was starting a fight. I swerved onto the narrow shoulder of the highway outside Blairstown and pulled to a stop. I was in love with Zoe. We were on our way to Washington so she could meet my folks, for God's sake, but here I was, exploding with jealousy. "She's *my* Aunt Caroline," I bawled. Suddenly a greasy ogre called My Insecurity had slipped into the back seat. The results were not pretty. Large technicolor exhibitions of pusillanimity never are. But what can you do? It came down to the fact that Zoe was out of my league. She was a star. I was an insecure beginner. Maybe I could get to her level, but I had to do it myself. I didn't want to live in her shadow.

Oh God, what a mess. The ogre raged while Zoe was, as she always was, generous and loving. In short order, I pretty well destroyed our relationship. Then we hugged each other in silence, rocked from time to time by a headlong whoosh of a passing semi. Then we told each other lies, but we both knew our time had ended. We would continue the trip to Washington and would see more of each other, but personally it was over. Fortunately for both of us, it was not over professionally. But that is a story for later.

———

Being back at Mrs. Van Horne's for the second season took some getting used to. Zoe was in Toronto filming for television, and Campbell was now living next door in a house he had rented for his wife Ann and their kids. I was a bit at sea, but not for long—there was too much work to do. In addition to my stage managerial duties, I had a semi-official role as head of workshops. This meant that anything that was done outside of the regular season was my responsibility. I hadn't been given a major show to direct yet, but I had taken a small step in that direction.

At the University of Minnesota, a popular professor by the name of Arthur Ballet was setting up, with help from the Rockefeller Foundation, an entity with a racy name: Office of Advanced Drama Research. It would produce several of the workshops we did and was also a source of new material. Arthur had a script he wanted me to direct called *And Things That Go Bump in the Night*—interesting, inchoate '60s writing by a promising beginner named Terence McNally. I thought it would be a good idea but then I came across a play about a man who loved a pig.

One day I was laboring through the great pile of scripts that had been arriving at the theater and discovered a long one-act called *Futz*, by Rochelle Owens. It chronicles the tragic fall of Cyrus Futz, a farmer who is on intimate terms with one of his pigs. Cy is hard-working and the gentlest of men. He just wants to be left alone with his porcine inamorata, Amanda, but the crazy redneck townspeople won't let him be. Ultimately Cy is lynched. However gamey the plot, the play is at heart a haunting tragedy about intolerance, given distinction by Owens's superb prose poetry—at times playful and satiric, at others wistful and dark.

Few agreed with my assessment. It became known as "Ed Call's Pig-Fuck Play," and most gave it a wide berth. I suppose there was something perverse on my part that drove the project as well. After two seasons of impeccably respectable classics, I felt it was time to kick up some dust for our third season.

Arthur Ballet was immensely helpful, and his organization underwrote a residency for Owens during rehearsals. Unfortunately, the timing was bad. When Owens arrived, I was busy with another workshop project. After casting *Futz*, I had to turn it over to another director.

After ten days, I began to hear that rehearsals were not going well, at least not as far as Owens was concerned. Since serving the writer was a great deal of what the workshops were all about, I felt I had to step in. With the other project out of the way, I was now able to do what I had wanted to do all along: direct *Futz*. It went together nearly painlessly. Owens started smiling again, and soon it was time to show it to the public. It was greeted by outrage from a considerable portion of the audience and some members of the press. I was hoping the piece would stir people up, but the passion of the vitriol was a surprise.

After the first performance, one of the troika, Oliver Rea, came to me with a "suggestion." He thought it would be a good idea, since the response had been so negative, for me to say a few words to the audience before the next performance. He wanted me to talk about the language, about how talented the playwright was, what a spiritual experience rehearsals had been...*anything* to blunt the response and stop the walkouts.

It seemed a reasonable request. I gave it a lot of thought, and then devised a statement, trying to keep it light and to the point. I told them about discovering the play and the collaboration with Owens. I warned them that they might find the subject matter hard to take but asked them to look beyond that to the real literary merit of the piece. Then I sat down. The performance went without a hitch, and no one walked out. I saw Owens afterwards; she seemed upset but said nothing.

Then I was confronted by an angry red bear. Campbell's eyes were blazing, his lower jaw thrust forward, his forefinger jabbing my sternum. "Never, *never* do that again!" he thundered. "Do what?" I asked. "Never apologize for the work you do. Never! Who are these people, that you must grovel for them, eh? Artists are dangerous, you silly twit! We should scare people; it's part of our attraction. It's what we're here for."

I had no answer. He was right. For someone like me, born with a deep-seated impulse to charm, it was an important warning. It's the wild side of being an artist that must not be renounced, however much society would like us to be corporate and domesticated. I couldn't make it up to Owens, but it was a deserved rebuke I've never forgotten.

Campbell and I had become "chums." During the first season, we were both living at Mrs. Van Horne's and seeing a lot of each other. He was a bit older than I and vastly more experienced. I found it easy to fall into a kind of kid-brother relationship with him (I had had a lot of practice being the youngest of my brothers), but he was like no older brother I had ever had. Under his blustery and pugnacious exterior was a true artist and thinker—a somewhat blustery and pugnacious artist and thinker, to be sure, but an exciting and original person to be around.

Memories of Campbell abound. Here's one on the light side. It concerns a skinny-dip he and Zoe and I took at the White Bear Yacht Club, in the early morning after the first Irvine Do. We were splashing happily about when a police car swerved up. As flashlights scanned the water, Zoe and I dove for cover behind the hull of a sailboat. Our companion did not. Suddenly over the shouted warnings of the police ("Not legal! Private property! Out of the water!") came a voice, a great, ringing, stentorian voice. It warned, "Put out that light! How dare you? We are guests on these premises! Put out that light!" But the beams stayed focused on the speaker. Then we watched in wonder as Campbell, *in purus naturalibus*, rose like a sea god from the waters of White Bear Lake and strode toward the policemen on the shore, water streaming from his great freckled bulk, a Jovian finger outstretched—a truly heroic moment. It should be on canvas, a large canvas; only an artist who combined the talents of Franz Hals and William Blake could do it justice.

By the time Zoe and I emerged from the water, all pruney and bent over, limping across the round stones on the beach, then making a quick dash for our clothes, Campbell and the cops were, if not friends for life, exhibiting a decent level of camaraderie. The first words I heard were those of commiseration. Campbell was "condoling in some measure" over the indignity of serious lawmen having to chase naked bathers when there was important police work to be done. We parted from the cops with handshakes all around and drove back to Minneapolis as the sky brightened.

Campbell was a consummate actor.

He had many strengths and a wide range. He played Lear and Othello and many other great classic roles. But for me, he was always at his best when his red-headedness was given free rein, when his sly, raffish joyousness was allowed to take flight. There are certain roles he did that just can't be done better. Falstaff is one; so is Volpone. And when he took a flier in the musical world, as he did in a 1969 Los Angeles revival of *My Fair Lady*, those who were lucky enough to see him know he was the definitive Doolittle.

He was a singer and dancer. A choreographer and a fencer. A director and an artist. As well as a pacifist and vegetarian, one of the most eloquent, voluble pacifist-vegetarians you would ever want to meet.

1965 Season: The Caucasian Chalk Circle

Theater people seemed to be coming from all over the world to find out what was happening in Minneapolis in those early seasons. Douglas Campbell saw to it that a fair number of them wound up, late at night, sitting around the kitchen table on the second floor of the big white house on Summit Avenue, jawing about theater and art. I listened and learned.

It was through Campbell that I got my first assignment to direct in the regular season. The plan was to revive *The Miser* in 1965. Campbell would be occupied elsewhere, so I was tapped to put it back together again. Since I had recorded all the blocking and run the show in '63, and both Zoe and Cronyn were returning, it was really a stage management job, not quite the directing break I was hoping for. Other productions for the '65 season were *Richard III*, to be directed by Dr. G, with Cronyn as Richard; *The Way of the World* with Zoe as Millamant and my old buddy Bob Milli, as Mirabelle, with Campbell directing. The final production of that season was to be *The Caucasian Chalk Circle* by Bertolt Brecht. No director had been hired. It couldn't be Campbell; he would be in Canada acting at Stratford.

I decided it should be me.

Hubris, sheer youthful hubris. I had scarcely a nodding acquaintance with the works of Brecht, but I didn't let that stop me. It was, in many ways, going to be the biggest, most complex production the Guthrie had yet undertaken. That didn't seem to bother me either.

Time passed. Every other day the name of some reputable director would hit the rumor mill, soon to be dropped for lack of interest or availability. Through it all, I kept reminding them that they shouldn't overlook the hometown product. I was still here, available, and a cheap worker.

The whole process dragged on for an ungodly length of time. I felt that the odds were getting longer and longer, when the impossible happened: I got the show.

When I had dreamed about it, it had happened like this: I was a painter of miniatures, exceedingly small miniatures. I had my little pots and my little brushes, and I created little gems the size of demitasse saucers. People dropped by the cramped little room where I was working. They looked over my shoulder and made admiring sounds. "Oooo," they went, and "Ahhh!" They said things like "You are really verrrry good. You shouldn't waste your talents on these little gems the size of demitasse saucers. You should work on something BIG." "Don't I know it," I would say, sourly, jabbing my little brush into one of my little pots. "But will they give me a chance, eh? Answer me that. Never! Here I am slaving away over these microscopic masterpieces and—" At which point the door bursts open, and in breezes a certain British knight. "Think you're so fucking good, do you? Well, let's see what you can do with THIS!" Then he turns back and wrestles in a blank canvas ten feet tall and fifty feet wide.

In reality it was quite different. I got the word early one evening, when Douglas came back to Mrs. Van Horne's. I was, as you might expect, wildly elated. We had to celebrate. So we went on a pub crawl down Hennepin Avenue. It was a long and happy night of noisy merriment that ended on the catwalk of a sign (advertising whiskey, appropriately enough) high above Hennepin Avenue with me bellowing to the street below, the buildings opposite, and the friendly twinkling starts that I was now "a Big Fucking Director!"

The morning after was harrowing. I had a miserable hangover but no time to nurse it. I had to attend a celebratory lunch with Dr G, Zeisler, Rea, and Campbell on the shores of the Apple River. As usual, Guthrie's instincts for the ritual touch were unerring. There I was told officially that I was the director of *The Caucasian Chalk Circle*. No strings. No co-director. Some of the principals had already been cast (Zoe was coming back and would play Grusha), but other than that it was all mine to make a mess or a masterpiece.

First, I had to deal with my own knowledge gap. I had a lot to learn about Brecht and Epic Theater, as well as that mysterious Brechtian quantum known as Alienation. I had to learn more about the open stage and how to use it. All that in addition to the considerable demands that the preparation of a bodaciously large production requires. Fortunately, I had the better part of a year to get ready. I would need every minute of it.

———

During China's Yang dynasty (1259–1368), Li Qianfu wrote a verse play named *The Circle of Chalk*. A popular adaptation of that play was produced in Germany in the 1930s called *The Chalk Circle (Der Kreidekreis)*, by the German writer Klabund (Alfred Henschke) . Set in China, it became the tale of a servant girl, the foundling she adopted, and their adventures together. It was a sweet, charming piece of chinoiserie. Brecht's adaptation of that story is renamed *The Caucasian Chalk Circle*, partly in contrast to that earlier version and also because he chose to set it in the Caucasus, specifically Russian Georgia.

Imagine the story as a fresco fifty feet long and ten feet high, a many-scened extravaganza teeming with vivid peasant life, painted in the style of the elder Bruegel and titled *Der Kaukasische Kreidekries*. It chronicles a medieval time in Gruzinya (the ancient name for Georgia), a time of cruel sybaritic rulers and cringing masses.

Let's begin our viewing at the far left, where we see a scene of chaos. A coup has taken place, and the ruling tyrant has been assassinated. The capital city Nuka is in flames, insurgents prowl the streets, terrified courtiers flee the royal palace. In the foreground a servant girl, Grusha, crouches, looking at an infant who lies on rich brocade. The infant is Michael, the ruler's heir, abandoned by his mother in her hysteria to escape. "Flee!" the other servants implore Grusha. "Save yourself!" But she cannot. She stays by the child throughout the night and then at dawn (the next scene) bundles him up and flees the city. In the distance we see two cruel Ironshirt soldiers, hunting for the infant prince and the reward that finding him will bring.

The story unfolds as we continue along the painting, following in vignettes the episodes of Grusha's fight into the Northern Mountains: bargaining for milk at a farmer's cabin, eluding the Ironshirts with peasant guile and her two strong arms. Then, kneeling on the bank of a mountain stream, taking the child as her own. She has just thrown away the rich brocade wrapping; you can see a corner of it sinking into the stream there at Grusha's right. She holds the naked infant upward in her hands and murmurs a prayer. Under the painting, we read: "The helpless girl adopted the helpless child."

In the next episode, we see her scrambling upward, the child securely bundled on her back, up a steep, rocky incline. The Ironshirts, still pursuing, are closer now.

Near the center of the vast painting, high in the mountains, a half-destroyed rope bridge sways over an abyss thousands of feet below—this is the Janga-Tau glacier! Grusha, with her child in her arms, at great peril, step by painful step, has made it across to the other side and safety, just before the bridge's collapse. Grusha, in the right foreground, facing somewhat away from us, holds the infant in triumph. In the distance, across the windswept chasm, the Ironshirts stand cursing.

The second half of the story deliberately begins at the extreme right of the painting and proceeds leftward to the big center panel. The first scene introduces the rogue hero, Azdak. In the dusty town square of a remote village, he is plying the trade of scribe. A rich landowner is dictating a letter. Azdak, sitting at a rickety table, writes diligently with his right hand while his left wanders up under the skirt of the landowner's toothsome wife.

The next view: after the revolt. It is dawn. Azdak is a small figure running along a path by a forest. He is on his way to the capital, bent on making a new start in the new regime.

Further on: Azdak in Nuka. We are looking at a courtroom where in the anarchy following the revolt, some drunken soldiers have decided that Azdak should be a judge. Several Ironshirts are stripping the robes from the corpse of his predecessor. Others have seated Azdak in the judge's chair and toast him with mock reverence.

Then several views of Azdak's form of justice: First, borne aloft in an improvised sedan chair, making his way along a country road, a bottle of vodka in one hand, the other outstretched, palm upward, ready to receive bribes. Next, a view of his court in session. Azdak, bored by the slow grinding of the wheels of justice, is hearing two cases at the same time. Pandemonium is depicted, with lawyers shouting, defendants tearing their hair, court officers subduing angry spectators, while Azdak presides nonchalantly, one leg thrown over the arm of his chair.

Further on: The sedan chair again. This time it is occupied by a frail peasant woman of great age. Azdak walks beside her, humbly. To one side, three rich farmers, the plaintiffs, glower and shake their fists.

Now we are standing in front of the final scene, at the center of the fresco, which brings the chronicle to a close and joins the two stories of Grusha and Azdak. Inscribed below is the title of this scene: *The Ancient Test of the Chalk Circle*.

Five years have passed. Grusha and the child have been arrested and returned to Nuka. The former ruler's faction has returned to power, and the Governor's Wife (the child's birth mother) now has gold and crafty lawyers to buy back a needed heir.

Azdak has been ordered to decide which of the two women will get custody of the child: the penniless servant girl who saved and cared for him, or the Governor's Wife who bore the child but abandoned him during the rebellion. Azdak stands on a platform in front of his chair. Before him, a small circle has been drawn on the floor in chalk. The boy, Michael, is standing in the circle, with Grusha on one side, the Governor's Wife on the other.

Azdak, having heard the arguments, has been unable to decide. He has devised a test. He tells the women that whoever pulls the child out of the circle will be deemed the real mother. The painting catches that moment just after Azdak has given the signal. Grusha has one of the boy's arms and is bending to the task. The Governor's Wife, dazzling in silver and pearls, has wrapped her long claw-like nails around Michael's other arm. They pull, the child whimpers...

So there is a taste of the people and events of the piece. This sprawling folk epic about the perils of goodness in a bad world, embellished with music and song, was the magnificent work of art I had been entrusted with. Nor was that all. The play had a framing device; it came in the form of a prologue.

The prologue takes place not in medieval times but just after World War II, "among the ruins of a war-ravaged Caucasian village." Representatives of two collective farms contend for control of a valley.

After some discussion, the matter is settled in an enlightened collectivist manner. Then an entertainment is announced. One of the farms is going to perform the ancient tale of the Chalk Circle.

Thus, if the play is performed as written, *The Ancient Test of the Chalk Circle*—the story of Grusha and Azdak—is a play within a play, a performance by a group of peasants, given to celebrate the resolution of a land dispute.

———————

Now in 1965, we were in the heart of the Cold War. Doing a play by that "Commie playwright" Bertolt Brecht was controversial enough. Some thought that the sight of earnest, idealized comrades forging their collective Marxist destiny might not sit too well with our audience. Every other production that I heard of had cut the prologue. I wondered if I should do the same.

Suddenly quite early on I was at an important creative crossroads. It really had less to do with offending the audience than with that age-old competition between convention and illusion in the theater, between the long strip of blue China silk that is waved flowingly and accepted by the audience as the mountain stream on the one hand and the real stream on the other, or the one as real as the scene director's art can make it with actual running water, phony rocks, and interesting waterside boscage. In the case of *The Caucasian Chalk Circle* I was being confronted with two radically different ways of doing the production.

Here is a single example, the scene at Janga-Tau where Grusha crosses the perilous rope bridge.

Shall we have skillfully painted Styrofoam mountains, fans blowing offstage, and recorded wind effects? Shall we try to convince the audience that what they are seeing is real? That the ragged span (superb prop-making) and the abyss below it (several open traps lined in black) are real?

Or shall we rely on the audience's imagination to propel the events? A ladder with an improvised railing nailed to one side is raised aloft and swayed on the shoulders of half a dozen peasants. This is now the bridge at Janga-Tau. The sound of the wind comes from half a dozen deep-lunged actors. And the abyss? It's there because the actors say it is.

So, two quite different choices, leading to two radically different productions: one (without the prologue) showy, realistic with some socko realistic scenic efforts; the other (with prologue) rather gauche and homemade, farmers making theater. Which to choose?

When in doubt, listen to the architecture.

I sat in the theater for twenty minutes, and the choice became clear. Those Styrofoam peaks and all the realismus? That approach was ideal for a proscenium theater. Producing the play the way the author intended not only meant performing the prologue, but also keeping the convention of the play within a play throughout. The peasant audience should surround the action, some members rising from time to time to take on roles. Now, this was nigh impossible on a proscenium stage, but not on the platform that Dr. G and Moiseiwitsch had devised, where the peasant audience, seated on the lower level that surrounds the stage on three sides, could be actively engaged as needed or utterly inconspicuous, just another row in front of the first row of the paying audience. Also, wouldn't the addition of those eight pages of Socialist Realism that make up the prologue add a depth to the production? If the story of Grusha is about the perils of goodness in an evil world, then perhaps adding the prologue would say something more—comments about the healing power of art after a time of terror and about the mysterious essence of theater, where from the earliest times people have taken objects from their everyday lives, be it a ladder from the barn or the discarded pelt of an animal, and transmuted them by simple and unsophisticated means into something different, something enchanted, something we recognize as art.

With the outline of a production scheme taking shape, it was time to think about casting. Zoe was Grusha. Lee Richardson would bring his smoky baritone and wonderfully menschy presence to the narrator of the piece, the Story Teller. The Fat Prince (jolly, devious) and the First Ironshirt (barbarous, violent) would be doubled by the protean Mr. Ruta. Ed Flanders, sardonic clown nonpareil, was perfect for Azdak. It was a strong company, top to bottom, and thanks to the wonders of repertory and the generous spirits of the artists, there were some small roles that I could cast with the likes of John Cromwell, Ruth Nelson, and Jessica Tandy.

Finally only a few small parts and the extras remained to be cast, and it was time for me to leave on my first trip to Europe. My itinerary read: New York, London, Berlin, Paris, DC, Minneapolis.

First a couple of weeks in New York, seeing shows at night and during the days sitting at a long oak table in the vaulted reading room of the lion-guarded library at the corner of Forty-second Street and Fifth Avenue, reading by the light of a green-shaded lamp, trying to get closer to Bertolt Brecht in all his roles: poet, playwright, and thinker.

It's a sorry fact that you don't hear much about old B. B. these days, but in 1964, almost a decade after his death, the reputation of his work was still extremely high. His great productions at the Berliner Ensemble—*Mother Courage and Her Children, The Resistible Rise of Arturo Ui, Chalk Circle, Life of Galileo,* and others—had electrified the theater world and became legendary demonstrations of his genius as both playwright and director. He was also an important and innovative thinker. His writings on what he called "epic theatre," on "alienation" (also called the "V-effect"), and other heavyweight dramaturgical musings were pored over in academia and were required reading for anyone who intended to direct his plays.

At the library I read his poetry with admiration, his plays with puzzled fascination, and his theoretical writings with tooth-grinding impatience. They just didn't seem to relate to the play I was working on.

I was being exhorted to rid myself of "flabby sentimentality" and enter the theater with a pure, critical mindset. There I would watch actors who weren't impersonating characters in the conventional sense; rather, they were "reporting" the characters in a detached, unemotional style. This was "a theater of the scientific age."[3] No more empathy. It would be as clinical as an operating theater and would lead not to tears and wet handkerchiefs but to enlightenment and action. I would be awakened to the social forces that brought about the hero's fall, instead of wasting my time blubbering over his sad fate.

Further, there would be supercharged moments in this theater, but these moments would be supercharged intellectually, not emotionally. "Alienation" was the term used to describe them; the actual molar-rattling German word is *Verfremdungseffekt*. Here I got completely lost. Maybe the Germans could help.

I flew to Europe both excited and nonplussed. I was beginning to understand the crux of Brecht's message. It wasn't that complicated. He was saying: "Don't feel—think." Fair enough.

But I was dealing with poor Grusha fleeing those nasty Ironshirts, her foundling clutched to her bosom, across the snows,

---

3   From Bertolt Brecht, 1949, "A Short Organum for the Theatre" in *Brecht on Theatre: The Development of an Aesthetic*, edited and translated by John Willett. (London: Methuen, 1964).

over that dangerous hanging bridge at Janga-Tau ("two thousand feet down!"). You want me to watch that and not feel? Come now. You need only add a dog, and Disney would option it.

———

Scene: East Berlin. Winter, 1964. Overcast. Damp. Cold. Surreal.

One day on my way to the theatre, I stopped to watch a traffic cop. He was trim, uniformed, standing on a small podium in the middle of an intersection. Precise military gestures of Stop, Go, and Turn orchestrated the flow of traffic. He had a presence, an odd grace. You felt he knew he was doing something important. I watched him for ten or fifteen minutes. In all that time, not more than a dozen cars passed. The gestures never changed. When I walked away, there was not a car in sight, but he went on semaphoring the nothingness: Stop, Go, Turn, Stop, Go, Turn.

Intimidating country boys called *Vopos—Volkpolizei*, the People's Police—were the cops of East Berlin. I was stopped one day by a prowl car. Four cops. I was invited to join them, so I sat in the back seat between two hulking Praetorians. The officer in the front passenger seat had my passport. From time to time he asked me questions in quite good English: Where from? Why here? And so on, in between long uneasy silences. After a half hour of driving around aimlessly, my passport was returned and I was dropped off. No explanation. I found out later that I had strayed off the beaten tourist path by a block or two. I didn't stray again.

Then the checkpoints, the breaches in the wall. Exasperating delays, and all around, those poignant faces that reflected the pain of a senselessly divided city.

My hotel was in West Berlin. I slept there, but most of my time was spent in the East at the Theater am Schiffbauerdamm, the home of Brecht's company, the Berliner Ensemble.

I saw some magnificent theatre—most memorably *The Resistible Rise of Arturo Ui*, Brecht's chronicle of the rise of Hitler as if it had happened in the United States and Hitler were a Chicago gangster. Ekkehard Schall played Ui (Hitler/Capone) with a manic comic panache that was at once scary and side-splittingly funny. The rest of the company was first rate: lots of vivid physical acting and lean, indelible sets.

The Caucasian Chalk Circle was not in the repertoire when I visited East Berlin. I was glad, in a way. These folks were so good, their productions so distinctive, that given the chance to see Brecht's own version of the piece, I might just have decided that the best way for me to serve the Minnesota Theatre Company would be to prepare a carbon copy.

If I could not see the production of *Chalk Circle*, I could see an impressively extensive record of it. I was taken to a comfortable study and seated at a table; several bulging picture albums were plumped down in front of me. These were the *Regie-buchs*: a detailed photographic record of the entire production. Brecht wanted to be sure that his ideal author's version of the play (that which Dr. G. and I had agreed so thoroughly didn't exist) would be available to directors like me, who might feel uncertain about his work and how to approach it.

I dove in.

It was most unusual, with so many photographs that it was as if I were watching a movie of the play, a movie dominated by one face, one divine moon of a face that belonged to Angelika Hurwicz, who originated the role of Grusha—a face so utterly lovable that my "flabby sentimentality" was irresistibly aroused.

Details of costuming and business were invaluable, and I wanted
to copy one scene outright. It takes place after Grusha has escaped
the Ironshirts and is forced into a disastrous marriage. The wedding
guests are crammed into an impossibly small room, smoke-filled
and clamorous, doing all the things that wedding guests might do:
drinking, singing, socializing, dancing, but all in subway-rush-hour
proximity. I later learned mine was not the first theft of this scene;
Brecht himself had stolen the scene from a Marx Brothers movie,
A Night at The Opera.

One of the dramaturges of the Theatre am Schiffbauerdamm,
Dr. Hans Bunge, was remarkably generous with his time. He spent
the better part of an afternoon with me and a translator I had hired,
trying his best to instill a knowledge of and appreciation for Brecht's
concept of alienation. It didn't take. As I remember, the translator
had a few "Ah! I see!" moments. Not me.

Back at my hotel one night, halfway through my stay in Berlin,
I was reading some of Brecht's poetry in a slim volume translated by
Eric Bentley. I came to a quite passionate antiwar poem. The subject
was the Trojan War; he mourned the destruction of a civilization,
the waste of young manhood, the horror, the suffering. It was laid
out on two facing sheets of the text and came to an anguished climax at the bottom of the right-hand page. Thinking it had come to
an end, I turned the page. I was wrong. There were three more lines,
to the effect that if there hadn't been the Trojan War we would not
have the Iliad.

I had stumbled on a key, feeling stupid that I hadn't seen it before. A great deal of what was vexing me about Brecht was simply
the ambiguity of a great artist, the ability to see all sides and every
nuance of a person, a political agenda, or a deadly conflict. That also
allowed him a certain delight in inconsistency and unpredictability.

It explained my confusion when I first entered the Theater am Schiffbauerdamm, expecting to see something jarring and antiseptic—blinding light, smooth metallic surfaces, a proper venue for the clinical laboratory that was to be that "theatre of the scientific age." What did I see? Gilded cupids, festoons of grapes, tiers of loges—in sum, the quintessential class-conscious playhouse in all its decadent splendor.

Brecht was a Communist, we were told, a dangerous radical whose last public appearance in the United States before he returned to Germany was in front of the House Un-American Activities Committee. Yet the truth is, he never joined the Party and showed a studied indifference to many of its concerns, and during the entire time he was running the Ensemble, this committed East German revolutionary kept an Austrian passport in his back pocket.

He wrote a short masterpiece called *The Measures Taken* in 1931. It was a so-called "learning play," intended to demonstrate the crucial necessity for discipline in political matters and conformity to the decrees of the Party. In performance, the lesson became dangerously ambiguous when the sympathy of the audience flowed to the nonconformist and away from the "good" comrades who followed the rules. This unintended (or was it? Brecht was known for his inconsistency and unpredictability) impact was so potent that the play was banned in the USSR.

Here was a poet who could rage against the cruelty of war and then—as easily as you turn a page—reverse direction and give it a slap on the back for creating great literature. And finally, here was a playwright who dashed off challenging manifestos calling for a New Theatre, a cold, hard theatre of the Mind and not the Heart, who turned around and wrote an irresistibly sentimental play about a Lady and a Baby.

I was onto the sly Mr. Brecht.

Some of the people who collaborated with Brecht started to look like him. They put on workers' clothes, got their hair cut short and brushed it forward, and wore distinctive round eyeglasses just like the Maestro. Eric Bentley, with whom I passed a pleasant afternoon in the leafy, lakeside Berlin suburb where he was living at the time, seemed to be one of their number. He was well known as the critic and playwright who had been an intimate of Brecht's from the time of his arrival in the US, as well as his longtime champion and translator. It turned out he had an excuse (sort of) for wearing the Brechtian regalia: he had devised a cabaret program in which he played the part of Bertolt Brecht.

I found he had an easier way of understanding our author than did the dogmatic Dr. Bunge. Bentley talked and I scribbled. I came away with many valuable insights and a wonderful parting gift. As I was leaving, he said, "Forget about alienation." I happily obliged.

From Berlin I flew to Paris. It was Christmastime. I wandered around the city, relieved to be back among clamorous, undisciplined humanity. I also saw some theater, notably a Brecht production right up there with the Ensemble's best: Georges Wilson and Charles Denner performed *Mr Puntila and His Man Matti* at the Théâtre National Populaire (TNP).

———

Finally, I was back across the Atlantic and down to DC to visit the folks and to get started on the nitty-gritty of preparation for *Chalk Circle*. After kicking back for a few days, I developed a routine. As my parents went upstairs to retire, I went downstairs to work. I had set up shop in the basement, constructing a rough model of the set and other toys. There I began to work out the moves for the thirty-five actors in their seventy-five roles.

The first line of *Chalk Circle* is spoken by a character identified as Peasant Woman Left. She says, "In those hills over there we stopped three Nazi tanks." After burning lots of midnight oil, ten days later I was still searching for the exquisitely correct way to get a score of representatives from the Collective Farm Galinsk on the stage. I was still a long way from "those hills over there."

My problems had been created by the structure of the open stage. I couldn't raise a curtain in the middle of the dispute, as was Herr Brecht's intention. I could, I suppose, have done one of those blackouts during which thirty actors clump-clump-clumped into place? No, no—that was too awful to contemplate.

One thing I had learned was that problems created by the open stage are, or can be, opportunities. I began to think about having the first collective enter in silence, tired, footsore, after a long trek. They are returning to the valley that was their ancestral home, where, more recently, as partisans, they harassed the Germans, burning their own fields and picking off patrols from the woods. Perhaps the body of a Nazi soldier has to be disposed of, mementos of their own dead are found, and so on. Something like that could give a charge to the opening and draw the audience into the situation more effectively. But after ten days, I had yet to get it right. "In those hills over there" would have to wait. It was time to head back to Minneapolis.

Back at the theater, it was a whole new life for me. It was nice being made much of in my new post as assistant artistic director, but at the same time I felt at sea: no stage managerial duties to perform, no lists to make. I can't say I missed it, but I did miss being around the company on a daily basis. It would be many months before rehearsals for *Chalk Circle* got underway. Meanwhile there was homework, homework, homework, and lots of meetings.

There was also, much to my delight, Pamela.

Pamela Ullman was a knockout: a classy brunette with a curvy, long-stemmed body, a derisive sense of humor, and a surprisingly bawdy laugh. A theater student at the University of Minnesota, she had accumulated, after three years of study, a rather indifferent academic record but some solid acting credits, both at the university and in summer theater at the Minnesota Centennial Showboat, a proper sternwheeler moored on the Mississippi River, and at the Stagecoach Theatre in suburban Shakopee, home of summer "meller dramer."

She had also acted for Tyrone Guthrie. The Good Knight had arrived on campus while his theater was a-building to direct Pirandello's *Six Characters in Search of an Author*. When he left a month later, there was a dazzling production in Scott Hall (the U Minn campus playhouse) and a young woman determined to work in the theater that was to bear his name. Like most of us, she took a step down to get there. In the summer of 1965, this willowy beauty was hired not for her acting ability, but as a truck driver and prop assistant. It was around the time the designs for *Chalk Circle* were going into the shops. The truck driving meant tooling around the Twin Cities in pursuit of whatever it was the shops needed that day, from goods at a fabric store to rusted leftovers from a junkyard (the latter for composer Herb Pilhofer's homemade orchestra).

When not behind the wheel of the Guthrie truck, she could be found in the theater, standing at a large table, hot glue gun at the ready, hacksaw, tin snips, hammer, saws, and wrenches within reach, fabricating the hand props the production required. Sometimes subtler tools were needed, as when she and Shirli Frank, her coworker took up needle and thread, some coarse muslin, a snippet of yarn, and a couple of buttons and created a touching, loose-jointed Michael Abashwili doll that would be the object of Zoe's fierce, loving care.

The table at which these women worked was under the stage in the trap room. Since it was between the lower-level dressing rooms and the tunnel entrances, it was a kind of thoroughfare for a lot of the company and staff. It soon became an irresistible magnet for the men in the company. I found myself lingering there more than once and thus began a relationship with Pamela that has endured to this day, during which I have been friend, lover, husband, estranged husband, ex-husband, and back to friend again, in which state I hope to remain until my final exit up left pursued by the Bear of Mortality.

I endured long, tense sessions with Lewis Brown about the costumes. He painted big, splashy renderings that were such intimidating works of art that I would get tongue-tied trying to criticize the costumes they depicted. I relaxed when he started doing pencil sketches.

He was great with the homemade aspects of the play within a play. Hundreds of tin cans were to be flattened and sewn to burlap tabards to make armor for the Ironshirts. Pots and kettles were becoming headgear, rakes were flagstaffs, and a rusted tractor seat was the start of Azdak's sedan chair. We decided the collective had gotten some professional help; a few rental costumes had come out from Tiflis (now Tblisi, the capital of Georgia) along with the Story Teller. It allowed us to justify the knockout regalia Brown had designed for Helen Harrelson as the Governor's Wife.

Herb Pilhofer was not waiting this time. He had already begun to compose the songs, for which the instrumentation was to be appropriately homemade. He commissioned curious stringed instruments of his own design, and an unlikely armory for the percussionist: many drums, to be sure, but not drums with skins, drums from automobiles—brake drums!

Since we were a repertory company, the cast of *Chalk Circle* was often to be found at the theater. Ed Flanders (Azdak) and I were palling around a bit. It was good to get to know him better while working on this major opus together. I found he had an Azdakian quality that I admired. I can only describe it as endearing social pugnacity. Let me explain.

We went on a pub crawl one night, in St. Paul. Near midnight (by this time I was well past the legal limit) he led me to a rundown bar with a singular clientele. They were all American Indians, probably Sioux or Chippewa, which are the principal tribes around the Twin Cities. It was crowded, but we found a couple of stools at the bar.

We were served. We stared into our beers. I was feeling uncomfortable, wondering what in the hell we were doing there, when Flanders, eager for some action, gave his neighbor's arm a backhand swat, then said with a kind of perky combativeness, "So what are you? Some kind of goddamned Chippewa?" I winced. Things got quiet, like that scene in a Western movie when all the patrons at the bar back away slowly, leaving the two gunslingers to settle matters.

Happily the silence did not last long. Suddenly the man grinned, then laughed. I can't remember the answer to Flanders's question, but soon he and James (I do remember the other man's name) were conversing in boisterous amity.

When the bar closed, James led Flanders and me and a half-dozen of his friends to his place. It turned out to be a memorable night of racial fellowship where White Man and Red Man sat down and talked (not too coherently, it should be noted) as brothers.

Such are the dividends of endearing social pugnacity.

There was another dividend. It started paying out the following morning. I had been doing some research on Russian Georgia. We have known it more recently as Dmitry Medvedev's cross to bear, trying to pacify factions that go by unfamiliar names like Ossetians and Ingushetians, but studying history revealed what a fascinating, mythic piece of real estate it is. Prometheus was chained to one of its mountain crags; nearby is Mount Ararat, where lie the broken spars of Noah's ark. Jason beached the Argo on Georgia's western shore before he went in search of the Golden Fleece. It is also a brutal crossroads where, from earliest history to the present, from Tamburlaine the Great to Adolf Hitler, waves of conquest and migration have left indelible marks of their passing and created an odd racial potpourri, a vivid amalgam of East and West.

So I was lying awake, thinking of the previous night's pleasures, when suddenly I jumped out of bed, dashed across the room, and grabbed a book of anthropology I had just checked out of the library. I quickly paged through it until I found what I was looking for: several pages of photos, head shots really, maybe twenty-five to a page. They were faces, Georgian faces, of tough, burnished people with black hair and high Tartar cheekbones.

"Will you look at that! Will you just look at that! These are the people I was drinking with last night. Hot damn! This is terrific. We've got to use them in the show. Out with all the pasty Scandinavians, and the blue-haired ladies from Edina. We want Sioux faces, Chippewa faces—an older race, a wiser race. And think about this! If it is our mission to sink deep roots into the community, what better way than finding a place on our stage for this criminally deprived minority."

In the car driving to the theater, my brain seethed. "This has to work. It's a natural and could be used in so many ways. The P.R. staff will love me. Hell, everyone will love me. It's a dynamite idea."

I rushed into our offices and made as many people as possible listen to my brainstorm. I rattled on excitedly about the night with Flanders, waking up, the book, and so on. "And what are we going to do? What are we going to do? We are going to fill the Guthrie stage with American Indians!"

A cool silence.

Finally, someone spoke. "Well, you know, you can hire them, but will they show up?" Murmurs of assent, eyeballs moving upward. Other comments were offered with a dead-eyed back-of-the-throat authority. They had to do with hard-set prejudices such as being sure all valuables were in a safe place, with the weakness for "fire water," and such.

I was amazed, mouth-agape amazed. Fortunately, my frigid interlocutors were not the people I would have to deal with in putting my scheme into motion. I looked elsewhere for a sympathetic ear and found it in Brad Morison, head of our public relations department. Thanks to Brad, I was soon going out a couple of times a week to one or another Indian political or social club around town. These were modest-sized organizations, usually meeting in a member's home. When the last items on the agenda (the coming pow-wow, the fund for unwed mothers, thank-you notes to 3M for the Weber Cooker) had been taken care of, it was my turn. I pulled down the projection screen I had lugged in earlier, found an outlet where I could plug in the movie projector, usually with a member's help ("There behind the sofa. Oh, watch the lamp!"), then threaded the film and started showing our twenty-minute promotional flick, *Miracle in Minnesota.*

I innocently assumed that showing this highly effective movie about how a British knight founded a lily-white, elitist repertory theater on their doorstep, plus a few encouraging words from me, would be quite enough to have them all clamoring to join the Minnesota Theatre Company. It didn't happen, but I was always received politely, sometimes quite warmly, and often invited to stay on for tea and cookies where carefully genial conversation sometimes took a swerve into hilarity, as happened when I became the object of some elder Indian lady's extravagant flirtation. It was partly send-up of the visiting honkey, me, but it made for a good table-slapping time.

One morning I went to the theater after what I thought had been a particularly successful meeting, to be met by a distraught Brad Morison. "What in the name of God did you do last night?" he asked. The tone of his voice implied that a major outrage had taken place. I was mystified. It had been a promising meeting, I told him. Some of the members showed interest in joining us.

He then explained to me that there was in the Twin Cities a pidgin language the Native Americans use that allows the various tribes to communicate with one another. Furthermore, they had this really effective telegraph that could get the word out to the entire Native American population in the blink of an eye. He then said a short phrase in that shared dialect. I heard a rush of sharp vowels interspersed with slashing consonants. A startling form of speech, to my ear. Brad told me that it dated back to the earliest days of contact with the non-Indians and was used to identify the killers, the exploiters, those who were dangerous to the tribes. Roughly translated, it means simply, "Give the White man nothing," but the connotations were far more ominous. "Well," he said, "you are Topic A on the Indian telegraph this morning, and the words that follow your description are—" and then I heard that same rush of croaking vowels and slashing consonants.

What could this innocent, well-intentioned White boy have done to provoke such wrath? I told Brad that nothing untoward had taken place. I did remember one guy who questioned me quite sharply, but I thought I had mollified him.

I hadn't.

Morison had a friend who was well connected in the Indian community. This friend started to make discreet inquiries. Before the end of the day we found out what had happened. When I was asked why I wanted to use Indians in the play, my reply contained the word "earthy." I wanted to cast Indians because they looked or were earthy. Something like that. It was an incendiary remark: "earthy" was what all those Eastern do-gooders had had in mind back in the nineteenth century when they took away the Indians' horses and told them to start farming; "earthy" was what the young Indians were trying to escape in leaving the reservations and coming to the Twin Cities; "earthy" was a word they regarded as racist.

I am happy to relate that after considerable effort our go-between was able to get my proscription lifted, so that after a few days I was able to continue my search. But whether because of the "earthy" imbroglio or simple indifference on the part of the people I was approaching, or both, I was only able to sign up two Indians for Chalk Circle. They were Mary Perez and Sophie White, two Sioux ladies who brought valuable skills and much-needed authenticity to our production.

I wanted the Michael Abashwili doll to bob along on Zoe's back when she trekked through the mountains and facing not to the rear but to the front. The designer looked grave and scratched his head as two costume assistants folded and refolded Zoe's shawl to poor effect. I appealed to Perez for help; she stepped in, and with a few graceful gestures the babe was properly wrapped.

After decades of meetings and countless centuries of tedious homework, after watching in a state of odd detachment as the

Minnesota Theatre Company opened three big productions—
Richard III, The Way of the World, and *The Cherry Orchard*—after
March became April and April finally turned into May and May
lurched into June, after plastering the walls of the rehearsal room
with my research—photos, reproductions of paintings, as well as a
big National Geographic map of the world that I had cut out into a
large circle with Russian Georgia at the center of the Earth—after
fretting endlessly about my opening remarks and sleeping fitfully,
the sun finally rose on June 23, 1965. The first rehearsal day of *Chalk
Circle* had finally arrived.

———

The company assembled at the appointed hour, three shows under
their belts, feeling good about themselves, relaxed, chatty. As I sat
coiled in a corner of the rehearsal room, prefatory remarks were
made by ... was it Peter Zeisler? I can't remember; only that he went
on for (to my taste) an ungodly length of time. Then I thought I
heard some words of introduction. There was silence.

"Now?" I asked.

"Now," was the reply. I lunged out of the blocks and was on my
way, spewing out the history of the Caucasus; the life of Brecht;
the greatness of Bruegel (Brecht's favorite artist); the production
history of *Der Kaukasische Kreidekreis*; the infamy of HUAC; the
greatness of the Berliner Ensemble; and how Brecht, that poor slob,
couldn't do his play the way he intended it to be done because of
the stupid proscenium stage. But we here on the miracle of the open
stage could do it right, as a play within a play with all of the actors as members of the collectives, sitting around the stage platform
watching the entire production, rising from time to time to take

part, so that not only would we be saying something about art and the nature of theater itself as well as the plight of Grusha and so on, and so on…at far too great length and probably not too coherently. But we were underway at last.

I settled down eventually, and rehearsals started to proceed in that deliberate way one rehearses in rep, where the director rarely gets the company for more than five hours a day because they are performing at night. The process was not marked by crises or tantrums or devastating lows followed by thrilling breakthroughs. I think for most of the company it was just a lot of tedious work. They had not been captivated by my exposition of the Grand Production Scheme. To many of them, the whole idea of the play within a play meant nothing so much as a lot of sitting around when they might have preferred doing their funny bits and then going home. Also, they'd been in rehearsal mode for a long, long time, most of them.

There was also this. In moving from ASM to associate artistic director, I had become the boss of my peers. That, a wise person told me a long time afterward, is one of the hardest rungs up the ladder, whether the business at hand is production of a play or frozen fish sticks.

So it was hard to get their attention. At times, the going got rough. I heard (not before the opening, thank God) that a delegation of actors appeared at Zeisler's office one day with the express purpose of getting me axed. He told them to get back to work.

But I was charging on, blithely ignorant of the negatives. I was too excited, working at last on this masterpiece, and working with Zoe.

I had written to her as soon as I knew that I was to be the director and she the lead. I told her that our past together could only be a good think that would enrich our collaboration and result in the best damn…. A great deal of that was wishful thinking on my part. But she made it come true.

After a week or so we were really getting into the thick of it. Zoe was a director's dream: flexible, responsive, superbly skilled, and working on a role she was born to play. I was beginning to find that whenever one of us got impatient with the direction, it was me. One example:

Grusha kneels beside the mountain stream, that strip of blue China silk being gently waved by our attentive black-clad prop men. She throws the infant's brocade wrappings into the stream. Then she christens the child (Pamela and Shirli's button-eyed doll) in the icy water. To Grusha, this ritual binds them as mother and son.

I had something in my head from religious painting, something I'd seen in an illustrated Bible. Was it Hagar and Ishmael? Maybe it was El Greco. There was a look I wanted, a ritual way of moving, yet it was eluding me, so I wasn't describing it well.

But Zoe was listening, intently. "Tell me again." "No, never mind," I replied. "You've already tried it three times. It's probably just wrong."

"Tell me again." So I tried to tell her one more time. And she did it.

Afterward I asked, "Zoe, what was it I said the last time that I hadn't said the first three times?" "Oh," she said, "I stopped listening. I was watching your hands."

At this particular time, rehearsals were not breezing along with anything like the Guthrie panache. They were, in fact, inching along with painful dullness. But the work was getting done. And with a splendid actress like Zoe determined to get my direction by osmosis, if need be, and with Richardson and Tandy and Flanders following my lead, the production I had imagined began to take shape.

It hadn't started to "work" in any real way; there was still too much resistance from the majority of the company. But as we began to run through (stumble through, really) certain sections, at least the architecture looked right.

Now, I think, would be a good time to write about the warm, supportive relationship that grew up between myself and Tyrone Guthrie during *Chalk Circle* rehearsals. How I was taken under the Knightly Wing and given the benefit of his sage guidance and insightful advice. Yes, it would be a good time, and it would also probably make good copy. The problem is that it would be a damn lie. It didn't happen. I couldn't even get him interested.

> ME. Dr. G, come on down to the basement. I'd like you
> to see the new set model.
> GUTHRIE. No, no, dear boy. It's all yours, I'm...
> ME. But I want you to see...
> GUTHRIE. I'm sure it's fine. I'm looking for Dougie.
> Have you seen him?

Nor was he available to look at the costume renderings, nor a bunch of Polaroids of my model characters in action. Nor would he drop by rehearsals.

It was really astoundingly generous. I can't help but believe that the pressure to "keep an eye on what Ed's up to" from the other members of the troika was great. And who could blame them? I was doing my best to shepherd this challenging piece, one that needed a strong directorial hand. Was I getting it? Dr. G made it clear he was not going to meddle. He was around, always ready to chat, but talking about *Chalk Circle* was of no interest to him.

Mind you, I didn't feel deprived. I don't think I wanted advice, and when I got it, I was not particularly gracious, I'm ashamed to report. In the entire process of tech rehearsals and previews, at a time when artistic directors can bombard junior directors with overbearing advice, endless detailed notes, midnight harangues, you name it, Dr. Guthrie gave me a total of two suggestions. I thanked him and promptly forgot about them both.

But whether I wanted it or not, advice was on the way. Charlie Weber arrived. He was "just passing through and thought he should say hello." Something like that.

Carl "Charlie" Weber (he's German, so his last name is pronounced VAY-ber) ran the theater program at Stanford University from 1985 through 2013. As a young director he had worked under Brecht at the Ensemble. He was buddies with all those actors whose pictures I had pored over in East Berlin. He knew Angelika Hurwicz! He was also the director of the most famous production of *The Caucasian Chalk Circle* other than Brecht's own; this was in San Francisco at the Actor's Workshop in 1963.

Weber was hard to resist—warm, charming, and endlessly informative about the play. He started attending rehearsals. Although he was supportive and liked a lot of what he saw, he just didn't understand what I was up to with the Prologue. It was so dreary and tendentious; why not cut it? Also I needed a revolving stage—how else could I suggest Grusha's journey? Brecht had had a revolving stage; he, Weber, had had one. Didn't I want one too?

On the third day he said "we" for the first time, as in "I think we should do such and such." *We?* I blanched.

Soon thereafter, a second delegation visited Zeisler's office—a delegation of one, me, to tell him how much I loved Weber, how valuable he had been, but that now was the time for him to get out of Dodge.

And that was that.

Now that the current season was over, the pace of our work picked up. We were now able to rehearse on the actual stage. The ground cloth was down, wonderfully coarse hemp spread over the entire stage, a good gnarly surface for our actor peasants.

And the set was in place: a modest-sized platform upstage with a second level at about ten feet—big timbers and primitive planking, a barn structure, all charred and half destroyed by flame and gunfire. Like the two-level staging innovation of the Renaissance theater from which it was derived, this unit had many uses. The upper level was home base for Richardson as the Story Teller (the narrator of the piece) and his three musicians, and it became the pinnacle from which Grusha leapt onto the bridge at Janga-Tau. At one point the lower level became the tight, smoky quarters into which all the wedding guests were crammed.

So a production was taking shape. The blocking had been done, the lines learned, and the scenes drilled. But so far, we had only seen it in bits and pieces. Now it was time for those make-or-break sessions when we put it all together and began to get a sense of what we had.

Because of the stop-and-go nature of rehearsals, I had yet to ask anyone to get into the positions around the stage from which they would watch *The Ancient Test of the Chalk Circle* as members of one of the collectives. Jimmy Lawless, after he finished his role as the Delegate in the Prologue, played the following parts: a Doctor, a Drunken Friar, an Invalid, and a Wealthy Farmer. He had yet to come to grips with the fact that whenever he was not acting one of those roles, he was a member of the Collective Galinsk, and what he did as Dimitri (or whatever name he chose for himself) sitting on an ammo box watching the performance, was just as important as what he did on stage. The paying audience would be watching a performance of that venerable tale, *The Ancient Test of the Chalk Circle*. They would also be watching the watchers in the performance of *The Caucasian Chalk Circle*. Lawless's commitment to this task, his intensity as a watcher, would make the difference between the performance of a diverting morality tale and the presentation of a society in the act of rebuilding itself through art.

I had to take them with me on that journey. Given my uncertain standing with much of the company, it was not going to be easy. I had to help them find a sense of mission. It seemed a big order for someone who felt at times like a harassed third grade teacher. "Allen, stop pinching Cicely." "Listen carefully, class, because this is going to be on the test." "Henry, stop that this instant."

Oh, woe!

With heavy tread, my charges slouched down the stairs that ring the stage to that lower area, just in front of the audience, where a jumble of crates and boxes awaited them. Once they got settled, it looked quite promising: they were like an extension of the real audience, surrounding the stage platform on three sides. I started blocking them in more detail, asking some of them to move off their boxes and onto the stairs of the stage platform, closer to the action, for some scenes. But when we ran it, it just looked like picture making without any emotional impetus.

We ran several sections without much success. The action on stage seemed to be working, but all this clutter surrounding it made no sense at all. Then late one night, when I was fretting about this dilemma, my dear old Aunt Caroline popped into my head. That made no sense either, until I realized that the conversation I was recalling had some bearing on my current quandary.

It was when she had come to visit me at Circle in the Square. After seeing the show (*The Quare Fellow* by Brendan Behan) she had told me how tepid my off-Broadway experience was ("a bit bland," you might recall), compared to the magical theater world of her youth, in the plays of Shaw and Ibsen. The disparity, she decided, lay with the audience, not the performances. "We thought we could change the world," she had said, "and that had made all the difference."

I decided to tell the company that story. I started the next day's rehearsal with pep-rally ardor. It was difficult to tell how the story was being received—there were too many averted gazes. I ended with a quote from Yeats that I had used in the program notes:

> All things fall and are built again,
> And those that build them again are gay...
> Gaiety transfiguring all that dread
> All men have aimed at, found and lost.[4]

"I know it's a big leap. I know it sounds like b.s. But you have to find that gaiety. Love Grusha and her story, celebrate the golden age of Azdak's justice, but most importantly find the gaiety. You have just survived a ghastly war, you've suffered unbelievable privations, you've lost dear ones, but you're full of hope. You feel you can change the world. That's the engine that should drive this production."

Then we ran Act One: the Prologue and all of Grusha's story up to the introduction of Azdak. It took forever, but there were some promising signs. I felt that maybe, just maybe, they were beginning to find their way toward the fire.

---

4   William Butler Yeats, "Lapis Lazuli," in *The Poems of W. B. Yeats: A New Edition*, edited by Richard J. Finneran (New York: Macmillan, 1933).

When it ended, I walked up on the stage to give a note to Richardson, who was still at his perch on the upper level. The whole company was there, some few on stage, the rest scattered around the house. Richardson and I were talking; my head was raised, he was bending down from his stool. I had my back to most of the company. I felt something odd, an emptiness. I stopped in mid-sentence and turned around. There were no murmurs, no horseplay, no whispered asides, just silence. Finally, they were listening.

Now things started to happen quickly. Now that they had caught the spirit, we worked faster, more creatively. Having the company around watching throughout also became a rich source of invention. When Grusha starts singing "The Song of the Four Generals" early in her journey to keep up her own and Michael's spirits, the company became the echoing mountains. "Four generals…" Zoe sang as she trekked around the stage. "Four generals…four generals…four generals…" echoed the company. They made the wind effect in the Janga-Tau scene and became the joyous crowd trailing Azdak's sedan chair.

There is an observer in the Prologue, the Man from Tiflis, a self-important bureaucrat who had come out from the capital to monitor the dispute between the two collectives (Don West with potbelly padding, in a shiny suit and dusty fedora). After the Prologue, an armchair was dragged on and put in the place of honor, down center. Perez escorted him there; a young girl brought him a bouquet. Smiles, laughter, applause. It got *The Ancient Test of the Chalk Circle* started with a nice sense of event.

We also worked up some business for the Man from Tiflis in the intermission. The Story Teller inveigles him, aided by encouragement and a few shots of vodka from some of the others, to do a small role in one of the Azdak trial scenes. We timed it so that when the audience—the real audience— filed back in from intermission, the Story Teller would be putting him through his paces. It was not what you might call a demanding role; he had only one line, actually. "Yes!" (It was an answer to the question "Did you seduce this lady"?) "Yes!" the Man from Tiflis would bleat, attempting to transform himself into the Lecherous Stable Boy. "Yes!" he would say, over and over, until the Story Teller was confident he had captured the proper note of rustic lubricity. All the while, Sophie was prodding him into a raggedy old jacket. His performance was an occasion for prolonged acclaim from both collectives.

We were working well. There was a hint of promise in the air.

———◆———

If you had come early to the Tyrone Guthrie Theater on the night of August 3, 1965, for the opening of *The Caucasian Chalk Circle*, you would have been surprised to see the performance beginning fully fifteen minutes before the announced time. The entrance of the two collective farms that I had started puzzling over in the basement of my parents' house had taken on a life of its own and become longer and longer. It now had a name, the Pre-Prologue, and a star, Tim Christie. Tim portrayed the stout heart who volunteered to be the German soldier, lying in a rictus of death amid the ruins of war. He was capable of performing prodigies of inactivity, lying on his back in full view of 1,400 seats, often for more than 45 minutes, until he felt the weight of a Nazi boot on his wrist and the rifle he held was wrenched from his frozen grasp.

You would have seen all this, and the rest of the long opening pantomime, had you arrived early. You might also have been aware of a nervous figure flitting up and down the aisles. This was the director. He was doing nothing especially useful, just getting in people's way.

Directors, although they hate to face this fact, are utterly superfluous creatures on opening night. Their work is done, and it is now in the actors' capable hands. The time has come to step aside. I realized this, but it didn't stop me from bustling about importantly, hailing friends and behaving with resolute boorishness until I was shushed into silence by some sensible members of the audience. I retreated to a cubbyhole near one of the rear doors and chain-smoked with Zeislerian intensity for the next three hours.

Soon the house lights dimmed, the doors whooshed shut, and Peasant Woman Left (Tandy) said:

"In those hills over there we stopped three Nazi tanks, but the apple orchard was already destroyed."

Sitting on my stool at the back, possessed by nerves, I had only one thought: "I can't stop it now; I can't stop it now."

The principal anxiety on opening night was time. One of the reasons the Pre-Prologue was done with house lights up before show time was because the first act was so damn long: well over two hours. I was confident, if anyone can be said to be confident on opening night, about Act Two. It was shorter for a start, it offered some surefire comic scenes, and Flanders was terrific as Azdak.

No, it was the first act that kept me dancing nervously on that stool. Would we lose them over that long pull? Zeisler had been grumbling to me about wanting some cuts. Others talked of crisper pacing. Just make it go faster, they said. I did nothing. I wanted to see the show I directed in front of an audience. But the anxiety was putting me in jumping-out-of-skin mode.

We seemed to be off to a decent start. By the time we got to the vigil scene, which ends with Grusha picking up the baby and stealing away, the audience seemed focused and intent. By the time Zoe stepped onto the bridge at Janga-Tau, they were gasping. At that point, we were just more than an hour into the act—still a long way to go.

Directors can be obsessive about time. They hound actors about pace and cue pick-up. A minute added to a ninety-minute act is time for extensive notes and maybe a "speed-through." These are real concerns and should be dealt with, but I wondered if wanting to "see the show I directed" was simply a smoke screen. Perhaps I didn't want to rock the boat, to disturb my new relationship with the company by becoming a drill sergeant. Was I just being weak?

Well into the second hour, there is a break from the melodrama. We come to a quiet scene, just Grusha and the boy. (Time has passed, and Michael is now being played by a child actor.) She's hiding out on her brother's farm; she's worried about Simon, her intended, who is a soldier. She sings a song, "The Song of the Center," a simple tune in which a girl entreats her lover not to be a brave hero and fight at the front line, but to stay in the center and survive. If there was one place where we would lose them, it would be in this scene.

When it started, I was tuned to the house more than the stage. During the whole scene there was nary a cough, nor the scrape of a single restless foot. I began to realize that we had arrived at a new place, somewhere I had never been before, a place where the rules change. Where the actors were now, time didn't matter. These people were so in thrall to Zoe, so enchanted with Grusha and her story, that there was no fear of losing the audience. They would not budge until they knew how it all came out. We could have gone on all night. I started to relax.

Soon Flanders was back on stage and, before I knew it, we were into the last scene. Grusha had just failed the test of the chalk circle twice. She wouldn't pull hard enough. "I brought him up," she cried.

"Shall I also tear him to bits? I can't." Then Azdak, satisfied with the results of his test, pulled Michael from the Governor's Wife and her toadying courtiers and led him by the hand to his true mother, Grusha.

Then there was a brief dance and finally, Lee's envoi, which connects Grusha's story with the dispute between the two collectives:

> But you, who have listened to the Story of the Chalk Circle,
> Take note what men of old concluded:
> That what there is shall go to those who are good for it,
> Children to the motherly, that they prosper,
> Carts to good drivers, that they be driven well,
> The valley to the waterers, that it yield fruit.[5]

Two weeks later, I came back to check the show; it was a matinee. After the performance I walked down into that lower area between the stage and the audience, where ten minutes earlier the collectives had been watching the test of the chalk circle. The house was almost clear. I had been chatting with one of the stagehands. He left, and I was about to cross up onto the stage when I saw a member of the audience who hadn't yet left.

She was a step or two above me, standing at the foot of Aisle Three, which sweeps from the top of the theater to the down left corner of the stage. She was in her early teens. Her eyes were side, staring. Her arms were at her sides. She was flexing her hands, rhythmically pressing her fingertips into her palms. She was looking intently toward the stage, looking but not seeing—as if she were

---

5   Bertolt Brecht, *Parables for the Theatre*, tr. Eric and Maja Bentley (Minneapolis: U. of Minnesota Press, 1948).

reliving the performance she had just seen, or desperately willing it to begin again.

"I want..." she said, tears in her voice.

"Yes?" I said.

"I want..." but it wouldn't come out. She chewed on her lower lip, still looking at the stage. When she spoke it was slowly, but with great intensity, almost a sob.

"I want...I want to be part of all this," she said.

Would she like to have a look around backstage?

"No."

Would she like to meet Grusha? Or Azdak?

"No."

I sat her down; we talked. Or rather, I talked, about how the Tyrone Guthrie Theater was *her* theater and maybe someday...and so on and so forth. She tried to listen, but it was impossible. She was still back there, still lost in the play. She just wanted to be alone with the memories. I let her go.

The troika were dancing; the Press was ecstatic; the actors were relieved and happy. ("Why didn't you tell us, you silly boy!" they said.) The houses were packed; the audience enthralled. It was all flowers and telegrams and flattering adulation, but nothing affected me quite so deeply as that young girl at the foot of Aisle Three, lost in a spell, pressing her fingertips into her palms.

"I want to be part of all this," she said.

PART III

The Genesis of a Theatre Director

Great events call for great language; sometimes only poetry will do. In the summer of 1944, I was seventeen. I had just discovered hitchhiking and Walt Whitman. The open road was beckoning. My friend Buzz Groden and I stuck out our thumbs in New England, bound for the "far Pacific shore." What better music to accompany us than:

> Afoot and light-hearted I take to the open road,
> Healthy, free, the world before me,
> The long brown path before me leading wherever I choose.[6]
> *Allons!*

And much, much later, when the miracle revolution was underway in the late '60s and new theaters were going up all over the country, we needed Walt with his continent-embracing voice to put the exhilaration we felt into words. We needed to hear thrilling lines of free verse exhorting us to "build our theaters at every dusty crossroads" and inspiring quatrains imploring actors and actresses who loved repertory to "flee Mannahatta's isle and flood the land

---

6   Walt Whitman, "Song of the Open Road," *Leaves of Grass* (Philadelphia: David McKay, c1900).

with transcendent art." Lots of long lines with an extravagance of exclamation points.

But Walt was unavailable. Carl Sandburg was still around, but he was busy doing commercials for American Airlines. They had hired him to celebrate the beginning of coast-to-coast jet service. Not so dumb, those guys at American Airlines.

In the early years of the Minnesota Theatre Company sculptors were commissioned to do works of art that would celebrate each season. At the time it seemed a good idea, but the results were neither apposite nor impressive. They turned out to be rigid, upright creations in wood, stone, or ceramics that seemed to have absolutely nothing to do with what they were supposed to be celebrating. I thought something more representational would fill the bill—like a big splashy panoramic canvas. And since I have only to describe it, not paint it, here follows (several decades too late) my contribution to regional theater self-aggrandizement. This timeless masterpiece shall be titled "Westward, the Thespians!"

A large canvas, thirty feet wide at least. Inside an exquisitely filigreed gilt frame is a vast panorama of the American West in the extravagant style of Albert Bierstadt. In this work, however, the people are not dwarfed by the stupendous scenery, but are larger than life—mythic. Center front, in the vanguard—Nina Vance, Zelda Fichandler, and Margo Jones, a trio of Sacajaweas, leather-skirted and moccasined, with beaded headbands that read "Subscribe Now!" They have tall walking staffs in hand and are striding forward leading the new corps of discovery: the Minnesota Theatre Company, a hundred strong—all broad-shouldered and beaver-capped, right hands raised, palms up, cup-like in the open stage salute. Across the rear rank a banner spells out their defiant cry: "Repertory or Death!"

At the head of this doughty band, Sir Tyrone; he is in buckskins, from the broad belt of which hangs his fur-clad tea thermos (90 proof). His hands grip the Ford Foundation banner pole with its hood device finial and the great classic flag with its crests of Aeschylus, Shakespeare, and Chekhov spreads out in billows above his head. His mouth is open wide—the great opera-trained voice trumpets a summons heard to the far horizon. And in the distance we see the answer to that call: Over a rise, all horn-helmeted, with mighty axes held aloft, march Allen Fletcher and his bold Northwestern Ibsenites; there along a creek bed charges Adrian Hall, urging on his wildly-painted Narragansett Braves; and high, high up, all Rolfed and Alexandered, dashing through a dangerous mountain pass, marked decks and derringers in their hip pockets, William Ball and his Frisco Con Men; and all the while, Chief Gordon Davidson and his many-hued tribe from LA's Valley of Smoke, attacked by arrows of the illiberal and intolerant, move relentlessly across the plain, but never slow their advance.

Far in the distance, forlorn and disreputable, a small, jagged silhouette on the horizon: the sordid, money-grubbing eastern Metropolis these artists have abandoned, where (if we could hear them) piteous voices cry: "Help! Oh, please help us!"

But what fills our eyes and stirs our souls are the heroic figures in the foreground and the mythic setting. Everyone on this monumental canvas is striding forward into the heartland, eyes shining with hope, forward into the dazzling light of a new artistic day!

———◆———

Down at the Tyrone Guthrie Theater in the fall of 1965, the dreaded day was upon us—the Knight was leaving. The three years he had promised were up, and (inveterate mover-on, he) now was the time to pack the bags for the final getaway. He would return, we were told, at some undetermined time in the future to direct a show or two, but his leadership as artistic director was at an end. Now it was our turn to "fuck it up," as he had so memorably put it. He was off, back to the homestead, Annaghmakerrig, County Monaghan, Ireland.

As the chilling winds of winter were gathering force, a great wave of emotion was sweeping through the Twin Cities. Solid citizens, not given to emotional public utterances, felt their eyes moisten as they dreamed of speeches they would make at the Testimonial Dinner. ("Let us raise our glasses to this Great Man, this Knight Errant who rode into our fair city and began...") Visions of banquets, gifts, keys to the city, maybe even a parade or two, danced in the heads of admiring Minneapolitans.

People of all sorts—cab drivers who'd never set foot inside the place, but liked the good tippers they took to the "Gunthree" as they called it, suppliers, teachers, hotel managers, restaurant owners, travel agents, landlords, not to mention every single soul who worked at 725 Vineland Place, wanted to express their deeply felt gratitude to the Good Knight.

Of course that was not to be, none of it. Guthrie detested such displays and was determined to sneak out of town unnoticed. He asked Oliver Rea to drive him and Lady Guthrie to the airport. Oliver was glad to oblige, but not before making an unannounced detour past the theater where the entire Minnesota Theatre Company was waiting under the marquee to give him a noisy sendoff. He and Lady G. took it in good grace; they got out of the car, and amid the tumult there were flowers from us and a few brisk words from him. They got back in the car; they waved; we waved. The car sped away.

A sad silence reigned under the marquee. We all sensed an era coming to an end. Suddenly, a one-line elegy surged through my mind, courtesy of that white Black Poet, Lord Buckley:

Finger Poppin' Daddy done gone ... done gone!

Brad Morison made a film about the first season and called it *Miracle in Minnesota*. The title could easily be dismissed as glib publicist's hyperbole. But Brad was right: "Miracle" was the right word. From nothing, in the blink of an eye, a major theater of revolutionary design had appeared in the middle of the American continent. An institution was born that would have a transforming effect on the culture of the Twin Cities and shape the aspirations of theater people all over the country for decades to come.

This miracle happened because of the long-shanked Irishman. Yes, he had two superbly gifted associates, but it was his vision, his energy, along with his knighthood and prestige that made it all happen. But this is hardly news. What is news because it is so rarely mentioned, and what may be his most significant contribution to this country, was the validation of the nonprofit principle—a rejection of the time-honored idea that the source of any given theater's finances must be the money taken in by the sale of tickets and nothing else.

I had come to Minneapolis in a state of high idealism about Theater (Big T) and its role. I had also come, as a good, hard-headed "Amurrican," convinced that if you produce good theater, then, by God, it will make money. The box-office take would support all financial needs. Subsidies, grants, government support? Intolerable! Effeminate and European—not to be countenanced in the good old U. S. of A.

The feeling was widespread. Truth to tell, some of the vanguard theaters, like Arena Stage in Washington, DC, and the Milwaukee

Repertory Theater, had become nonprofit organizations and were making discreet steps in the direction of deficit financing, but the principle had yet to be accepted by the general public. Symphony orchestras, art galleries, opera and dance companies could float majestically on a sea of red ink, but the Theater, that renegade of the arts, was determined, on pain of death, to turn a profit.

Guthrie had a different notion; his message went something like this: "We must be allowed the luxury of failure! This theater has an obligation to lead the way artistically, and to do that it must at times be daring and experimental. Now 'daring and experimental,' though it may be the life blood of the institution, does not guarantee financial success. We are experienced theater artists with confidence in our taste and skill. Nevertheless, some of the projects dearest to our hearts might turn out to be risible fiascos, but they might also be our greatest triumphs." (As his daring production of *The House of Atreus* would prove a few years later.)

"If we must turn a profit and that profit can only come from ticket sales, then in choosing our repertoire we will return again and again to what we know works, to the kind of product which will succeed at the box office. The result will be solvent mediocrity and artistic death.

"If what we are trying to build is a theater that can stand alongside the symphony hall and the opera house, a place where you can see great acting in compelling productions of great plays, then like the opera and like the symphony we must find the agencies, the grant-giving bodies, the benefactors who will support us. We must be liberated from the tyranny of the box-office balance sheet."

The theater he founded with Peter Zeisler and Oliver Rea was evidence of that liberation. In 1963, the Ford Foundation embraced Guthrie's message and donated $270,000 to the about-to-be-formed

Minnesota Theatre Company, a sum meant to sustain it, along with the box-office revenue, through the first three years of its existence.

For over a century, symphony orchestras, art galleries, opera and dance companies had, in addition to the revenue from ticket sales, been enjoying the benefit of financial support that came from patrons, foundations, and industries. Now the prejudice that had barred the theater from such support was slowly evaporating, in large part because a British knight came over here and talked sense to the Americans.

By 1965, when Guthrie stepped down as artistic director, the theatrical landscape in America was undergoing a slow but relentless seismic rearrangement. Theaters were popping up all over the country; what is now called the regional theater movement was in full swing. Scores of theaters were being founded, and their creators didn't think twice before devising budgets that projected earned income (ticket sales) as well as unearned income (grants, gifts, donations, etc.). If the board objected to the unearned part, there was the example of that British knight who had set up shop in Minneapolis. This is an important part of his legacy.

So our leader escaped without his gold watch. Well, that's the way he wanted it. Okay, Dr. G, but we must not forget what you did nor forget to celebrate it.

That rarely happens. Theatrical endeavor is, as we all know, writing on the water. Nothing lasts. I am told that nowadays young Minnesotans going to the theater that bears his name imagine Guthrie, if they think of him at all, as some rich midwestern grain merchant who got naming rights to a theater in exchange for dropping a lot of loot on the city.

Within the American theater world, however, Guthrie remains a formidable figure. His productions may fade from memory, but the two major theaters he built on this continent will survive along with the theatrical daring their architecture insists on. His witty, often profound, and profoundly readable prose will continue to delight and inform. And that bright plume, his panache, lives on to this day in those semi-fictional anecdotes, a special category of theater yarn—the Tony Guthrie Story—puzzling perhaps to the civilians, but catnip to the pros. (They need a seriously good mimic to put them across, however.)

There's the one about Tony (he's always "Tony" in these yarns), wildly enthusiastic after seeing a performance of some great classic, the cast of which was rich with the storied ladies of the English stage: Sybils and Peggys and Judys and so on.

So he went backstage to spread some joy. He made his way to the ladies dressing room and began tossing flowery and extravagant praise left and right. The ladies positively cooed in response.

But he stopped suddenly, because he found himself face to face with the one actress whose work in the play he detested. The dressing room became quiet. Then:

> TONY *(extravagantly genial)*. Oh, hello there, Coral!
> *(Pause. Then brightly)* How's your mother?

Or this one, which takes place at the Old Vic after he has just driven his company through a grueling twelve-hour technical rehearsal. He stands center stage, winding a ridiculously long scarf around his neck. The company, limp with fatigue, is scattered around him on the floor like so many sweaty puddles.

> TONY (in a voice that is ever so chipper, beaming with
> the ardor of a stagestruck beginner). Fun getting up
> a play, isn't it!

Or this one I heard from Douglas Campbell, who was an eye-witness. The scene is the open stage at Stratford, Canada. Tony is seated halfway back in the auditorium. Campbell is a few seats away. Tony has been directing the trial scene from *Merchant of Venice*. James Mason, the film star, who is playing Shylock, has just said he preferred not to do a piece of business Tony suggested.

> Tony (hugely indignant, to Campbell in a loud stage whisper). Fucking amateur! Won't prostrate himself!

All right. Enough of that. They really do need a great mimic. You were warned.

But here's a different kind of Tony Guthrie story—not one about him, but an illustration of the stories he could tell about others. I mean, think of the raw material he had! A generous supply of the major stars and famous theater-makers of the mid-twentieth century! So did he ever tell that marvelous story about *Candide* the time when Lillian Hellman tore a fire hose off the wall and aimed it straight at scenic designer Lennie Auerbach? Or the priceless one about *Arms and the Man* at the Old Vic, when Larry Olivier made an entrance wearing Ralph Richardson's nose from *Cyrano de Bergerac*?

No. Nothing like that. Never.

I was around him for the better part of seven years, and the only theater story I ever heard him tell the company was an odd one about some obscure leading lady who fell off a tall stage platform and landed on the leading man's thumb.

All this was deliberate, this anecdotal reserve. He wanted us to feel that what we were doing was the most important artistic adventure on the planet, not some colonial experiment forever in the shadow of the Old Vic's glory days. No, these times here, in Minnesota, *these* were the Glory Days.

And few of us knew what those days cost him. Guthrie had suffered two serious heart attacks prior to starting the Minneapolis enterprise, but the creative energy never flagged.

But here Campbell intrudes on my thoughts: "A little dirt on the shoes will make him more human, you know." Campbell speaks to me with the authority of a thirty-year collaboration—no actor knew Guthrie better. Campbell is gone now over a year, as I write this, and still cruelly missed; but never one to keep his peace, he is at my elbow to remind me not to be so damn idolatrous about "the old fart."

"Okay, okay," I respond, "Rest, perturbed spirit—I'll get to that later on. For now, how about this memorable put-down from one of his countrymen: 'Tony Guthrie is without doubt the greatest director on the face of the Earth—when there are more than six people on stage.'"

"Better," says my spectral friend and dematerializes.

I am sure there is a fair amount of vanity involved in seeing to it that a playhouse that bears your name gets off to a good start, but looking back, it seems to me nothing so much as a gift, an astoundingly generous gift. If there were a card attached, it might read: "To the Yanks, from Sir Tony, with admiration" ... or it might even read "with love."

"Grrrrr!" is heard from the beyond.

Guthrie Theater's 1966 Season

During the run of *The Caucasian Chalk Circle*, Doc Whiting, head of the theater department at the University of Minnesota, wrote me a note saying, "In a lifetime of theater-going I have never been more moved or overpowered than I was by *Chalk Circle*." Richard Christiansen (*Chicago Daily News*) spoke of "virtuoso theatricality."

Variety called it "a triumph," not only for me but "for designer Lewis Brown and composer Herb Pilhofer." Zoe Caldwell was "incomparable" and Ed Flanders "superb." Martin Gottfried (*Women's Wear Daily*) called it one of the greatest theatrical events of his life and concluded his review with the following panegyric: "All the splendid fury of theater—real and important theater—is in this play and this production."

Now, facing the 1966 season, a huge question loomed: "What the hell am I going to do for an encore?"

This was not for me to decide, of course; that was Campbell's job as the newly installed artistic director following Dr. Guthrie's departure. He took scant time in announcing the 1966 season.

The repertoire for our fourth season would consist of:

Skin of Our Teeth, Thornton Wilder's raffish ode to the imperishability of man

As You Like It, W. Shakespeare's delicious romantic comedy

The Dance of Death, bleak, deadly marital warfare rendered by that unhinged Swede, August Strindberg

The Doctor's Dilemma, George Bernard Shaw's acerbic skewering of the medical profession

Four of Eugene O'Neill's one-act plays about merchant seamen combined under the title *SS Glencairn*

This rich collection of approved classics was crammed with juicy acting roles.

I got the nod to direct the Shakespeare, which was to have sets and costumes by Ms. Moiseiwitsch. Another succulent plum had fallen into my lap. I expressed suitable gratitude, but secretly I was uneasy. I was no longer a lowly ASM, aflame with ambition and with nothing to lose. I was now, because of the crazy success of *Chalk Circle* and my recent elevation to *associate* artistic director, an established practitioner in the field. Suddenly it was taken for granted that I possessed a mastery of any number of theatrical styles and periods: Commedia del arte? "Of course, I can do that. Want to see my *lozzi?*" Restoration comedy? "All that profound superficiality! Let me at it!" Shakespeare? "Ah, well, the very foundation of my art."

Alas, it was not true. Neither my education (1 received a D in the one directing class I took), nor my experience (mostly summer stock) nor my curiosity (1 didn't really like to read plays all that much) had prepared me to be a master of the classical repertoire. I knew my way around some Shakespeare, yes, but most of it was martial Shakespeare—the history plays. Once again I had some lost ground to make up and some fancy footwork to do before I was ready to expound my vision of *As You Like It* to as compleat a theater artist as Tanya Moiseiwitsch.

———◆———

My second favorite place in Minneapolis is a body of water with a somewhat affected but evocative name—Lake of the Isles. Not far from the theater, in a residential area of generous lawns and tall trees, sits this gem of a lake, dotted with a few wooded islets. All around the shore, carefully trimmed grass grows to the water's edge; a path set back from the water follows the shoreline. A leisurely circumambulation lasts an hour or so; it's a walk I've taken innumerable times alone and in company, in all kinds of weather.

As you stroll along (on a summer afternoon, say) the prospect changes. Sometimes the far shore is not more than a couple of stone-skips away; then as you walk, an island marches slowly past; and when you look again, that far shore is a quarter mile away—it's a whole new Renoir vista, with picnickers on the grass and red canoes sliding across the water. That view gives way to others, and those others to still more as you thread and curve along the shore. At one point the path rises, loops over a bridge, then dips back down to the lakeside.

A friend once told me that the reason I liked it so much was because I couldn't see it all at one time. It seemed an odd remark at first, but then I realized he was exactly right. There are many lakes in and around the Twin Cities—you drive to the shore and there it is, the entire circumference is revealed: no surprises. Lake of the Isles is full of surprises.

There is only one way to see its entire shore, and that's by flying over it. I did that once. There I was, looking down from a thousand feet, wondering what that strange body of water could be, just over the hill from the theater. "My God, it's Lake of the Isles!" But it was a shape I had never seen before or even imagined. I could see it all: its odd irregular outline, all scallops and curves wandering around several dime-sized islands. I stared and stared. How could something so familiar look so strange?

Eventually this led, by some loopy mental process, to my seeing Lake of the Isles not just as a body of water, but as a metaphor, a metaphor that could be used describe a director's strategy in investigating a playscript.

Let me explain: In starting work on any given script, I adopt two points of view simultaneously. One is walking along that path down by the water encountering the play in sequence. The other is looking down from overhead, trying to get a sense of the whole. Let us deal with the first one first. I put on some sensible walking shoes, a little trail mix in my pocket, fill my canteen, and off I go. And I don't forget a copy of *As You Like It* because that's the script I'll be working on.

Before I've gone too far, here is Act One, Scene One. I find a young man, Orlando, complaining vehemently. His older brother has pocketed his inheritance and forced him into a life of servitude. Adam, an old servant, listens patiently. Orlando's first line is "As I remember Adam, it was upon this fashion bequeathed to me …" Upon what fashion? What's he referring to? A glance at the notes shows me there's some textural conjecture to sort out. And what are these men up to? I need to devise some activities that reflect the disorder in the household: Orlando, sweaty, overworked, reduced to the status of a field hand, hauling heavy sacks or piling up firewood—something strenuous. Adam, above him, a house servant, preparing the Master's soft boiled egg or polishing his riding boots, something of that nature. Then Oliver, the Master, the older brother, enters—arrogant, peremptory. What is the source of his animus? How far physically can I let this confrontation go? Or should it not be allowed to get physical at all?

I turn a corner and come upon a new vista. It's Scene Two, with the girls, Rosalind and Celia. Perhaps Rosalind should enter first, evincing sadness (Papa's been banished). Where is she coming from? Is there a party or a dance going on in the distance? Do we hear the music? Maybe something lively to contrast with her spirits? Then Celia bustles on and tries to cheer her friend up, and then we get that difficult word play about Fortune and Nature. How to make that live? And why does Celia call Fortune a "housewife"? And who is "Nature's natural?" And so on.

One after the other, each small section of the play is examined in great detail. In this perspective I am dealing with the play scene by scene, line by line, and as is often the case with Shakespeare, word by word.

But now I move away from the lakeshore, with its buzzing mosquitos of textual inquiry, and go aloft for a different perspective. I exchange my hiking gear for some sporty togs, and I find myself in the basket of a colorful hot air balloon, tethered several hundred feet above the lake. With my eyes I trace the meandering shoreline. I sip champagne and think deep thoughts, like "What is this play about?" adding perhaps per Sir Tyrone "… to me?"

On the shore I am narrowly focused, almost blinkered. "What does this character want *now*?" "We will need a music cue to reinforce this moment, and it should happen *now*." "Rosalind falls in love with Orlando *now*."

In the balloon, there are no *nows*. Thoughts glide across my mind—I wonder a lot. I wonder, what is the role of artifice in this play? Who is artificial? Who is real? How real is Rosalind in her disguise as a boy? It's all very satisfying and soft focus, because of the distance and because I'm not down there dealing with the nitty-gritty. Contradictions just drift away. I'm able to make interesting generalizations. Who cares if they are a little inaccurate? They sound good from up here, and the actors will be impressed.

Suddenly I'm back on the shore. Mosquitos, gnats, chiggers; it's brutal.

I splash on citronella, push aside a branch and there it is, the Forest of Arden. I run into an odd bunch of old gents who seem to be on an endless camping trip, led by the banished duke. One of their number, a gloomy old soul by the name of Jacques, is about to launch into the Ages of Man speech: "All the world's a stage" and so forth. Gotta be careful here. This is one of Shakespeare's top ten solos. How do I handle that aria? Or rather, how do I handle that speech so it becomes something someone says and not an aria?

And so it goes. Down on the shore for the difficult spade work, digging into the text—then up to the balloon for the titillating intellectual panoramas.

Eventually, I get smart and rig a long string with a tin can at each end so that shore and balloon perspectives can communicate. That's when the most valuable work gets done. The high-altitude perceptions start to inform the goings-on at the edge of the water. In the process the shore gets some guidance and becomes less frantic, and the balloon burns off some of its gassier intellectualizing and becomes truly helpful.

The point I am trying to make, having tortured this poor metaphor to death, is this: There are only two vantage points from which to perceive a text, and neither is complete without the other. What eventually becomes a production is some mysterious amalgam of the two viewpoints.

Here's another example. There are two ways of describing *Hamlet*:

#1— "Hamlet is a play about a man who could not make up his mind. (This was Laurence Olivier's view.)

#2—Hamlet is a play, the first line of which is "Who's there?" and the second line of which is "Nay, answer me. Stand and unfold yourself," and the third line is … and so on for five acts.

A long string connects those two descriptions. Dancing on that string that is what directors do. This dance, this distillation is not a place from which you can see the play—it's air, a volume of air with string curving through it.

I did some capering on that precarious filament and began to find my way into the world of *As You Like It*. Such an uncertain adventure, full of missteps and misapprehensions, but bit by bit some of the characters were beginning to come to life for me. One big challenge was deciding where to put all the characters. What period, which environment would serve them best? I didn't much care for Elizabethan clothes; moreover, Dr. G's experiments with changing the periods of Shakespearean plays were an invitation to think in terms of some bold coup de théâtre. But what? Where? How?

One day I was up in my balloon, sipping VSOP and looking moodily over Lake of the Isles, without an idea in my head, when suddenly that ghostly Douglas Campbell showed up, buzzing around me in his ultralight aircraft.

CAMPBELL *(throttling back)*. Having trouble, are we?

ME. Yeah.

CAMPBELL. Just want to plant a seed. Ready?

ME. Shoot. *(He zooms in close, circling around me.)*

CAMPBELL. American South—just after the Civil War.

ME *(unable to suppress a laugh; it seemed an absolutely hare-brained notion that only a Brit could come up with)*. You're kidding?!

CAMPBELL *(shouting as he flies off toward the theater)*. Dead serious. Just think about it!

ME. I will, Douglas …

… I thought, *but not for long*. I soon went back to poring over my art books with reproductions of Gainsborough, Fragonard, Watteau (the usual suspects), but none of it took. That night at home, I sat down to read the play through again. Before I had finished, the outline of a production scheme was taking shape in my head. Campbell was absolutely right. Here was a lush, romantic environment for the play and one that American actors would take to with delight: *As You Like It* in America, in the Deep South in 1866.

As I read with the post-Civil War period in mind, some fascinating choices appeared. Those men on the endless camping trip that so puzzled me—could they become Confederate soldiers, unable to pick up their shattered lives after Appomattox, who had taken to the woods with their comrades? And Jacques, more than just a verbose eccentric, could he become one of those great warrior generals, like a Lee or a Jackson—the great battles done, he prowls the forest wrapped in bitterness and disillusion?

One scene sprang vividly to life. It takes place in the Forest of Arden, halfway through the play, when Orlando, mad with hunger, stumbles upon the soldiers' campfire. After an initial skirmish, he is welcomed and offered food, but he refuses to eat until the soldiers promise to welcome the "old poor man/ who after me hath many a weary step/ limp'd in pure love." "Go find him out," says Duke Senior, leader of the renegades, "and we will nothing waste 'til your return." What an interesting intensity there will be when "the poor old man," the servant Adam, in this version a Black former slave, is carried to the campfire by Orlando and welcomed by the southern warriors. Truly, the Forest of Arden, which Shakespeare seems to intend as a kind of earthly paradise where rank and social status count for little, would become an enviable commonwealth.

Adopting a Southern locale meant facing the problem of accents. But was it a problem? Hadn't certain scholars been maintaining for years that if you want to hear English spoken as it was in Shakespeare's day you should go to Appalachia, not the British Isles?

Almost more important than the sound, however, was the culture of the South, where a colorful use of language and a love of poetry seemed part of everyone's inheritance.

In my wildest dreams I could never imagine *Our Town*'s George Gibbs dashing through a New Hampshire forest, nailing bad poems in praise of Emily Webb's elbow to all the hardwoods in sight—but down South, in a moonlit forest, moss-hung and secret, filled with the song of owl and cricket, lover (Kermit and Miss Piggy, certainly and yes, maybe even George) can go slightly crazy. As I read the play, I found, as if born to the place, Shakespeare's Orlando, dashing from live oak to cypress papering the forest with his doggerel masterpieces.

> Run, Orlando, run, carve on every tree
> The fair, the chaste and unexpressive she.

I immediately wrote to Moiseiwitsch (who was still in England) about these strange visions I was having. I passed on the name of an artist I thought she might like: George Caleb Bingham, who painted American frontier life with a Renaissance palate.

Her return letter referred to my "bombshell," but her curiosity seemed to have been piqued. Finally, she conceded the Southern idea might be a "good prospect" and was willing to proceed just so long as I didn't make her read *Gone with the Wind* for research. Meanwhile she was packing.

Soon she would be in America, and we could go to work.

Nowadays, what used to be called "the design process" is less a process than a sweaty, frenetic whirl that consists initially of getting Director Sam, who is in Minneapolis, say, and Designer Susan, who is in San Diego, together in a hotel room in Denver for six hours, at the end of which the designs for *The Glass Menagerie* or whatever their project, are well underway. The fact that Director Sam has never met, much less worked with, Designer Susan before is of minor concern. They're pros after all, they can work it out.

Following that one flying visit, the rest is snatch, grab, scribble, and endless phone messages:

"Where are you?"

"Unicorn *must* be three inches tall."

"Cut Blue Roses projection; too obvious."

"Call me in San Jose on Tuesday."

and Fed-Ex more items, and email more people, and then— whap! It's first rehearsal.

"Change the size of the bookcase?! Impossible, it's already built."

This is not a healthy way to make art, but in regional theater today, sometimes, it is the only way. To make a buck, designers have to keep to lunatic, insomniac schedules that would make most workaholics look like slackers. Moreover, they have to take work wherever they find it, which means Show A may be in Milwaukee and Show B in Atlanta. As a result it can happen that when he or she is in Milwaukee working twelve hours a day on Show A, while trying to design Show B at night on some wobbly table in a cheap hotel room, the cell phone beeps—it's the production manager of Show C in Chicago, who needs all the working drawings by Thursday so his soon-to-be-idle shop crew has something to occupy its time. That's why designers have been known to fall asleep standing up.

Once upon a time I had a collaboration so fulfilling, so creatively rich, that I hoped it would become the model for all that followed. To begin with, there was time, blessed time, not only to do the creative work at hand, but also for the careless pleasures of getting to know one another—time for a dinner or two and even a movie. And then there was the lack of distractions: no other deadline save …

But I'm getting ahead of myself here. Let me tell it from the beginning. This is the story of my collaboration with Tanya Moiseiwitsch on our bayou version of *As You Like It*.

We began in deepest winter. Moiseiwitsch had just arrived in Minneapolis for the '66 season and had settled into her impossibly tiny but enviably cozy apartment over Oliver Rea's garage. Our relationship (Moiseiwitsch's and mine) had warmed appreciably after that disastrous start when I'd picked her up at the airport several years earlier. I had tried my best to please her when I was a stage manager and had been rewarded a couple of times when, coming upon me hammering away at that backstage piano on my Guthrie-inspired course of self improvement, she sat down beside me on the piano bench, and we tried a four-handed piece. Mind you, this was Tanya Moiseiwitsch, daughter of Benno Moiseiwitsch, a world-famous concert pianist. I was incapable of anything much above the level of "Tony, the Pony" and *Sprightly Pieces for Beginners*, but we had a great silly time—our first attempt at collaboration.

On a January day, I tramped through the snow to her place. I was shivering, no doubt partly from the cold, but from apprehension as well, since I was about to start work with one of the most famous designers in the world.

That first afternoon, no deadline loomed, no production manager hovered nearby awaiting results, Moiseiwitsch's phone was not about to ring with some urgent inquiry from Stratford, Ontario, or if it did, it would not be answered. We had tea and talked. We talked about art, we gossiped, we told stories. As I remember there wasn't a word spoken about William Shakespeare or *As You Like It*.

It wasn't until the second afternoon in our snow-covered hide-away that Moiseiwitsch and I delved into some research—Bingham paintings and Brady photographs of the Civil War. We also began to talk about the set. How do we get a suggestion of rural Dixie onto our open stage? It must be something minimal but eloquent, in keeping with her and Dr. G's design philosophy.

We spent several days exploring different possibilities. First there was a network of moss-hung branches over the playing area. This evolved into a singular, outsized tree, but after a while its rigidity and some difficult engineering problems began to oppress us—out it went. Next we dreamed of water, a large swath of stage floor opened to reveal the dark waters of the bayou; we amused ourselves with fantasies of Orlando throwing Charles the Wrestler in the drink and other jolly aquatic japes. But soon we realized we were beginning to devise *A Play About a Pool*. We went on to what eventually became the solution: a simple ground cloth of grasses and moss covering the top level of the stage; a stylized hillock down left; some hanging moss; and between the two upstage backing units, a dilapidated breezeway embraced by an ancient, gnarled wisteria vine. (This was for the look of it, but also for Rosalind and Orlando to climb on.) We reviewed the play page by page, and it seemed to answer all scenic needs. Moiseiwitsch's rendering of the set turned out to be exactly what we hoped for—minimal, but Deep South romantic.

Working on costumes was remarkably different. Where Moiseiwitsch's pencil was out and sketching every idea we came up with for the set, it budged not at all when we shifted our focus to the clothes. Moiseiwitsch was only interested in knowing what I thought about each character in as much detail as possible. I would arrive each morning thinking I might see a scribble or two that she'd made the previous evening but there was nothing. I was asked to keep on talking about Jacques or Touchstone or whomever was next on the dramatis personae.

Mind you, it was flattering to have my brains picked dry by the charming Ms. M., but there was a limit. Finally, when I had exhausted every insight I had had about every character in the play and was beginning to babble senselessly, she cut me off. *Ah,* I thought, *now I can go home and she will start sketching.* No, that was not on the schedule for the day. Very gently, but very firmly (Moiseiwitsch's gentle firmness could be very convincing), she told me I was going to read the play to her. "What!" I exploded, "that's crazy!" "No, no," she told me, it might give her some insights I hadn't put into words. "But," I said, "it's … it's …"

Eventually, gentle firmness overseen by dark Russian eyes prevailed, and I read her the play—the whole damn play! I thought I could get away with an act or two, but she was listening so intently that I read through to the end.

> ME. Proceed, proceed. We will begin these rites,
>   As we do trust they'll end, in true delights.
> *(A pause. I close the book and turn to her. She nods her head slowly a couple of times as if a conclusion had been reached.)*
> MOISEIWITSCH *(rising briskly).* All right. You can go away now. I need to do a few things. Come back on Friday.

Rejection! And it all seemed to be going so well. A gaping pothole on the highway of love? Well, not really, but it was odd suddenly to be on my own, wandering around, bumping into things, trying to find something to occupy my time for the three days until our next meeting.

Finally, it was Friday. I tramped Moiseiwitsch-ward. I was tense. She greeted me warmly and sat me down in the comfortable chair, now situated so the winter sun would pour in over my left shoulder. In front of the chair was a small table, and on that table a neat three-inch stack of renderings. The costume designs for *As You Like It* awaited my approval.

My approval?

Yes, she wanted to know exactly what I thought. Had she gotten anywhere near what I had in mind? What did she need to change? Or should we throw out the lot and start again? Apparently there were to be no disputes, no wrangling like those endless bouts with Lew Brown over the *Chalk Circle* designs. I was the director.

"You're on, Edward, speak up."

I looked at the first group of sketches. I said nothing.

There is a feeling that comes over me in the theater sometime (all too rarely, actually). The play has just begun and I'm watching the first few beats of what will be a fairly lengthy evening. Something about the shape of things, the colors, the sounds, the first few moves fills me with pleasure. I have a sense of being in the presence of immense competence and exquisite taste. I lean back in my chair with a sigh. "More, more, I prithee, more. ..."

I had that feeling as I began looking at Moiseiwitsch's sketches. Finally, we spread them all out on the rug, and there it was—the world of our southern *As You Like It* had been peopled. I could see the influence of the Bingham palate and some of the Brady photographs. Moiseiwitsch profound sense of character had created a wonderful gallery of vivid individuals, all authentically of the period. But there was something more, something that took it further:

a grace of line, a sense of form and texture that gave it a dreaminess, a certain unreality. Some of it was in the details, touches that often would not be discerned by the audience but that were so evocative to the actors. One such were the patches of moss growing around the golden epaulettes on the jacket of "General" Jacques. Magical!

If I had any criticisms, they were minor and could be taken care of in the fitting room. All I really wanted to do was run down the hill to the theater and show everyone what Moiseiwitsch had been up to. But she would have none of it. There were renderings that should be altered because of my remarks. She would take care of that.

So twenty-four hours later, fifteen days from the start of it all, director and designer slid and capered down the snow-covered hill to the theater, beaming like proud parents, on their way to show off their new progeny to the world at large.

Despite my success, despite a fairly positive outlook, there was still some small, tentative part of me that was the plodder, that skinny, bucktoothed kid who was always on the outside, always looking to older brothers for approval and support. But this wouldn't do; my ambition was propelling me into situations in which my voice had to be preponderant. Leadership had to be learned. Time, I began to see, should not be wasted with competing aesthetics, as had so often been the case in the past. If you direct, you lead. "Shut up and listen," period. Moiseiwitsch in her generosity showed me the dance. She allowed me to lead, she followed, and since our tastes were similar, the entire process was a delight. Can you imagine what a shot in the arm it was to a journeyman director like me to be deferred to by a talent like Ms. Moiseiwitsch's? To discover that my taste was on a par with a truly world-class talent? I have always treasured the memory of our work together and had hoped it would be the model for all the projects that followed, but that has rarely been the case. There have been many joyful collaborations, to be sure, but none on a par with Moiseiwitsch's and mine. It's impossible—there's never the time, never the money, never the lack of distractions.

The cast of *As You Like It* was a promising group of young actors, some of them just entering the profession, all at the start of what would be very distinguished careers. Ellen Geer brought her wit and her wistful blonde beauty to the role of Rosalind. Her bumpkin admirer Orlando was played with great charm by a young actor/singer who had just bopped down from Canada, named Len Cariou. That most loved of actors, James J. Lawless, recently plucked from the ranks of the Guthrie apprentices, was Orlando's evil brother Oliver, and Patricia Elliott, a striking young brunette with a wonderfully smoky voice, was his vis-à-vis, Celia. A wisecracking former Navy X-ray technician turned actor, Ed Flanders, played the clown Touchstone. Helen Carey, newly hatched from a Catholic college, was our definitive bayou minx, Phebe; a callow youth, all blonde and cherub-cheeked, just out of the Royal Academy of Dramatic Art, Michael Moriarty was her touchingly wilted but ever hopeful swain, Silvius.

Add to this youthfest some members of the strong acting cadre of the Minnesota Theatre Company, like Bob Pastene, Paul Ballantyne, Don West, Ken Ruta, Sandy McCallum, and others, and the cast of *As You Like It* was complete.

I had anticipated some painful early rehearsals. I thought the company would have a difficult time adjusting to the changed mise-en-scène. Not at all. They plunged in with relish, and in a short while, the sound of Southern-drawl Shakespeare seemed natural. Sometimes the felicity of the accent would make us explode in amazed laughter, as when Helen Carey, playing Phebe, waving her improvised palm-frond fan, acting ever so ladylike despite her bare feet, drawled out to the lovelorn Silvius: "Thou hast my love, is not that neighborly?"

The production moved fairly painlessly toward its opening. When we got on the set with the addition of costumes, music, and lights, some real enchantment ensued. As we moved into Act II (The Forest of Arden) we seemed to have found that world, moonlit and mysterious, where our Shakespearean wanderers could discover new selves and let love drive them crazy. And the soldiers in their tattered Civil War duds with their frayed battle flags lent a poignant dignity that was a telling counterpoint to all the youthful ardor.

If there was a problem, it was with the director. He had done just enough Shakespeare to know his way around, but not enough to get beyond what might be called the "badminton and croquet" stage of Shakespearean direction: That's when you can't resist embellishing poor Will's works with stunning directorial touches. You think you're being ever so clever, but all it does is distract the audience from what is being said and make the cognoscenti cringe. I did understand the tone of the piece, and think we found a lot of it. There were no actual croquet or badminton matches, but I seem to have a memory of … oh, never mind.

Then we opened.

The critical reception was split and surprisingly emotional. For every eloquent denunciation ("a mundane and dismal swamp," Stanley Kauffman, *New York Times*) there was a compensating bouquet ("Bravo to them all for a bold and often brilliant venture," Richard Christiansen, *Chicago Daily News*). Most importantly, the audiences seemed to have a jolly time. And the photographs I have of the production serve to remind me that whatever the final verdict, *As You Like It* looked gorgeous.

Creating a Theater, Bill Ball style

Do you thrive on stress? Are you excited by the idea of hanging by your creative fingernails over the yawning abyss of theatrical disaster? Will you be amused when your contract seems to indicate that you will be acting in two different plays that perform at the same time in two different theaters, and it isn't a mistake? Do you like taking classes at midnight? In a single season, would you like to play eight major roles and understudy ten more and still find time to attend classes in voice, Alexander technique, transcendental meditation, theater games, and something called "rapid rate of utterance." If this were the mid-1960s and you found all the above irresistibly attractive, you would seek out a director by the name of William Ball, who was soon to become one of the most significant figures in the burgeoning regional theater movement.

I was lucky enough, following the success of *The Caucasian Chalk Circle*, that Ball sought me out. I would soon be between the '66 and '67 seasons at the Guthrie, so the timing was perfect to direct for him at ACT. He asked me what I wanted to do. I allowed as how I knew little about Samuel Beckett and it was high time I learned. Would he let me direct one of his plays? "Of course," Ball replied, "Come and visit, and we'll work it out."

After studying at what was then the best theater school in the country, Carnegie Tech, Ball had spent a decade accumulating a fiercely impressive directing résumé. It included notable gigs at Stratford, Connecticut; Stratford, Ontario; Arena Stage in DC; and theaters elsewhere; a passel of operas at New York City Opera; and numerous award-winning productions off-Broadway. He was becoming the hottest young theater director around. Broadway beckoned, but he turned his back on all that and set about forming his own company. He called it the American Conservatory Theater

(ACT). I went to visit them at their first digs, in Pittsburgh, where they were performing a modest (for Ball) repertoire of six plays.

The work I saw was hugely impressive—skillfully directed productions full of theatrical panache, with some dazzling performers. Two daring young men in particular caught my eye: René Auberjonois, who at twenty-six was playing King Lear, and as his Fool an equally young Robin Gammell. They worked extremely well together and were also, I learned, very good friends. With Ball's permission, I asked them to play the leads in Beckett's *Endgame*, the opening night of which I've described above.

"White heat" is a phrase that comes easily to mind when writing about Bill Ball. There is just no better way to describe the titanic creative energy that was powering the American Conservatory Theater. When I first worked there, Ball asked more of actors, designers, technicians, and staff than seemed in their power to give, but somehow they found a way and gave it, then came back for more. Under his leadership, in a single season more productions were mounted, more classes held, more costumes built, more props constructed, more news releases released, more creative breakthroughs witnessed, more audiences sent home in a state of glowing satiety than in a decade at a more rational institution.

At the source of all this exhilarating madness were a couple of simple precepts. The first was: Idleness Is the Enemy of Art. It was Ball's fervently held belief that artists, actors in particular, thrive on pressure. When an actor was up to his neck—with too many roles to play, too many classes to absorb, when he was barely able to keep his chin above the rising waters, that was when he could do his best work, answering the challenge and drawing things from his creative unconscious he didn't know he possessed. Ball asked the impossible because he thought it could lead to what is unexpected and original and, under the best of circumstances, to what is inspired and sublime.

The second precept had to do with training. It is the source of the word "Conservatory" in American Conservatory Theater. Ball believed that a diploma from a university theater department, a certificate from an acting school, or anointment by a Method guru was only the beginning of a theater artist's education. The training of an actor should be a lifelong process that continues after his entrance into the profession and goes on without interruption during his entire career.

Bear in mind that actor training at this particular point in time (mid-60s), if it existed at all, was woefully deficient. Universities had yet to acknowledge the fact that they were training actors, not, as they insisted, aspiring teachers. That commonplace of today, the M.F.A. acting program, didn't exist; there are now hundreds of them. Two of today's most notable theater academies were not even in the business. Julliard was solely a music school; at Yale, theater was extracurricular. Moreover, a great deal of acting training was in some version of the Stanislavsky method—admirable to be sure, but often taught to the exclusion of other skills and techniques.

What Ball set out to create, much like what Dr. Guthrie was building, was a company that could do it all—perform the best plays of the classical and modern repertoire; a group of actors who could range over the works of Shakespeare, Molière, George Bernard Shaw, Ibsen, and Chekhov, but also be at home in French boulevard farce or Italian commedia, as well as taking on some of the moderns like Arthur Miller, Edward Albee, and Sam Shepard.

And this tall order was only half of the enterprise. The other half, the conservatory half, would make possible the actor's continuing search for mastery; it would be a place immune to the pressures of rehearsal or performance, where the company could explore different styles of acting, different ways of using the voice and the body, as well as acquiring useful skills—fencing, for instance, or sight-reading music. At the same time, they would be encouraged to read widely and add to their knowledge of *all* the arts.

The early life of the company was peripatetic. I directed *Endgame* in Pittsburgh, but the production opened in Ann Arbor on the campus of the University of Michigan. The company played other gigs—in California at Berkeley and Palo Alto, in Connecticut at Westport and East Haddam. All this movement was advantageous; enthusiastic word of mouth and positive press coverage was coming from all over the country.

By 1966, in the midst of what *Time* magazine was calling a national "cultural explosion,"[7] every major city in America wanted its own version of the Tyrone Guthrie Theater. And here was this fabulous outfit, ACT, on the loose, wandering the country, looking for a home.

Bill Ball was an engaging guy, pink and boyish despite a receding hairline. His luminous eyes were glowing, and his contagious laughter was heard a lot that summer, for he was in an amazingly enviable position. Today his counterpart would be the billionaire owner of a hot NFL franchise who was looking to move his football team to the city that came up with the highest bid. Eager civic emissaries were arriving weekly to woo him. Phoenix was offering to build him a theater. Chicago already had one and a pile of money besides. San Francisco had theaters, cheap office space—and cable cars! The tumult grew, the rumors flew, but finally a decision was made. ACT was going to San Francisco. Initially there was talk of splitting the season with Chicago, but it never came to pass.

---

7   *Time*, Dec 2, 1966, "Box Office: Exploding the Explosion," http://content.time.com/time/subscriber/article/0,33009,836598,00.html.

San Francisco became (and remains to this day) the home of the American Conservatory Theater.

———◆———

René Auberjonois darted a look at Robin Gammell. Auberjonois was not happy; he was in rags, rather elaborate rags, seated in deliquescent splendor on his throne chair, center stage. Gammell, seething like a manic rodent, stood quivering by the garbage pails down left. The play was *Endgame* by Samuel Beckett. Auberjonois was Ham; Gammell, Clov. It was ten o'clock in the morning. These two actors were beginning the final dress run-through before the opening later that day. The director (me), mindful of his actors' energies and the unusually long day ahead of them (*Endgame* didn't open until midnight), had asked them to take it easy; the production was ready. We only needed this one last run-through to refine some light cues and work out a few other kinks. It was really for the benefit of the technical people more than the actors. "So remember," I said, "You've got a very long day ahead of you. Keep the pace we've set, but use as little energy as possible." The actors nodded gravely. It was sound advice.

But now they were five minutes into the play, and Gammell was gunning his acting engine in an annoyingly provocative way. That's why Auberjonois had shot him that look. Though the best of friends, Auberjonois and Gammell were furiously competitive with one another. So Auberjonois eased past him on the inside lane, then Gammell sped around the far turn, and *VAROOM!* Away they both went, full tilt until the final fade-out an hour and a half later.

Since it had become a real performance, the director started taking notes. And having taken notes, he had to give them. And the director having given them, the actors wanted to "do" them, so they wouldn't have to be remembering notes on opening night. This meant an extra half-hour of rehearsal, following which they scooted upstairs to their dressing rooms, got out of costume and make-up, wolfed down some sandwiches and then got back into costume (seventeenth-century, this time) and make-up for the matinee performance of Molière's *Tartuffe*. Auberjonois played Tartuffe; Gammell, Damis. A long afternoon of delicious conniving and romantic hijinks to the tune of exquisitely crafted rhyming couplets, all received with happy gratitude by an adoring audience. Applause! Applause! Applause! Then whoosh up to the dressing rooms, off went the costumes, off came the make-up, slap, slap, slap (Skin Bracer), and then it's time for a snack and rest. Ahhh, but wait—it was Saturday! The restaurant that delivered was closed. Damn! They dashed out, finally found a greasy spoon that was open. Gobble, gobble, gobble! Raced back to the theater, jumped into their tuxes, dabbed on just a hint of make-up this time, and got ready for the evening performance: that popular British revue, forerunner of the Monty Python troupe: *Beyond the Fringe*. Offbeat Limey humor, crisp timing, frightfully amusing send-ups. Ha! Ha! Ha! Finally, applause! applause! applause! Zipped up to the dressing rooms, tore off the tuxes, and dove into the decaying rags and the festering Ivan Albright make-up. Then a final touch—adding color to the oral cavity with vegetable dyes swirled around in the mouth: a screaming blood red for Gammell, a cadaverous dark blue for René. Then trip! trip! trip! down to the stage. Places! Auberjonois got seated in his throne chair. He draped "Old Stauncher," the bloody cloth, over his face. Gammell stood down left. They could hear the muted tumult of a young, excited house on the other side of the curtain. Work lights flicked off, stage lights on. The curtain rose in silence. Clov began a lengthy pantomime during which he reeled painfully, stiff-legged, around the set looking out of windows and staring down into garbage pails. Each new sight was followed by a nasty snicker. Finally, sagging with fatigue, he looked at the audience and said:

"Finished, it's finished; nearly finished; it must be nearly finished."

But it wasn't; it was midnight and the opening of *Endgame* had just begun. For the next hundred minutes, Gammell and Auberjonois lit up the night like two neutron stars with big-scale, irresistibly magnetic performances that drew a rambunctious, late-Saturday-night audience ever closer to the ambiguous world of the play—drew them to rapt silence, to wild laughter and perhaps to a new thought or two, finally, to warm, prolonged applause.

And when it was over, as the clock was edging toward 2:00 A.M. and the curtain had fallen on the last of many calls, after they got out of costume and make-up one final time and back into civilian clothes, did that mean it was time for bleary-eyed good-nights and trudging off to bed? Not on your life. They were still up, still ready for more. "Hey," chirped Gammell, "where's the party?"

Welcome to theater, Bill Ball style.

———————

In October of 1966, with the blessing of the Guthrie brass, and after codirecting O'Neill's sea plays with Campbell, Pamela and I took off for the city by the bay to be part of ACT's explosive first season in California. Sixteen productions, at two theaters, in just twenty-two weeks.

It is a right pleasurable activity, looking back after all these years, to relive a time when I was young and immortal and truly blessed in my professional life—burning pure and gemlike, constantly on the go. I remember that when the actors were working, the idea of sitting down in the rehearsal room seemed a slacker activity. The same in the theater itself. For years I had purple bruises just above my knees on each leg from colliding with seat arms in the semi-darkness. Always up and moving, rushing to meet the next challenge. We were all drug addicts, really, but we didn't need a pusher; the drug was adrenalin.

I have always loved the rhythm of my chosen profession—that long arc of increasing tension building to the climax of opening night. I find its varying and often irrational demands extremely congenial. They seem to suit my personality.

I always did my damnedest to see that nothing got in the way of that rhythm. Paying bills, doing the laundry, answering Aunt Minnie's latest letter—no time for that. I was a 24-hour-a-day occupant of Ibsenville or Shakespeareland or wherever the playwright (vile kidnapper, he) had taken me. Needless to say, the effect on personal relationships was not felicitous.

Even when I was an artistic director, if I was in production, I would try any subterfuge to duck business matters, publicity campaigns, fundraising, etc., so I could concentrate solely on making an insanely delectable piece of theater.

Also I became as superstitious as a baseball player: "Get a haircut?! Are you mad?!"

Into the Wild Blue (Theatrical) Yonder:
An Exercise in Extravagant Self-Dramatization
I savor the leisurely beginnings: studying the script, writing notes from time to time, leaving gaps for dreaming, sometimes strolling about, saying the text aloud. In

daydreams, these activities morph into the preparations for a trip, a trip by air over water to an unknown land. I study my check lists and write up a flight plan.

Soon it's time for final visual inspection. I circle my League of Regional Theaters aircraft; she's a LORT Two-oh One-oh, not known for beauty or speed, but a dependable flying machine I've come to love. I reach out and give one of the starboard struts an affectionate shake.

Now Teddy, my loyal mechanic, runs up panting with a clipboard (the cast list). I look it over as I settle the white silk scarf around my neck, elated to see that all my first choices have signed. Next, a brisk thumbs-up for Teddy, and I vault gracefully into the cockpit. Down come the goggles, calls of "Switch on!" and "Contact!" and then Teddy gives the propeller one mighty heave. The motor wheezes and then CHUNK, CHUNK, CHUNKs into life, and soon my fragile canvas-clad biplane is wobbling over the grass toward the runway, past the preblocking pylon and the design conference windsock.

I swing around deftly at the end of the long ribbon of macadam. Then it's time for engine run-up and final instrument check. As the engine crescendos, I turn back to have a look at the ailerons and see a dozen members of the staff who have broken loose and are dashing toward me, waving and shouting. They stop twenty feet away at five o'clock, their clothes wildly buffeted by the prop wash.

"Do you like this ad?" Molly screams, holding some tasteless graphic over her head. "When are you going to choose those extras?" yells Russ.

I advance the stick and the plane answers, inching slowly forward, steadily gaining speed—10 miles per hour, then 20 ... but the staff is charging down the runway after me! "Have you written the program notes yet?! Don't you realize the fate of the theater depends on you?" Now they are all shouting at once and the engine is getting louder as it struggles to gain speed; bone-rattling vibrations begin. "Mrs. Bumble, our most loyal volunteer, had a miscarriage!" "We found a dead skunk in the shop!" "What are you going to do about the parking?!"

"I can't deal with this right now!"

Meanwhile, the speed is picking up: 60 ... 70 ... 80 ... With both hands I pull back slowly on the stick, the rehearsal room door swings slowly shut, the plane rises slowly from the planet Earth. At once the rattling stops, the yelling dies away. I'm airborne! First rehearsal has begun and I'm airborne! In a new element, all those quotidian cares left behind. Life is only this flight into the unknown, making a masterpiece of literature come to life. I execute some crazy aerobatic maneuver, spiraling as I roar upward, wild with joy. What a gift I have been given—to make this journey few have made before.

Hour (it seems like weeks) pass. My mood and the sky darken. I begin to hear sounds that make me uneasy—a certain wheezing of the engine (a cranky leading actor?) and an ominous rattle of the airframe (design problems?). But there's no time for that! I'm over water and there is no turning back.

Night comes, and with it cruel crosswinds and a ceiling of impenetrable clouds. I can't get my bearings. The compass is sticking. I'm buffeted this way (by the producer) and that (by the actors), but I grit my teeth like Snoopy in pursuit of the Red Baron and plunge on. I fly by the seat of my pants. Only instinct guides me.

Finally, the winds calm, the clouds thin, and by the light of the first run-through I see the reassuring outline (familiar from the charts I've studied so intently) of the coast I've been aiming for—long sought, feared lost—but there it is at last below me. I'm over land. I've survived! Now it all seems possible.

Soon it's time to descend. I swoop down easily, but suddenly I'm in a dense fog of previews. Lost again! And now fatigue is beginning to take its toll. I drain what's left of the black coffee in my thermos and chain smoke cigarettes that burn deliciously as I inhale.

Ahhhh!

On, on I fly, keeping my valiant craft steady at a safe altitude—but now the fuel gauge is nearing empty, and I am still in the fog's grip. I can't hold out much longer. Then, through the fog I see a hazy glow several miles ahead. Can it be? Yes! As I draw nearer, the lights show the outline of a runway. My God! It's Paris–Le Bourget Airport!

The fog is clearing. It's Opening!

I throttle back and descend toward the lights. My work is almost done. Then my hand on the stick begins to shake uncontrollably. My eyes fill with tears of happiness and relief. "Not yet, you fool!" Somehow I gather what's left of my strength for one last effort and glide down to a perfect three point landing, then collapse into the arms of the waiting throng. Cheers! Rave reviews! Medals! Kisses! Champagne! Then I am driven into the city, speeding down streets lined four deep with madly cheering French citizens.

Finally there is the Ritz Hotel, where, on a down-soft four-poster, a twenty-year-old Brigitte Bardot, naked and eager, awaits. The flight suit falls from my body and I leap into her arms. Then we madly tussle and tenderly caress until the light of dawn paints the window sill, then we fall entwined into the benison of sleep.

Incredible challenges! Hairsbreadth escapes! Unbelievable daring!

Then finally: the soul-nourishing rewards!

And that, my friends, is how to put on a play!

If, that is, you've got the right cast, and if there's enough money so that the brilliant design by the if-brilliant designer can be realized, and if you can inspire the company and if … and if … Until all the "ifs" get tired and go home, leaving you to do your work.

Before things got ugly in Chicago in the fall of 1968, before tear gas and sirens filled the air around the Democratic National Convention, there was the 1967 Summer of Love in San Francisco. The intersection of Haight and Ashbury streets became the epicenter of a startling new culture of long hair, drugs, antiwar protest, and rock and roll. For myself, I barely noticed; I was otherwise engaged that spring, for twenty blocks away Bill Ball and Company were setting up shop on Geary Street. The American Conservatory Theater was about to rock San Francisco.

"16 Productions! 2 Theaters! 22 Weeks!" was the proud boast that could be seen on brochures, posters, and taxi signs for the 1967–68 season. The two theaters were the Geary, a 1200-seat proscenium at 450 Geary Street, and the Marines Memorial, another proscenium, this of 600 seats, up the hill at Sutter and Mason.

The sixteen productions were to be *Long Day's Journey into Night, Our Town, Tiny Alice, Tartuffe, Under Milk Wood, Charley's Aunt, Endgame, Dear Liar, Six Characters in Search of an Author, Arsenic and Old Lace, Death of a Salesman, Man and Superman, The Torchbearers, The Seagull, Beyond the Fringe*, and a program entitled *A.C.T. One-Acts*.

From the knockabout farce of *Charley's Aunt* to the grim family warfare of *Long Day's Journey*; from that dram of ratsbane called *Endgame* to the cool martini of *Beyond the Fringe*—now that, friends, is what might rightfully be called, in the best tradition of season-ticket-brochure prose, "a dazzling theatrical cornucopia!" But was it doable? Was it even sane? For the first season in Minneapolis we did a repertory of four plays, and even our later seasons had no more than six. And, bear in mind, all these shows were to be in rotating repertory. We had a colossal mountain to climb.

The 22-week season was to run from January 21 until June 18. Concurrent with all the production activity (it would mean three or four openings a month) was the training program where Bill's theories of continuing education for the actor could be realized. This was not to be some ancillary activity that would be tacked on toward the end of the season when the pressure of all the openings had passed. No, training would start on the first day of rehearsal.

To get some idea of the fever of activity these grand schemes engendered, it might be useful to take a look at a rehearsal schedule. I happen to have one handy. It is for a spring day in 1967. Whoever typed it (probably Bobby Bonaventura, ACT's scheduling genius) had to use legal-sized paper that was turned sideways and ruled into eight columns, each column representing a different location— these were the two theaters mentioned above as well as half a dozen rehearsal rooms of varying size in a building across the street from the Geary Theater.

On the day in question there were rehearsals for six productions: *Under Milk Wood, Man and Superman, Long Day's Journey into Night, The Seagull,* and *The Zoo Story.* In addition to these rehearsals there were the conservatory activities. When actors were not rehearsing, time did not lie heavy on their hands:

- Voice classes for fourteen actors—not all at once mind you; these were individual sessions—one actor and one teacher, with each session lasting 45 minutes.
- Dialect class for twelve actors—45 minutes each.
- Singing lessons with Robert Weede for seven actors — one hour per student.
- Guitar lessons for eight actors—40 minutes each.
- Sessions for ten actors with Frank Ottiwell, the Alexander Technique trainer—each for half an hour.

That was only the daytime schedule. After a dinner break came the performances: *Tiny Alice* at the Geary and *Endgame* up the hill at the Marines Memorial.

It was a regimen that kept us on the move. We swarmed like lemmings over that slightly seedy warren of rooms across the street from the Geary Theater, former home to massage parlors and tattooing dens that was now the ACT HQ, short of sleep, excited, exhausted, but thrashing onward. We played theater games, we meditated, we took special classes at odd hours that Bill gave. I remember one on dynamics that led to insights I still profit from and a legendary session on laughter that started at 11:00 P.M. and went on well into the small hours of the morning. We also rehearsed plays, sixteen of them, and somehow the whole damn thing came to pass, just as the season brochure said it would.

The season opened on January 21 with Bill's memorable production of *Tartuffe* in an elegant translation by Richard Wilbur; it had been a staple of the repertoire from the beginning, but now with René Auberjonois as a deliciously villainous Tartuffe and Sada Thompson inimitable as the wily comic servant, Dorine, it was at its best. San Francisco was enchanted!

The following Wednesday a real surprise—Bill's insolent, inventive, all-stops-out theatrical rendition of Edward Albee's cryptic opus, *Tiny Alice*. San Francisco was astonished!

Then two nights later Jerome Kilty's staged version of the George Bernard Shaw/Mrs. Patrick Campbell correspondence titled *Dear Liar* with Sada and Michael O'Sullivan irresistible as the immortal pen pals. San Francisco was charmed!

Then it was my turn.

I would like to go on in this breathless mode, tripping from triumph to triumph, but we've got to take a pause here to confront my work and its shortcomings. I directed three productions that season: *The Torchbearers*, *Seagull*, and a revival of *Endgame*. It's not that I had to hide under the seats or anything, but Bill set a pretty high bar; I never felt that my own work came near clearing it.

Time for some marks for my directing prowess:

The Torchbearers—A charming, at times hilarious, light comedy about an amateur theater group of high ideals and inept accomplishments, a forgotten gem by George Kelly that I had great success with when I directed it at Equity Library Theater in New York. I let myself be talked into some casting mistakes and was not at my best. Grade: C

Endgame—This time Auberjonois played Clov and Ken Ruta was Hamm. They were splendid, but somehow that special rapport between Auberjonois and Gammell in Ann Arbor was missing. Grade: B plus.

The Seagull—A play I have loved since birth. And why not? The author is Anton Chekhov and the subject is us: theater folk. This was the sort of naturalistic material I rarely got a chance to work on, but Bill, ever the gambler, turned me loose. I had a wonderful cast led by Ellen Geer (Rosalind in Minnesota) Angela Paton, Ray Bieri, Richard Dysart and Austin Pendleton; it looked good—evocative sets by Stuart Wurtzel, dynamite costumes by Ann Roth—a handsome production that caught the mood of the piece but often short-changed the substance. Grade: C-

Not stellar on my part. But these were minor speed bumps on the long victory lap that was the first ACT season in San Francisco. Soon there were more superlatives for Jerry Kilty's production of Shaw's *Man and Superman* (two productions really, for it included the Hell Scene often done alone as a full evening of theater); and for Allen Fletcher's *Death of a Salesman* with Dick Dysart, deeply moving as Willie Loman; and for another of Bill Ball's chef d'oeuvres *Six Characters in Search of an Author*. Then a final soufflé: René Auberjonois shamelessly hilarious as Fancourt Babberly in Ed Hastings's production of *Charley's Aunt*.

Toward the end of the season, local and national critics were filing their summation pieces:

"The single most important happening in San Francisco's theatrical history," *San Francisco Examiner*

"A season of playgoing that should make it the envy of any community in the country," *Chicago Daily News*

"There is more excitement in a weekend with ACT than a month on Broadway," *Los Angeles Times*

"The most recklessly imaginative and technically adventurous of all repertory companies," *Saturday Review*

The final performance was to take place on June 18 in the Geary Theater; the show was *Tartuffe*. Because of the huge success of the season, plans were afoot to mark the event with some sort of ceremony following the performance. Various notables were to be approached about speaking. The chairman of the ACT board should begin it all, followed by various worthies—the mayor, the president of the California Theater Foundation, and so on. Then Bill was to talk about next season, chatting about the plays and plugging subscription sales. Then, to end it all, there would be a final curtain call—not just the *Tartuffe* folk but all the notables and the whole ACT company.

In the usual way of such things, the artistic director, after his remarks, would gesture to the wings. Then the Company, some in costume, some in mufti, would straggle out onto the stage. They would smile and wave; they would bow in serried ranks. There would be some embraces; eyes would water, and then that would be it. Curtain. End of season.

Ball had other plans. Speeches would be brief and few in number; most importantly there would be no undisciplined meanderings for a final call. What he wanted was a celebration of the entire season, a recapitulation of the audience's journey through the repertory of sixteen plays. Stunningly illuminated and accompanied by exquisitely appropriate music, the cast of each production, in full costume, would stride triumphantly down the raked stage of the Geary to take their bows. All sixteen casts, one after another. No matter whether the stage managers tore their hair with the complexity of it all, or the wardrobe ladies threatened a job action because of all the quick changes. No, it had to be done: The-Great-Mega-Sixteen-Production-Walk-Down-Get-'Em-On-Their-Feet-Screaming-and-Stomping-Curtain Call Extravaganza!

Bear in mind that no one in the history of the theater has ever staged a curtain call with the consummate skill that Bill Ball brought to the task. (An outrageous statement, I know, but it's true. Trust me.) Each was a small masterpiece of exuberant theatricality, and when you put sixteen of these gems back to back, when you delight an audience with their choreographic originality and at the same time give them a delicious reprise of the amazingly varied theatrical feast they've been consuming for the past 22 weeks, well, then it is time for standing ovations, for stamping of feet and for bellowing "Bravo!" until the rafters sway.

The famous scene designer of the '20s, Robert Edmond Jones, disillusioned with Broadway commercialism and theatrical taste-lessness, was wont to wail: "Where is the glory of the theater?"

Glory. Big word. Not a commodity in great supply in any age. But in the spring of 1967, in the city of San Francisco when Bill Ball and his Merry Pranksters came to town, there was glory abounding. I know. I was there.

Driving Down the Coast

With my gig at ACT finished and ten days of freedom before I had to start work in San Diego, Pamela and I decided to rent a car and drive down the California coast on Route 1, that macadam roller coaster that glides over sea cliffs and swoops around mountains revealing breathtaking panoramas on a heart-stopping ride down the edge of the continent.

On the first night we stopped not far south of San Francisco. Pamela needed to call home; I decided to take a walk on the beach. Such a wonderful way to unwind—the soothing rhythm of the surf, the long line of the horizon, all those healthy ions bubbling in the air. Late afternoon. The clouds scattered near the horizon promised a memorable sunset.

I stopped. Something was very wrong. The sun was going to set into the ocean!

Not rise out of, but set into—I'd never seen such a sight! I felt like the mama hen who adopted the abandoned duckling and then went bananas when they were walking by the pond and one li'l duckling decided to go for a dip. *"You're not supposed to do that!"*

A moment's thought and my wobbly gyroscope righted: I was on the opposite coast, facing west, not east. But the look of it ... so different from what I was used to.

You can imagine the scene: A Long Island beach at the end of a summer's day. The sun descends behind the houses, the light goes dead, and suddenly the water seems colder. The last of that ragged parade of the sun-drenched, weighed down with beach chairs, blankets, umbrellas, and empty ice chests, trudges up the weathered steps and down the long walkway to the parking lot, leaving a few scattered holdouts on the once crowded, noisy sands. At such times it is hard not to feel a slight pang of absence or loss. This is what a near-deserted beach at sunset symbolizes, is it not?

That's true if you're facing the dark green Atlantic, but now I was on the far side of the continent, staring slack-jawed at the Pacific, watching that big yellow disk slip into the sea like a voluptuous starlet easing herself into a perfumed bath; a wavering honey-colored light spread over houses and people and turned the sea foam into golden froth. This was no time for pangs of sadness and sentimental musing. Oh, no, this was West Coast magic time, and that great cosmic light designer had slipped a little Golden Amber (Roscoe #15) into Old Sol's gel frame, and the world was looking absolutely succulent.

Then the Nereids appeared. Two stunning young girls, blonde, tanned, and topless, wild with teenage high spirits, dashed from the surf with happy screeches. Once on the sand, they danced around each other, laughing, teasing, utterly indifferent to the fully-clothed, somewhat wide-eyed male not 15 feet away. Then they scampered off with exuberant shrieks and disappeared up the stairway to a nearby beach house.

I stood there dumbfounded, feeling like some pallid, ink-stained Dickensian bookkeeper who nods off at his desk and wakes on a beach in Tahiti.

Welcome to Southern California!

Today the state is a vibrant, vexing part of the national scene, but when I grew up on the East Coast in the early middle years of the last century, California was as little known and distant as the moon. The few who had ventured that far dismissed it as vacuous and superficial. The usual take was reflected in an oft-quoted re-mark of playwright George S. Kaufman, who, when asked what life was like in California, replied: "Great, if you're an orange."

This is what I knew: In the north, there grew a lot of big trees— sequoias they were called. One was so huge they'd cut a tunnel in the trunk and cars could drive through; I'd seen a picture of that. In the middle of the state was a beautiful city called San Francisco, built on some hills. You could ride over those hills on funny cable cars. There was also lots of fog and a long time ago a terrible earthquake.

In the south was sunshine. It was the place where the movies I went to two or three times a week were made, and though I adored Ingrid Bergman and tried to slide my upper lip over my teeth like Bogey, the entertainment their films provided was simply diversion. Good taste, real art, was the property of the east and resided in centers of culture like New York, Boston, and Philadelphia. Though by the time I was eighteen, I had hitchhiked the length of the state, I hadn't added much to my knowledge and subtracted nothing from my prejudices. It took the long stint at ACT to begin my re-education; that process was to continue in San Diego where in a week, I was to begin living on the beach and directing *Twelfth Night* at the Old Globe Theater.

A Water Baby Arises

I was three.

It was too hot on the beach, so I went swimming— at least I tried to. I toddled at top speed into the waters of the Long Island Sound and promptly sank. Thrashing wildly, choking, sputtering, I was soon delivered by Charlie, the lifeguard, from the perilous 12-inch depths and into my mother's arms.

This is a story my mother told me; I remember none of it. My mother, Agnes, hoped that this incident, which happened in late August, would be forgotten over the long winter. Indeed, everything seemed to indicate that such was the case.

The next spring she decided to try a test. On the first really warm day, she put me in the car and we started off. After a short ride down a familiar street she made a turn, a turn that to me could only mean one thing: we were headed for the Rocky Point Beach Club, site of my dunking the previous summer! Suddenly I erupted in deafening wails. She had to turn back before we'd gone half a mile.

But Agnes was not one to give up easily. She was quite athletic, loved the water herself, and was damned if any child of hers was going to be denied its pleasures. She began a campaign of loving, maternal bamboozlement that was to last an entire summer.

Step one was making that turn-off to the beach, but not before assuring me that "Oh, no, no," we weren't going to the beach club—she was turning onto this road because it was a shortcut to the village. This turned out to be true, but it took several repetitions before my blubbering subsided. Other seemingly innocent journeys disguising her hidden intent followed. By mid-July she had me feeling comfortable driving past the beach club. Later in the month we were stopping in the parking lot, "just waiting to pick up your brother," I was told; when I became uneasy, she started reading me Pooh stories.

By careful increments, I was being coaxed to the water's edge. The closer we got, the more difficult I became. When she got me into the beach club, I wouldn't get into my trunks. A week later, I would get into my trunks, but wouldn't go anywhere near the water. Given her unwavering purpose, however, the day of full immersion soon arrived. The following vignette is from my own memory.

Scene: The almost deserted pool at the Rocky Point Beach Club, August 1931. (We couldn't return to the scene of the crime because jellyfish had taken over the

Sound.) Late afternoon, a glassy blue-green sky,
water shining on duckboard. From the deep end of
the pool come those tight vibrating thumps as a div-
er leaps from the slightly saggy, hemp-covered div-
ing board and arcs into the water; he swims to the
ladder and dives again and again.

Halfway down the pool, at one side, there is a shrill com-
motion—a small boy, daring mightily, leaps from
the edge into the water and his mother's arms; they
laugh and splash around playfully. With her help, he
scrambles back onto the edge and jumps again, and
then again and again, and again. And each time the
daring, then the laughter and the silly splashing.

And thus was a water baby born. What a wonderful
gift my mother had given me!

———————

Two names are to be found on the letterhead of most regional theaters, each followed by a title. The names might appear in a line at
the top or in a column down one side. There are numerous variations to these titles, but by and large they fall into two categories.
The first belongs to the creative leader of the organization, usually
known as the artistic director, sometimes producing director, and,
rarely, general director. The second is the name of the person who
looks after the business side of the enterprise, usually identified as
managing director or simply manager.

These two people are responsible for the totality of what any given
theater is and does. Usually from somewhat different backgrounds,

they are, whether the two of them like it or not, joined at the hip for the duration of their mutual employment. They have to get on. Although, as the letterhead indicates, the artist is predominant, the manager is his most important ally. Their good relations and support for one another, their successful division of the great pie of responsibility, their willingness to achieve productive resolutions of the inevitable conflicts and work together for the common weal, may be, in the long run, the most important factor in the creation of a successful theater company.

Without John Houseman, no Orson Welles; without Nemirovich-Danchenko, no Stanislavsky—like that.

It is odd that this relationship—which has so little to do with the art itself—should be so important in an artistic institution, but it is so. At the Tyrone Guthrie Theater in the spring of 1967, that relationship between artist and manager was in alarming disarray and building to a crisis.

Guthrie had departed his namesake, leaving, as the poet Edwin Markham said, "a lonesome place against the sky."[8] Into that space, swaggering like a bumptious Henry VIII, arms akimbo, ready to take on the world, bounced Douglas Campbell. Now it was his turn; he had been heir apparent long enough. As was Guthrie's wish, the Board had named him the new artistic director.

But wait! There was someone else in that void between the trees at the crest of the hill. Yes, lurking ominously nearby, half hidden by the bushes, was our own éminence grise, Peter Zeisler, the managing director. You knew it was him because of the jets of smoke issuing from the boscage. (Zeisler, in an effort to curb his two-pack-a-day cigarette habit, had taken up the pipe, but to the alarm of all,

---

8   Edwin Markham, "Lincoln, The Man Of The People," *Lincoln and Other Poems* (New York: McClure, Phillips & Company, 1901).

he inhaled his Meerschaum with the same ferocity as he had his Marlboros.)

To complete this cartoon, we need only add Raggedy Eddie Call, smiling toothily, doing his I-Can-Charm-Anybody-Into-Doing-Anything routine, trying his damnedest to reconcile the second Tudor monarch and Cardinal Richelieu.

But this is only wishful thinking; I was out playing in California as the conflict unfolded; moreover, the importance of this matter not only to the Guthrie but to the state of regional theatre in general, deserves a more serious treatment than my lame facetiousness allows.

So, in another vein:

Douglas Campbell. Peter Zeisler. Say the names aloud. Hear the difference? One is sort of glottal and earthy, the other a narrow sibilance. The sound reflects the natures of the men, and those natures were diametrically opposed philosophically, temperamentally, artistically, you name it. They shared only one thing: a consuming love of theater.

Campbell believed, and believed passionately, that theaters like the Guthrie must be run by the artists. He believed the artistic director should have all the power—not just in creative matters like choosing the repertoire, casting, and selecting designers, but in matters fiscal and managerial as well. This latter role would be supervisory in nature, perhaps would consist of no more than veto power, but Campbell felt that without both these reins in his hands, he would be unable to guide the destiny of the institution.

The managing director did not share these sentiments. Zeisler did not approve of Douglas' elevation to artistic director, did not care for Campbell's choice of plays, had scant respect for him as a director, and was deeply pessimistic about what the future held with Campbell in charge.

As this time, Zeisler was regarded by many as something of a miracle worker. It was he, after all, who had played the principal role in guiding the Minnesota Theatre Company from idea to reality. In some ways he had been the most important of the original "glamorous troika." Having labored ceaselessly in the cause, he had a huge stake in its continued success.

And thus the impossible new collaboration began.

That wonderful list of plays that Campbell had announced for the '66 season, despite the best efforts of a strong acting company, failed to ignite critics or audiences. Sententious Sunday think pieces started to appear in the press warning of "museum theater." Mr. Kauffman in the *New York Times* professed admiration for the ensemble but felt some of our actors lacked the chops for the big leading roles. Most damaging of all were the statistics, which showed a significant drop in both subscriptions and single ticket sales.

Some of the second guessers thought Campbell should have made a stronger move to get out of Guthrie's shadow, should have made some chancy play choices that made the press people all tingly, writing about Campbell "confounding the naysayers, and striking out in a bold new direction"—stuff like that. "He is such a gutsy, two-fisted, free-swinging kind of guy; why isn't it happening?" some asked.

Well, it didn't happen for a simple reason. Campbell lacked the desire—not the guts, mind you, but the desire. Campbell was comfortable in Guthrie's shadow; his taste was similar to Dr. Guthrie's taste. How else could they have worked together so successfully all those decades? He loved the same theatrical literature that Guthrie loved and wanted no more than to continue Guthrie's mission of making that literature live on the stage. He had certainly chosen a superb list of masterpieces to do it with. Yet in the eyes of many, they fell short in production. Perhaps expectations were too high. Or it just might be that achieving high praise following directly after the mythic Sir Tyrone was an impossible task.

Important here to remember that Campbell was an actor, a Player, if you will, in every atom of his body. Being a director was a sideline. Thus his directorial work was brisk, lucid, and theatrical, but lacked, as we all lack, the Guthrie panache. The 1966 repertory of the Minnesota Theatre Company would have wowed 'em in any playhouse in the land, but in the eyes of the cognoscenti, it just wasn't good enough for the flagship theater the Guthrie had become. As the season ended, Campbell's leadership was under a cloud and Zeisler was about to make his move.

Managers enjoy one great advantage over artistic directors: They speak the same language as members of the board. The Board of Directors—the mysterious seat of ultimate power in any artistic institution, is usually composed of business types. The manager is also a business type; they are cut from the same cloth.

The artistic director is of another breed. He needs to be creative, inspiring, even visionary. He needs to be able to light up the boardroom with descriptions of the artistic distinction that will be achieved under his stewardship, and then deliver a decent approximation of same on the stage. As long as he does so, his position is secure. But if the work falters and the audiences start to dwindle, the board will turn to someone it can trust, to its natural ally, the managing director.

The Board of the Tyrone Guthrie Theater held such trust in Peter Zeisler that in early 1967 it vested him "with ultimate authority over artistic as well as administrative matters." Campbell had received a stinging vote of no confidence. It was an indignity he could not countenance, and soon thereafter he resigned.

———

Sitting on the sand at Mission Beach with my inescapable companion, the legal yellow pad, I tried to write out what I felt and where I stood in this imbroglio.

Sometime during my stint in San Francisco, I had had a stunning insight: My relationship to the leaders of the theater in Minneapolis represented an idealized version of my own family. Here was Dr. G, the Guvnor of course. Douglas Campbell was Don, the loving, unpredictable brother, and Peter Zeisler was Jack, the shrewd, manipulative one.

We've all heard that a need for family often attracts people to the theater, but this kind of one-for-one equivalency astounded me. I wondered how much it had to do with my early success in Minneapolis, as well as the subsequent lack of it in San Francisco. I felt a longing to get back to work with a trio of men who so obviously had my best interests at heart.

My debt to and affection for brother Campbell were undiminished. Yet Zeisler—difficult, mysterious Zeisler—was a brother as well. He was the one who had hired me in the first place, the one who sponsored the workshops that allowed me to strut my directorial stuff. And when *Chalk Circle* was in rehearsal and Dr. G was uninterested and Campbell was in Canada, it was Zeisler in his secretive way who watched my progress indirectly through seconds, guiding me away from some land mines and facing down that angry committee of actors who wanted me fired.

One thing became clear to me as I wrote: The Guthrie Theater was my creative home; I wanted it to stay that way. If throwing in my lot with Peter Zeisler was the only way to do it—so be it. I knew that my choice would put my friendship with Campbell at risk, but

I was willing to chance that. Ambition was driving me. Only the work was important.

In returning to Minneapolis, I was returning to turmoil, and it would be years until I fully realized the debt I owed Zeisler. At that point I only knew I would be facing the turmoil with a producer I could trust.

The Old Guard's days had always been numbered. Before long, those of us who back in 1963 had stamped the snow off our boots, walking into that over-bright rehearsal room and into a new world of theater, would soon be going our separate ways. We were granted only three seasons with Dr. G in that marvelous old tub, the Great Guthrie Pleasure Palace. Daddy Tyrone had left, and my two brothers were duking it out for control of the theater.

Elsewhere on the national scene, by age 29 Mel Shapiro was becoming a hot young director. His home base was at New York University, where he was already head of the acting program, but he also directed around the country, at Arena Stage, Stanford Repertory Theater, and the Old Globe. These productions were attracting attention. One of those who took notice was Peter Zeisler, who brought Shapiro to Minneapolis with the idea of creating a new troika to head the theater, consisting of himself, myself, and Shapiro.

Shapiro and I were to direct plays and share with Zeisler some of the splendid burdens of management. We would be billed as producing directors.

There would be no artistic director.

Unbeknownst to me yet, Shapiro and I were to become an odd couple. A waggish friend once suggested that if the producing director thing didn't work out, we might consider a career in stand-up comedy. There was certainly an Abbott and Costello polarity in our physical makeup. There I was—a tall, skinny WASP, irredeemably preppy, square and bright-eyed as a Mormon; and there was Shapiro, a short, round Jew, New York to the core, droll and cynical as Touchstone.

Even more pronounced was the difference in the way we approached directing. I was all outside; Shapiro was all inside. I directed with my eyes. Staging was my obsession. I believed that the solution to any actor's problem lay in finding the perfect position for him on the stage, or the perfect move, or the perfect gesture, where he should be in relation to the other characters, where they should be, et cetera, et cetera.

Oh, I was listening, but not well, not deeply enough. I think a great deal of what I have learned in my career has to do with listening—daring to close my eyes so that my only contact with the event is hearing the text being spoken. But even now, my listening only goes so far. It monitors the plausibility of the reading, questions the choice of stressed words, tunes into the fast/slow, loud/soft music of dynamics, picks up the effect more than the source of the effect.

There is another kind of listening some directors are capable of, the kind of listening that vaguely apprehends the externals but is more focused on going deeper to find the emotional weather at the heart of the process. An almost mystical affinity, it allows such directors to grasp, at any given moment, the actors' feelings in relation to the material he is attempting to embody. Shapiro is that kind of listener, that kind of director, which is one of the reasons he has been such an outstanding teacher all his life, as well as a director.

———◆———

3755 Ocean Front Walk, Mission Beach, San Diego, when I first saw it, was a somewhat weathered, three-story apartment building

trying to bring some picture-window class to the gathering of surf-
ers' shacks that surrounded it. The facade was decorated with tall,
narrow diamond shapes, painted yellow, that gave it a sort of car
wash panache. But whatever its architectural shortcomings, it lin-
gers in my memory as an oceanside villa of rare enchantment, a
fantastical snuggery on the sands, where Pamela and I played for
most of the summer of 1967.

Craig Noel, the lovable, avuncular producing director of the
Old Globe, had invited me to direct *Twelfth Night* at his theatre.
I accepted happily, with one condition: I had to live at the beach.
I was only partly serious, but following our arrival in San Diego,
damned if Noel didn't drive Pamela and me out to Mission Beach,
just north of the city, to look at some possibilities he'd heard about.
After rejecting a few, we arrived at 3755, where there awaited a
two-bedroom apartment on the second floor with a tiny balcony
and big picture windows facing the restless Pacific.

It was hard to believe such stunning good fortune. With any encouragement I could go on at great length about body surfing in the
Pacific; about the sunsets; about heroic little fish called grunion that
come ashore to spawn; about my farcical attempts at board surfing;
about beach parties at night, gathered around the fire ring; about
waking at first light, looking over Pamela's sleeping form through
the big picture window at "a grey mist on the sea's face, and the grey
dawn breaking"[9] and seeing a quartet of sea birds, their great wings
moving easily, almost in unison, cruising south, a hands-breadth
above the shore break.

But enough of these indulgences. On with the show!

On the huge mesa that is known as Balboa Park, near dramatic
Spanish Renaissance buildings created for an exposition in 1915, in

9   John Masefield, "A Wanderer's Song," *Salt-water Poems and Ballads* (New York: MacMillan, 1916).

the corner of a generous green lawn, shaded by palm and eucalyptus, stands a charming approximation of Shakespeare's theatre, the Globe.

At dusk, accompanied by the murmur of doves and the cry of peacocks from the nearby San Diego Zoo, a skinny youngster in a somewhat wilted Elizabethan costume clambers out onto a platform over the theatre's entrance to address the crowd on the grass below. These theatregoers in their new tans and crisp summer finery have just witnessed fifteen minutes of heavy-footed Elizabethan dance performed by a large group of marginally spirited teenagers, cavorting on the greensward in doublet and farthingale, to strum of lute and wail of recorder.

The skinny youngster perched over the entrance checks his costume one last time; rings his crier's bell; then, in a genial shout, delivers some doggerel lines meant to entice the ticket-holders into the playhouse. They begin:

> Hark, ye gentles, hark ye all! Now's the time for curtain
> call [*sic*]
> Masked and 'coutered in the wings
> The actors wait; the play's the thing
> And when you hear ... [*and so on*]

This was the Old Globe Theatre as I knew it in the late '60s and through the '70s. Unlike the Guthrie or ACT, so recently arrived fully formed, so sleek, so complete in every detail, theater in Balboa Park, like many of the theatres that would be heard from in later years, was in the midst of a long evolution from amateur to professional status—from a modest classical festival to the formidable institution (three theaters, numerous Broadway transfers) that it is today. In 1967, the Globe was midway on that journey, part amateur, part professional. In the winter, professionals supervised a community theatre. In the summer, it transformed into a professional Shakespeare festival with a warm amateur heart.

And how we did love working summers at the Globe! What was it? Love of Shakespeare and sunshine? Yes, that and the love of being young and lucky enough to work on a masterpiece in very happy circumstances, watched over by Noel, this genial magus who put it all together with such a deft touch. If Guthrie was the internationally renowned chef de cuisine who created astounding classical dishes while frazzling the entire kitchen staff, then Noel was the virtuoso pastry chef, whipping up wonders with modest means, while inspiring love in all, from sous-chef to dishwasher. He always tried to sneak you an extra dessert.

There was an easiness about the place. Actors from the east, released from the rigors of New York, let down their guards, became both more daring and more accessible. For some it was like discovering again why they went into theater.

I remember a photo call for *Twelfth Night*, four of the leads in full costume. We went to a beautiful garden across from the theatre, a place of fountains, graceful terra-cotta benches, and vast flower beds. We started setting up shots near one of the fountains, contriving all those dreary manufactured poses the press department needs. "That's it, Katherine, put your hand on Orsino's shoulder. George, don't look at the camera, look at her … Yes, yes, I know the sun is hot, but try not to squint. Ready?"

Click!

Then someone suggested that since the photographer was using color film, why didn't we get the flowerbeds into the shots? Then someone else proposed that we put the actors in among the flowers.

That seemed slightly odd, not to mention destructive when some-one said "Why not put the actors on top of the flowers?" "That's it!" Sudden scurryings to the theatre followed. "Stools, we need stools!" Stools appeared and were carefully insinuated among the blooms. Finally, there they were, the leads of *Twelfth Night*: Sir Andrew (Joe Maher), Viola (Katherine Henryk), Orsino (George Backman), and Feste (Don West), having enthusiastically joined the game, all spaced about, each an island of jocundity floating on a sea of red dahlia.

Click! Enchanting. Things like that happened at the Globe.

This openness, this collaborative spirit really saved me as a di-rector. I had come to San Diego full of enthusiasm and good will, but ill-prepared to direct *Twelfth Night*. I just hadn't had the time for the exacting homework I like to do—little time to dig into the difficult Shakespearean text and no time at all to get started on the blocking.

It is a situation all directors have to face some time or other, when, through lack of self-discipline or some mischance of sched-uling, you have to go into rehearsals with a relatively empty head. At such times you have to keep your wits about you, trust your in-stincts, and get on with the work. And also use every second of free time to catch up.

With *Twelfth Night*, I was immensely aided by the congenial atmosphere at the Globe and the creativity of the superb cast that Craig had assembled. Given the circumstances, I had to let go of some of my more controlling impulses, and as a result each of the actors, having contributed more to the process, felt a greater sense of ownership of both their own role and the production itself. The result of all this was a great success. I could scarcely believe it; I hadn't suffered enough.

So with *Twelfth Night* humming along and me not due in Minneapolis for several weeks, there was time for swimming and sailing and day trips to Mexico and zoo visits and all the delights of San Diego, delights made more intense and poignant because the idea of going back to the Guthrie Theatre was beginning to fill me with dread.

———————

Guthrie Theater's 1968 Season

When I arrived in Minneapolis toward the end of the '67 season, I found, to my relief, that the leadership dust was beginning to settle. The big conflicts were past. The new troika of Zeisler, Call, and Shapiro had been contracted. Campbell would stay on to act some major roles, but his artistic leadership was at an end. At this time, our personal lives were taking us in different directions, so Campbell and I rarely met, which was probably for the best. Needless to say, the few encounters we did have were awkward. We needed to talk it out, but neither of us seemed to have the will.

My tan soon paled, and the echo of the Pacific soon faded in my ears. I didn't mind; I had an exciting new role and new responsibilities that were not mine alone but that would be shared.

It took time to sink in, the fact that the giants had really departed and we were on our own. Henceforth, no blaring trumpets would sound. Neither cherubim nor seraphim would hover expectantly over 725 Vineland Place to hear *grreat Doooglas,* the Mighty Scot, reveal the *grrrand and consuming worrrrk* that lay ahead. And the awesome Tyrone, whose thundering voice once rocked the very walls of our castle, was silent—withdrawn, brooding moodily on his windblown Irish isle.

The great vastitude of the 1968 season lay before us. What would it be? What philosophy would buttress it? What works would be performed and who would perform them? It was all up to Zeisler, Call, and Shapiro—the Pep Boys had taken over the Guthrie Pleasure Palace.

Another ambitious wrinkle for the Guthrie Theater troika to incorporate was the expansion of our scope that year. In addition to executing our first national tour, we planned to program events at two new venues: a three-play repertory at the Crawford Livingston Theater in St. Paul and smaller experimental works at a nearby studio theater, The Other Place.

We set to work. The first major task was picking the six plays that would be performed in the Tyrone Guthrie Theater. The discussions started at some intersection of philosophy, taste, and box-office appeal. Then other concerns took over, like who did we have to play what?

We decided it was high time our company honored Henrik Ibsen, the man who invented modern theater, by producing one of his plays. Given Minneapolis's large Scandinavian community, we also thought an Ibsen play might make good box-office sense. But which Ibsen play would it be? After tossing several titles around, we settled on the exact play rather quickly. Imagining Bob Pastene in the leading role of the doomed architect, Solness, led us to the choice of Ibsen's own *King Lear*, a play called *The Master Builder*.

Then, of course, we had to find roles in the rest of the season for Pastene, some large, some small.

Multiply that process by twenty actors for the main stage, then add to that the rep we were planning to do in St. Paul, as well as a dozen or so attractions at The Other Place, and you begin to see the multidimensional jigsaw puzzle we were dealing with.

In spite of the difficulties, I remember choosing the plays for that season as a time of pleasurable excitement—new buttons, new levers—heady stuff. All this power was shared, but I didn't mind that: less pressure.

Twelfth Night would open the season. I was to direct, or so I thought, until it was revealed that the gods had other plans. I was sidelined for a time with hepatitis and had to turn the show over to Rob Lancaster, who put together a splendidly funny and touching production.

Next would come *Serjeant Musgrave's Dance*, John Arden's gritty antiwar play. Shapiro was to direct.

Then *The Master Builder*, Ibsen's meditation on youth and age. Pastene, now a veteran of five seasons with the Minnesota Theatre Company, was the aging architect, Solness, and Lauri Peters, a radiant young blonde new to the company, would be his fatal muse, Hilda Wangel.

The above three plays would open in mid-June. Later in the summer I was to get another crack at Bertolt Brecht with *The Resistible Rise of Arturo Ui*, Brecht's parable about A. Hitler's climb to power. In this mock-heroic parable, Hitler is Arturo Ui, a two-bit thug who claws his way to the top of '20s gangland Chicago—all in blank verse.

We wanted to end the season with an American comedy, but we couldn't find the right one. If it fit the company, it didn't suit the balance of the repertoire; if it was right for the rep, we couldn't work out the casting.

Until Shapiro asked, "Did you ever hear of a play called *Merton of the Movies*?"

Bingo! A sly, endearing, almost forgotten 1923 comedy by George S. Kaufman and Marc Connelly, filled with the glitz and panache of silent-era Hollywood, *Merton of the Movies* tells the story of Merton Gill, a humble, bumbling clerk in a hardware store in Simsbury, Illinois, who dreams of, and achieves (although not quite in the way he intended), riches and fame as a cowboy hero on the silver screen.

We may have wavered for a few minutes, thinking that perhaps this piece might violate our oh-so-serious theatrical mission, but then we remembered that Dr. G was always trying to shoehorn *Three Men on a Horse* into the rep. Moreover, we had in our company the best character juvenile on the continent to play Merton: Michael Moriarty.

So, with the above and a few other choices, we had our season. But it was just a beginning—cast lists and a pile of contracts. The real work was over the horizon. Meanwhile, down in the theater, the '67 season was winding down. It was destined to end not with a whimper but an enormous bang.

———————

Tyrone Guthrie, keeping his promise to come back to direct from time to time, blew into town and was turning some scary creatures loose on the open stage. Huge, dark, tattered, implacable, they seemed like nightmare apparitions from the dawn of time. He had gone back to the Greeks and chosen as a vehicle for his genius not a single play but a trilogy of plays—*The Oresteia* of Aeschylus, a 2500-year-old work, honored as one of the seminal masterpieces of world drama and, like most seminal masterpieces, never performed. But now, John Lewin, an actor in the company and a comer as a playwright, had wrought a supple adaptation of the piece that he called *The House of Atreus*, and the Minnesota Theatre Company, thirty strong, all masked and shod with cothurni, was bringing it to life.

The great warrior king Agamemnon returns in triumph from Troy, his chariot shouldered onto the stage by adoring subjects, while his queen, Clytemnestra, waits in the palace, fingering the axe with which she will hack him to death. Thus the blood curse of Atreus grinds on as wife murders husband; then in revenge, son Orestes kills mother; until out of the darkness, like bats at sunset, the Furies swarm.

This horrific tale (five hours in performance) ends finally in the quiet of an Athenian temple. The gods come down to earth to put the scattered affairs of men in order. On the Acropolis, a court is established, and in that grand-daddy of all trial scenes, Orestes is freed from the Furies' torment. The gods end the curse of inherited guilt, and the concept of justice tempered by mercy begins to soothe the fevered brow of man. One critic called the work a chronicle of "our passage from savagery to civilization." Just back from San Diego, I watched a performance. The stage I thought I knew so well had become strange, somber, brutal. I heard unusual poetry, odd musical sounds; the chorus swirled. There were performances of great daring by actors wearing masks that seemed to be made of rusted metal and dried blood. Gods stalked the earth; a huge statue came to life.

I hadn't been in on the rehearsals, but I knew all these performers. Campbell was inside the big statue. There was Robin Gammell in a prophetic frenzy as Cassandra. And the giant god Apollo? That was Lee Richardson in plasterer's boots and a huge golden sun mask. But it made no difference. Nothing could mitigate the jaw-dropping wonder I felt at that dark, boldly theatrical pageant of mankind's struggle with his darkest impulses.

Tony Guthrie, master of the light touch, flippant ironist ("ever so expert with the gossamer wit, don't you know") had stripped off his shirt, kicked off his tennies, and taken a dive into the great the-atrical mosh pit where, with a champion's fury, he had mud-wres-tled the treacherous Greeks into submission. He emerged with a dirty laurel wreath on his head, a wicked grin on his face, and the theater's biggest hit. Un-fucking-believable!

———————

In 1941, as a twelve-year-old, newly arrived in DC, I started explor-ing some of the monuments of our nation's capital—the Smithsonian Museum, the National Archives Museum, Arlington National Cemetery and the Tomb of the Unknown Soldier. Sometimes on these forays I would hear the shrill newsboy cry of "Extra!" as some new war panic erupted. Then one sunny Sunday, Pearl Harbor hap-pened. My brothers went to war. I was too young; I stayed home.

In summers on the Atlantic beaches, World War II seemed re-mote. The big waves crashed as they always had, but sometimes as the water surged near, I noticed that the foam looked oddly yellow, and when the wave receded, its furthest reach was painted on the sand with a thin line of grimy black oil—memento mori from the local U-boat commander.

I spent the summer of 1944 at Westhampton Beach on Long Island sun-drunk, infatuated, thoroughly absorbed with teenage lu-nacy. Once in a while, I would stop and stare at the horizon and try to imagine brother Don, then age 23, dodging bullets ("the flying Schwiebak," he used to call it cavalierly in his letters home) and leading his platoon across France. These memories came back to me as I began work on Bertolt Brecht's Hitler parable.

The Resistible Rise of Arturo Ui is a fascinating mutt of a play, difficult to label. Ostensibly, it is a violent, brass-knuckled saga of

a brutal gangster's rise to power, but it is written in blank verse—
in George Tabori's superb translation, often hilarious blank verse.
Early in the play, Arturo, still low man on the totem pole, swears
vengeance with the following iambs:

> I'm gonna take him for a ride, Ernesto,
> As soon as I get credit for a car.

Shakespeare gets mangled when one of the grocers whom Ui is
trying to shake down complains:

> What's artichoke to him or him to artichoke?
> Several scenes echo *Richard III*, and elsewhere we have:
> Friends, countrymen, Brooklynites, lend me your ears.

Given our Damon Runyon tradition of lovable lowlifes, given
the way we Americans can hug the most bloodthirsty mobsters to
our collective breast, and given Brecht's witty mock-heroic satire,
there is a danger that this piece can become merely an entertainment and not the cautionary tale the author intended. For it is the
"resistible" rise, remember? We have to wake up and act before some
stupid but implacably ambitious thug hijacks our government and
its power makes him invincible. At the very end of the play, a brief
epilogue makes this point chillingly clear. The actor who has imper-
sonated Ui, having stripped off his Hitler mustache, warns us:

> Don't yet rejoice in his defeat, you men!
> Although the world stood up and stopped the bastard,
> The bitch that bore him is in heat again.[10]

10   Bertolt Brecht, *The Resistable Rise of Arturo Ui: A Gangster Spectacle*, adapted by George Tabori
      (New York: Samuel French, 1972).

Yes, I wanted to exploit the *Guys and Dolls* side of the play for all it was worth, but if it was done to the detriment of the grim admonitory intent of the piece, the production would be a failure. My brother Don, who became an authentic hero of World War II, had been killed in an automobile accident in Paris a couple of years before I started work on *Arturo Ui*. I wanted it to be a production he would have admired. I intended to dedicate it to him.

Brecht's script calls for headlines to be projected on the curtain at the end of each scene, headlines that make clear the Ui/Hitler parallels. Thus, after Ui has a grocery store torched to convince the merchants of Chicago that they'd better sign up for his "protection service," the headline reports the Reichstag fire of 1933. The German audience for whom Brecht was writing would hardly have to be reminded of that infamous event, but Americans would need some help, particularly young Americans to whom the history of the '30s and '40s was nearly as remote as the Ice Age.

Film became my answer. Newsreels and documentaries would render in gritty black and white the real German history behind the gang wars and show us again those unholy faces: Hitler, Goering, and Goebbels, all of whom had counterparts in the play.

Film would also help cover the fifteen scene changes. I saw it going like this: Scene ends, an ominous chord is heard, actors freeze, an amplified voice speaks the headline, then blackout on stage for the scene change and start the film—but where? How to manage projecting two-dimensional film, pancake-flat film in our three-sided theater?

Enter Richard Hay, whose inspired set design somehow effortlessly melded the architecture (in this case, the large rectangular panels that hovered over the stage) with the walls of the set and in the process created a three-sided screen for Adolf and Co.

With that problem out of the way, we could turn our attention to the next step: finding the appropriate footage and acquiring the rights to that footage. Not easy. Next, the nightmare of technical rehearsals needed to integrate the film into the production. The folks who were supposed to know about such things warned us that teching film requires a huge amount of time. One expert told me that you can't double the tech time or square it; "you must cube it," she warned ominously.

Enter S. Leonard ("Lennie") Auerbach, and the film was found, edited, scored, and folded into the production with a minimum of fuss. And as I had hoped, those looming images became a disturbingly eerie counterpoint to the events on stage.

To realize the serious purpose of the play, headlines help. The episodes of film help. But the real onus of the task falls on the shoulders of the actor playing Arturo Ui. He's a Hitler caricature with a Brooklyn accent. Although the play takes place in Chicago, Ui, as he often reminds us, is really a "loyal son of Brooklyn." As such, he is, or can be, exceedingly funny, particularly in the early scenes when he's so powerless and inept. But as his power grows, he must begin to make us uneasy; finally, he must terrify. The demands of the role are immense and unique. There are few actors who can cut this kind of mustard. Fortunately, we always knew who Arturo would be, as he was already a member of the company. His name is Robin Gammell.

Robin, who was that memorable Clov in *Endgame* at ACT, had joined the Minnesota Theatre Company in 1967. He had played leads in several productions, most notably Arthur in Mrożek's *Tango*, and two female roles, Cassandra and Electra, in *The House of Atreus*. In signing up for Arturo, I think it is not an exaggeration to say that he was taking on the role of a lifetime. He had all the necessary comic resources for the piece, as well as the classical chops to handle the blank verse; most importantly he was capable of projecting the furious animal mania that was driving the character. From the start of rehearsal, it was obvious Gammell was going to deliver the goods in a major way. In the final weeks of those rehearsals, despite the technical complexity of the production and my unreliable health (still not quite recovered from hepatitis), it all came together with surprising smoothness.

When we opened, it was all roses and champagne. Gammell and I owned the Twin Cities. John Harvey of the *St. Paul Dispatch* wrote: "Arturo Ui, in the amazingly agile and versatile person of Robin Gammell, is a funny, timorous, hysterical clown who grows before one's eyes into a figure of reptilian menace."

Don Morrison of the *Minneapolis Tribune* was not officially a theater critic, but often in his lively general-interest column you could find the most perceptive remarks about the work at the Guthrie Theater. He had chewed me out for *As You Like It*, but this one really turned him on. Gammell's performance was:

> an authentic tour de force, one of a handful of sustained virtuoso performances that have electrified the stage of the Guthrie—which tends to offer strong, solid, craftsman-like acting rather than skyrockets like this.
>
> Comparisons are too tricky to say that Edward Payson Call's production of *The Resistible Rise of Arturo Ui* is the best thing done in six seasons at the Guthrie Theater, which has ranged over a very diverse spectrum of plays. But without question this is the most exciting—and, because of its contemporary theme, perhaps the most gut-punchingly relevant.

"Relevant"—a beautiful word to read if you earn your bread in classical theater where the reaction can often be admiring but remote, tepid. Precede it with a mouth-filling adjective like "gut-punchingly" and the show's creators begin to think that the impact they so earnestly hoped for might be a reality.

So, we were feeling pretty good about the production—a tad smug, maybe. What we didn't know was that the relevance meter was about to go through the roof. A couple of weeks after the opening, we watched the TV in horror as Chicago Mayor Richard Daly's police made a vicious attack on the antiwar demonstrators who had gathered in several Chicago parks to work the 1968 Democratic National Convention. In a night of tear gas, billy sticks, and blood, hundreds were injured. Only the tragedy at Kent State University eclipses it as the nadir of domestic events during the Vietnam War.

The effect of what happened in Chicago on the audience at *Arturo Ui* was immediate. The theater became electric with a new kind of tension, a tension that came not from the production, but from the audience. It was sizzling inside them as they came through the doors.

Suddenly, unexpectedly, I was encountering the spirit that my Aunt Caroline thought was lacking when she saw *The Quare Fellow* at Circle in the Square back in 1958—the spirit of people who were deeply committed to political action, people who "thought they could change the world."

These folks in the Twin Cities were solid citizens, not even sympathetic with, much less given to, radical politics. But they were coming to the theater enraged by the events in Chicago, and they saw a play about the catastrophic cost of political indifference. This was theater at the barricades. These people vibrated. The laughs were all there, but it was a different kind of laughter: harder, more observant, more in sync with Brecht's purpose. They didn't applaud, they cheered. I stood at the back watching, and from time to time my shoulders jerked as the chills went down my spine.

Don's Homecoming, 1951

Finally, Don was coming home.

Following his training at Fort Benning, Georgia, in 1944, my eldest brother Don Jr. had gone into combat in France as a replacement officer, just before the beginning of that ominous Nazi breakout with the unfortunate name, the Battle of the Bulge.

Replacement officers did not have a healthy survival rate. Most soldiers go into combat for the first time side by side with comrades, men they trained with and have come to trust. They take care of one another. Going green into combat, utterly alone at such a young age, being called upon to lead tough, battle-hard troops must require strength and prowess we noncombatants can only dream about.

It turned out that my charming, movie-star handsome, hard-drinking, womanizing brother, after only twelve weeks of training in Georgia, had what it takes on the field of battle. He led his platoon through the Bulge and into Germany until V.E. (Victory in Europe) Day and accumulated a distinguished record and many medals in doing so.

My mother, desperate to distract herself from the worry that consumed her when she knew Don was in combat, had taken a job in a department store. Now she began to relax. He was safe and would soon be home.

But he didn't come—not even on leave. He stayed in the Army, became fluent in German, started working to resettle those orphans of the war, the displaced persons, DPs as they were called. He fell in love with an Austrian girl. Months passed, then years. He was not coming home, and we didn't know why. We were becoming a family of four.

Then, in 1951, Don returned to the States. Outwardly unchanged, he nevertheless seemed deeply troubled.

He was always a heavy drinker, but now it was getting out of hand. He had a few narrow escapes in his car. Not only his family but the Army was worried about him. He was now working for Army Intelligence, and however effective he was on the job, rumors started to get around about the heavy drinking off duty. Word was passed to Counter Intelligence.

Don's favorite watering spot was Martin's Bar on Wisconsin Avenue in Georgetown. One night when he had had a few too many, he found a stranger sitting next to him. They fell to talking, became friendly; soon Don was buying him drinks. Then the stranger made a bad mistake—he got a little too curious about Don's work and asked too many questions. My brother clammed up, but the stranger persisted. Then came some ambiguous proposal and a hint of rewards, at which point Don pulled him off the bar stool and punched him out. The stranger was shown the door. Don went back to his drink and the Army stopped worrying.

But not the family. He seemed to be on a long and difficult road back, and none of us knew how to help.

We were, of course, very curious about his war experience, but he didn't want to talk about it, until one memorable night.

Our family home was now outside Washington, just off Massachusetts Avenue, two miles past the District Line—the burgeoning suburbs of the '50s. It was an evening in late summer, warm enough to "eat out" as the Guvnor decided, which meant dinner on the back porch. All five of us were there. As the dinner ended, without any prompting Don began to talk—to tell us about his war, of the men he fought with, of his trial by fire as a replacement officer, of being wounded when he stood to shoot covering fire for some of his men, then after a hospital stay returning to his unit, now billeted in a tiny French village, to find a homemade banner had been draped across the main street. "Welcome back, Lt. D. M. Call Jr." it read. He was a replacement officer no longer.

He had been speaking for some time now. The sun had set, the twilight faded, and then it was dark, pitch dark, save for a few fireflies at the back of the garden and the ember at the tip of his Camel cigarette. He would take a drag; his face glowed briefly, then disappeared. But his voice went on in the darkness. We listened suspended in some way, unable to move or speak, clear the table, turn on a light, do anything but listen hypnotized to my brother's chronicle of his time on the battlefield— just a voice in the darkness, then the inhale, a soft glow, then darkness and the voice again. ("And I alone have escaped to tell you."[11])

---

11 Job 1:15

Later in the war, with the "Krauts" on the run, his unit moved toward yet another French village. At its southern edge, some people were waving frantically, trying to communicate the fact that the Germans were at that moment hotfooting it out the other end of town. Don floored the accelerator of his Jeep; he and his sergeant rocketed through the town to a rise on its northern edge. Most of the enemy were out of sight, but two Germans, dashing away across a hay field were within range. My brother took out his submachine gun and shot them dead.

I tried to imagine that scene—bright sunlight, blue sky, the field, the Germans running—*bup, bup, bup, bup, bup, bup, bup,* they fall down; then silence. The war, the real war, not the Hollywood war, not the Shakespeare war, but the real war had come home to the suburbs. No one spoke. From the depths of the garden came a whispery buzz and the eerie glow of the fireflies.

"My brother took out his submachine gun and shot them dead." I have always wondered if I could have done that. I think I would have failed; I was not cut out to be a warrior. We all have different roles to play—he was Dimitri Karamazov, I'm Aloysha. It could be that I would not be sitting at this table in a quiet garden outside Seattle writing these words if my brother and his fellow GIs had not taken out their submachine guns and shot them dead. Viva Karamazov!

Then it was time for the satyr play: his long tale ended with a surreal, almost farcical story of the end of it all. In Don's sector for most of June 7, 1945, there was not much gunfire. There had been rumors of surrender, so neither officers nor men wanted to take any chances, but nothing official was heard. Finally, sometime after nightfall, word came from headquarters: unconditional surrender! But the celebration was cut short by new orders—Don's battalion was to accept the surrender of the better part of a panzer division. The Germans had been ordered to take their tanks to a nearby sports field. These huge machines of death, which had so recently struck fear in every infantryman's soul, were now lumbering down the hill to the floodlit field, single file, like so many amiable circus elephants. And then the men of my brother's company, dangerous warriors all, having dropped their M-1s, shouted and gestured like so many overexuberant parking lot attendants and bullied the beasts into orderly ranks. The war was over.

After a long silence, my mother turned on the porch light. We blinked stupidly and concentrated on clearing the table.

In the winter of 1968, the Minnesota Theatre Company took its act to Broadway. A national tour, long talked of, had become a reality. At last the world at large would get a chance to see what we had been up to in the heartland. We were taking two shows: *The House of Atreus* and *The Resistable Rise of Arturo Ui*. First stop, New York City.

Oh, the excitement we felt! Oh, the disaster that awaited!

We were to play the Billy Rose Theatre (now the Nederlander) on Forty-first Street, south of Times Square. On one of our first days in town, I went to the theater to have a look. There were no rehearsals, so I wasn't needed, but I couldn't stay away. Could you blame me? My first real Broadway show. I just wanted to drink in the magic.

I slipped into a seat at the back of the house. John Jensen, who had devised a clever way to adapt our open stage sets for the Billy Rose proscenium, was watching the load-in, seated at a tech table halfway back in the orchestra. House and work lights were on, and the crew (maybe a dozen strong) was scattered about—a few in the house (electricians), most of the rest at various places onstage.

It was not going well. The IA (short for the stagehands union IATSE: the International Alliance of Theatrical Stage Employees of the United States and Canada) had not quite caught the zestful high spirits with which we had come to town, and it was showing in the pace of their work: deliberate sliding toward to glacial. I couldn't quite believe the activity, or rather the lack of it, on stage.

One creature in particular caught my attention. Ragged clothes on a skinny frame, a wizened face, and an attitude that can only be called sullen outrage combined to produce in me the following insight: The IA (Local #1) had added a new specialty in addition to flyman, electrician, prop man, and so on, which might be called the Beckett vagrant.

The specimen I was observing seemed to be involved in a behavior best labeled "creative inactivity." He would linger down right, sitting on the lower rung of a ladder, fiddling with a piece of rope or a length of wire; ten minutes later he'd cross the stage, moving quite quickly, and find a box or barrel, sit down, and continue fiddling. These activities were punctuated by remarks of vulgar derision directed at anyone who chanced nearby. From time to time he was called on to fetch something by the electricians in the auditorium.

At this point he would stop fiddling, rise, cross down center, peer out into the house, then yell: "Hey, Solly (or Jimmy, or whoever), I got your crescent wrench (or gaffer's tape, or whatever) right HE-AH!" On the "HE-AH" he would grab his crotch and shake his manhood vehemently, then explode in laughter and wander off to look busy someplace else.

If the demonstration I had just seen was any indication of the quality of the labor force, we were in for real trouble. As it turned out, however, there were enough skilled workers around who, given the proper encouragement (John Jensen and Peter Zeisler letting loose with some well-chosen expletives), saw to it that we were ready to open on time.

Besides, our apprehensions had gone elsewhere. A particularly vicious flu virus was loose in the land. Now referred to ominously as the pandemic of 1968, we knew it as the Hong Kong flu, and as the openings approached, it was laying waste the Minnesota Theatre Company. At any time during the engagement in New York there would be several cast members coming down with, several members in the throes of, and several recovering from that plague. Buckets were placed strategically in the wings for the emergency use of the afflicted. Grim.

With the Hong Kong flu barely under control, another scourge struck: the locusts. As night fell on Friday, December 17, they swirled around Times Square, a black chittering cloud that dimmed the neon signs in its path, then shot off in the direction of the Billy Rose. Patrons ducked in fear as they swept through the lobby and into the auditorium, where strong audience members froze in terror and beautiful ones shrieked, unheard over the ungodly rasping of the swarming host. Then suddenly, as if on a signal, the desiccated twitching of the wings ceased and they floated down, slowly, in silence, downward into those thrones of literary eminence, the aisle seats.

It was the opening night of *Atreus*, and the critics had arrived.

The number one bug—biggest proboscis, deadliest sting—was Clive Barnes of the *New York Times*. When he wrote his review, his first words were surprisingly mild and apologetic. The warmth of Christmas season lubricated his carapace; his claw made graceful curlicues of the letters. He confessed he felt wretched, just wretched to be a naysayer. "Oh, dear!" he began, "I feel like one of nature's Bob Cratchits, forced by cruel circumstances to play Scrooge." How understandable it was for actors to come to New York for "visibility and validation," he wrote. And what a worthy enterprise this tour was and how other companies must indeed visit in order to enrich the New York scene. "But why, oh why," he asked, feelers twiddling beseechingly, "did the Minnesota Theatre Company bring *The House of Atreus* to New York? I could have wished that it had brought almost anything else."

Then he struck; the ragged claw shot forward, digging into the paper; the venom oozed: What he had seen was "a bundle of stage tricks that gets more laughs out of a Greek tragedy than any other production I have previously encountered. ... Any feeling for the trilogy's original tragic passion is obscured completely by the willful and tawdry gimmickry of the production." The actors were called "grotesque puppets." Worst of all, men played women's parts and played them badly.

Douglas Campbell as Clytemnestra was a "second-rate drag queen." The show at its best resembled "nothing so much as a ballet by a bad choreographer," filled with the "twists, tricks, and twirls" of the typical Guthrie production which, he said, continuing the holiday imagery, "had more business going on in it than Macy's and

Gimbel's on the night before Christmas." After a few backhanded compliments, he scratched out the production's epitaph:

"Guthrie's self-seeking excesses destroy the classics."

The rest of the reviews, if less carelessly venomous than Mr. Barnes's, were universally negative. The company reeled on groggily through a week of dwindling attendance.

Then it was the evening of December 22, *Arturo Ui* was opening, and the Billy Rose was full. The director paced nervously at the rear of the house. Had they come to cheer or jeer? We would soon know.

The show began. The reaction to the initial scenes was promising, and (wonder of wonders!) by intermission it seemed as if we had captured them, or most of them. l watched the second half amazed.

Despite all the setbacks, the damn show was better, tighter than it had been in Minneapolis. Laughter was rolling in like waves off the Atlantic. When it came time for curtain call, the director was almost dancing in the back of the house. We'd fucking done it! The warmth of the ovation, the looks on the actor's faces, bespoke a change in fortunes for the beleaguered Minnesota Theatre Company.

Now it was time for Gammell's call. He entered alone upstage; the applause swelled; he strode forward. Two steps separated him from the company now spread out in a line on the forestage below him. As he negotiated those steps, looking down briefly before raising his eyes to savor that tiered panorama of adulation, I got the unmistakable feeling that I was watching history. At that moment Robin Gammell was walking into theater history in a major way. For two hours he had kept a difficult New York audience hypnotized, acting a great role in an epic play. Who knew what lay ahead? Now he and the company would really soar off the launching pad, into the empyrean.

Chug … cough, cough … burp … rasp …

Not to be.

"Hey, Robin, I got your reviews right HE-AH! Heh, heh, heh!"

Another volley of negative articles was leveled at the company. Gammell came out okay, but the production was "surprisingly flat" (Richard Watts, *New York Post*). "Brecht is old hat" (John Chapman, *Daily News*). The director "missed the whole tone of the play" (Martin Gottfried, *Women's Wear Daily*). Our actors were "insufficiently committed politically" (Robert Pasolli, *Village Voice*). And so on and so on.

The one surprise was from the *New York Times:* a rave, an absolute love letter! But our press agent told us to forget about it—it wasn't written by Clive Barnes (where was he anyway?) but by a second stringer, and a new second stringer at that. It wouldn't count for beans. We also got a strongly favorable review from Harold Clurman in the *Nation*, but it didn't appear until after we had left town.

I should tell you that the effect of the negative reviews on the company did not us lead to a reappraisal of our work or our commitment to the Guthrie enterprise. Well, that's not quite true; it did in a way, but not in the way you might think.

For my entire life to that point, New York had been *it*. New York was Theater. Period. I wanted a theater career, so New York was where I'd aspired to live and work, for I knew in a deep way that only New York could validate my endeavors. Well, I had just shown New York my best work, and the old figgo was my reward.

You would think the effect of that would be wailing and gnashing of my teeth. Not at all. I was surprised to find that my head had gotten radically rearranged in the last six years. I had spent that time aboard the Guthrie Pleasure Palace, and New York was losing its aura. It had become just another town, the first stop on our great national progress. The New York stranglehold was loosening. The original troika's dream was coming true.

We did have, however, some important concerns. What effect would the small houses that would result from those awful reviews have on our company, which had been accustomed to playing two enthusiastically received SRO productions? What effect would it have on the balance sheet? And perhaps most importantly, what effect would it have on the folks at our home base in the Twin Cities? After only six years in the community, was our audience about to have some second thoughts? "You know, Mildred, if those New Yorkers don't think that much of them, it just may be …"—is that what they were beginning to say?

Thankfully, it was not. First, we heard about some reassuring calls that came to Zeisler's office, indignant calls from the home front in the "how dare they?" vein. They were from playgoers who see the best of theater in both New York and London, who knew quality and knew that "their theater" was absolutely first rate. Then the press weighed in. That estimable noncritic, Don Morrison, with carefully controlled ire, wrote a singularly effective skewering of the New York critical fraternity that concluded with the following:

> I lived long enough in New York to know the smuggest smart-ass encountered there is also the most limited provincial—who is bound to the soil within walking distance of 5th and 50th and who walks in peasant terror of anything that does sprout in those stony acres.

I think there is a time in the early life of any theater (perhaps any artistic institution) when it bonds with the community it is trying to serve. Prior to that time, it could go under with minimal fuss, the strongest reaction being a half-hearted rescue attempt, an editorial or two, and a bundle of letters from tearful subscribers. *After* this bonding takes place, however, the organization is, by unspoken consent, woven tightly into the fabric of the community, accepted just as a relative is accepted in a family. Now its failure will not be tolerated. For the Minnesota Theatre Company, that bonding came after six seasons of varied artistic success, and was brought about, ironically enough, not by the creation of some dazzling theatrical triumph, but by the disastrous critical reception of our work in the City of New York.

So feeling loved and reassured, we took off for Los Angeles and the second (and last) stop on the tour—the Mark Taper Forum, that gem of a theater set in a murky green pool at the Los Angeles Music Center.

After chill, inimical, plague-ridden New York, Los Angeles beckoned s a warm treat. After bundling up against the crosstown blasts, now off came layers of clothing. We looked around us. Flirtation was in the air—at restaurants, in elevators, on the sidewalks, even when you stopped your car at a red light, for God's sake. Oh, "the talk of those turning eyeballs."[12]

In this bewitching atmosphere, it came to pass that the tawny temptress of the Angel City held out her arms in welcome, and we of the Minnesota Theatre Company, free at last from New York and its manifold miseries, ran to her like happy school children on the first day of summer vacation. She crushed us with joyous ardor against the ample real estate of her soft, warm, surgically augmented bosom. And for the first time in weeks, we sang!

---

12   Walt Whitman, "Song of the Open Road," *Leaves of Grass* (Philadelphia: David McKay, c1900).

The Taper had an open stage with half the audience capacity of the Guthrie Theater. The production of *Arturo Ui*, which had gained in effectiveness in New York, took another step upward in Los Angeles. It had to do with the positive mood of the company, in large part, but there was another factor—the size of the house. There was something about cramming those violent mock heroics into a smaller space that made the production more insistent, more dangerous.

The critics expressed approval—among them Dan Sullivan. As a second-stringer for the New York Times, he had dared to write a rave for *Arturo Ui*. Now as the newly-installed drama critic of the *Los Angeles Times*, he enthused with an eloquence that led what became a wave of critical approbation and audience acclaim.

We were becoming a very happy bunch, enjoying LA and its pleasures during the day and the Taper and its excitement at night. We didn't really need any more kudos, but it happened that the most gratifying praise of all was edging our way.

On the other side of the murky green pool that surrounded the Taper sat the Ahmanson Theatre, a big, barn-like proscenium house where distinguished foreign visitors sometimes took up residence. In January of 1969, the premises were occupied by that august British assemblage, the Royal Shakespeare Company. Like the Minnesotans, they'd bought a brace of big productions to Los Angeles (with Helen Mirren, Ben Kingsley, and Patrick Stewart in the repertory): Shakespeare's *Much Ado About Nothing* and *Dr. Faustus* by Christopher Marlowe. The previous year, the RSC brought over *The Taming of the Shrew* and *As You Like It*.

It seemed that our proximity made comparisons inevitable. The result was that lingering by the murky pool at intermissions, at cocktail parties, even on Santa Monica Beach, if you listened carefully the comparisons were being made. And even among members of the RSC, pound for pound, iamb for iamb, thrill for thrill, the folks from the Land of Ice Fishermen had won the day.

Guthrie Theater's 1969 Season

At the end of the tour we returned to Minneapolis to work on the 1969 season. The company did not know it at the time, but it would be our final voyage on the Guthrie Pleasure Palace.

Major productions for that season:

- *Julius Caesar* by W. Shakespeare. Edward Payson Call to direct.
- *The Beauty Part* by S. J. Perelman. John Lahr was our literary manager at this time. He talked us into doing a piece that had been a vehicle for his father. Unfortunately, Bert wasn't around to give us a hand. Philip Minor to direct.
- *The Homecoming* by Harold Pinter. Quiet but deadly familial warfare courtesy of England's hot new playwright. Joseph Anthony to direct.
- *Mourning Becomes Electra* by Eugene O'Neill. Our Nobel playwright's turgid post-Civil War retelling of the Atreus saga—the same tale that, in its Greek original, Dr. G had made a hit of two years earlier. Mel Shapiro to direct.
- *Uncle Vanya* by Anton Chekhov. Dr. G to direct. It was to be his last production in the theater that bore his name.

It turned out, given the several show shops the Guthrie now operated, that my final contributions to the Minnesota Theatre Company could be toward the surprising end of the spectrum. We brought in a little-known gem by Jean Anouilh called *Ardèle* and two Indian plays—one modest-sized but authentic, dealing with real events in American Indian life; and the other Latin American, large and flamboyant and about as authentic as a Radio City Music Hall extravaganza.

First the Anouilh, which was performed in our outpost in St. Paul, the Crawford Livingston Theater. The leading roles are familiar to us from his other plays, notably *The Waltz of the Toreadors*: General Saint-Pé, that ever-vexed roué, is there, along with his shrill, paranoid wife ("1 whose breasts were famous throughout Paris!") and, at the center of it all, that charming bon vivant, Count Gaston, a role I offered, much to my confrères' alarum, to James J. Lawless, who had been playing small parts as a Guthrie apprentice. There was no reason to worry, however, as within days Lawless showed us he had all the right stuff—the wit, the charm, and a captivating light touch.

Thus began a major career in the regional theater that ended with his premature death in 2000, a loss that all of us who knew and loved him mourn to this day.

———

Thomas White Hawk was born in South Dakota, on a small Sioux reservation called Rosebud. His young life unreeled like a feel-good biopic. He was the model of the American Indian brave who somehow avoids all the pitfalls of reservation life: the drugs, the alcohol, the petty crime. His early promise earned him white sponsors, and he was sent to Shattuck School, a Minnesota military academy where he not only excelled at the academics but was also a star athlete. Then it was on to South Dakota State on an athletic scholarship, while back on the reservation they waited for word of his triumphs.

It never came. Halfway through his freshman year, something inside Thomas White Hawk snapped. He broke into the home of a jeweler in the little town of Vermillion, and a hallucinated night of mayhem followed. The next morning the police found a frying pan full of blood on the kitchen stove, strange markings in blood on the walls, and elsewhere in the house—the bodies of the jeweler and his wife.

After a short trial, White Hawk was sentenced to death, but because of the aberrant nature of the crime and his otherwise flaw-less life, a successful citizen's movement began with the object of commuting his sentence to life imprisonment.

In spite of, or maybe because of, the prejudice I encountered when I attempted to cast American Indians in *Chalk Circle*, I want-ed to get our sometimes-stodgy theater involved. The result was a commission to a young Twin Cities writer, Fred Gaines. He called the play that resulted *The Ghost Dancer*. Using parallel scenes, we de-veloped the similarities between White Hawk's hallucinated ram-page and the ecstatic Sioux ceremony known as *The Ghost Dancer*. Much of the material was documentary accounts by the Sioux, in an exalted, biblical style, of the prophesies of that dance: how the ghost shirts would protect them from the white man's bullets, how the feathers of their regalia would lift them to the sky as a great tide of earth swept westward, burying the white man and all his works. Then they would float downward to a land reborn—the land as it was in the old times—and the buffalo would run once more.

Interspersed were factual accounts of White Hawk's life that evolved into the madness of the crime. The White Hawk story end-ed with two murder scenes: the Ghost Dancer narrative with the round-up of the Sioux dancers, and the Wounded Knee Massacre of nearly 100 years earlier.

The play had a brief run at our 200-seat experimental theater, The Other Place. Although the national *Saturday Review* found it "both an intelligent and excitingly relevant piece of work," it was not admired by many others, even an object of derision to some who dismissed it as shallow and meretricious.

Well, they may have had a point. But I was unfazed. How else will we learn, save by trying? If we do stumble in an early attempt, won't we have learned something for the next time around? How about this: However enlightened my do-gooder motivation, I should not have proceeded without the support and approval of the folks I was trying to do good for. At a minimum I should have found an Indian coauthor for Fred, as well as a proper Native American to play White Hawk. Honkeys with headbands just didn't cut it.

Another consideration: This burgeoning nationwide drama movement was now being called "regional theater." Not a glamorous title, granted, but a useful one, tying us, as it did, to some specific acreage in the continental expanse. Well, what use is regional theater if it is not truly regional—if it does not deal with the artists and issues of the region it serves?

Further: In the late '60s the simple fact of these new theaters' existence was enough to celebrate, but as time passed wouldn't we want to find out what makes us unique, what sets us apart from all those other playhouses? If not, we may succumb to deadly similitude—producing identical lists of new plays, recycling a few classics, and putting up *A Christmas Carol* every year to top off the coffers during the holidays.

I thought we all should have resolved to mine the strong vein of geography, history, and culture that surrounds the blessed demi-acre of God's green Earth on which each theater stands. For me in Minnesota all those years ago, I had only to listen to the sound of the names surrounding me:

Mesabi, Mississippi, St. Croix, and St. Cloud. The Sioux, the Chippewa, the Voyageurs. Grangers and Populists. Hubert and Fritz[13] and F. Scott Fitzgerald. Old Mr. Pillsbury and Babe the Blue Ox.

Seeds of songs yet to be sung.

———◆———

For myself at that time, *Ghost Dancer* having closed, my work for the Minnesota Theatre Company was coming to an end. After seven amazingly brief and fruitful years of excitement and growth—of living, loving, and learning (the three Ls)—having matured from a bumbling aspirant ("Oh God yes, he's charming, but is there anything in there?") to someone who could be called a director, now one gigantic task remained: the socko finish. My vehicle: *Julius Caesar.*

The *best*, it had to be the *best*. Nothing else would do. I had to create a wondrous gift for the good folks of Minnesota, something that would bring the whole seven years to a close not with a whimper, but a *BANG!* A theatrical experience of hugely wide appeal:

Hurry! Hurry! Hurry! Yes, there'll be a new show in town next year, folks, but *this* is your *LAST CHANCE!* Only one more spectacular extravaganza and the Tyrone Guthrie, Zeisler, and Rea Circus Big Top will be coming down for good!

---

13   Minnesota politicians Hubert Humphrey and Fritz Mondale

I dreamed of devising an event that would send the audiences streaming from the theater, crazy with excitement. I fantasized them storming the box office, clawing at the wickets, money yanked out of their pockets as they bought tickets for all their friends, all their relations, and "that nice Mrs. Erikson from Duluth who *must* see this *miracle!*"

In case there was reluctance, I daydreamed gumshoes being hired to escort the unwilling ("Get in the car, buddy, or else!"), arriving at 725 Vineland Place just in time for curtain.

I'm getting a bit barmy here, but seven years? Seven years! Isn't that some sort of significant biblical period? Feast or famine!? The symbolism is getting intense … parallels streaming through my head.

I'm in England somewhere. It's Wimbledon! Center court. I'm serving. It's 6–3 in the fifth. I have McEnroe on the ropes. The game score is 40–30. One more ace and the cup is mine! I do one of those fist pumping circuits of the court. "Yeah! Yeah! Yeah!" and the crowd goes NUTS! The more I showboat, the madder John gets. Good.

I take a really long time with the Ritual of the Balls, manipulating three of them slowly, deftly in my palm in that phony search for the fuzziest. Finally I throw one away, pocket the second and step to the service line. From ear-splitting yells, the crowd goes dead silent—the kind of quiet you can eat.

John's doing that side-to-side rock, trying to keep his temper under control. A final look at my opponent, I toss the ball up and … away we go!

Where? *Where are we going?* GUATEMALA!

I had some free time before preproduction of *Julius Caesar* began, so Pamela and I did some traveling. An invitation had come from our friends the Kleins, Bob and Maxine: she a well-known director of experimental theater; he an executive of an NGO, working out of Guatemala City. They invited us to join them there for a couple of weeks.

Guatemala is a beautiful country with all the variety of climate and terrain you find in Mexico, contained within a piece of Central America no bigger than a single Mexican state. Yes, small and gorgeous. And when Pamela and I visited there in 1969, it was at war—an invisible war, for the most part, but war nevertheless, with insurgents operating in the countryside and death squads working the city, wiping out a whole generation of young leftist intellectuals. This backdrop didn't add to our comfort level, but Bob and Maxine seemed unfazed by all the mayhem, which tended to reassure at least one of their guests.

One day Maxine saw Pamela and me off on a floppy-winged old DC-3, bound for the ancient city of Tikal, deep in the Yucatan jungle. The airport turned out to be several hundred yards of dirt road where jungle had been cut back far enough to make room for the wings. At that time, Tikal was an archeological site where the work was just beginning to show results. There were several steep-sided pyramids almost completely excavated (bone-white against the dark green jungle) along with some dwellings and many of those large stone tablets called stelae. And all around, a strange irregular topography: man-made works that time and the jungle hid. Here, a steep hill covers a pyramid—the only visible evidence being a ruined temple at the summit, locked in the embrace of huge vines thick as a man's waist. Behind every upward slope, a palace; every hillock, a dwelling.

After three days in that most mysterious of places, I came out of the jungle with a raging fever—delirious with visions of a whole new way of producing *Julius Caesar.*

Out with those extravagant togas! No more marble—hammer it all to dust! Screw all that classical folderol. The mise-en-scène: a brutal Latin American dictatorship in the early years of the nineteenth century where a decadent oligarchy rules, led by Caesar, who has stolen many of the symbols of Mayan culture for his own aggrandizement. He rules over a cowed, desperately poor native population. The conspirators are Mayan. Brutus becomes an Indigenous intellectual, a man of the people, a literate Zapata dreaming of leading a democratic revolution. Can you hear the music? Tense, insistent Spanish guitar and thundering Mayan drums! And the sights! At Caesar's assassination, black obsidian knives flash in the sunlight—a Mayan blood sacrifice. The Soothsayer—a sightless brujo led by a dirty child. Caesar's ghost—a massive Day of the Dead puppet, stalking the battlefield.

There's a certain amount of tinhorn producer in the above paragraph, don't you think? In Hollywood, I believe they call it the pitch:

> Can't you see it, Morrie? A blood-red sunset. A thousand refugees streaming down to the shores of the Rhine. In the background, the deadly Panzer tanks! Then we cut to a close-up of the kid, searching desperately for his baby sister ... Then we hear a wail ... Then ...

Yeah, guilty—but as we agreed before, a necessary part of the job description.

And there were deeper reasons (beyond wanting to lose the togas and sandals) that were making me contemplate a change of scene. Aside from the obvious delights of blue skies and sandy beaches, as well as a colorful and diverting civilization, I have always felt a certain unease when I ventured south of the Rio Grande.

Maybe it's the greater poverty, or that haunting indigenous look. Also the bullfight's ritual slaughter And celebrations like the Day of the Dead, when people go to the graveyard not to grieve or to pray, but to *dance!*

Yes, death somehow feels closer south of the Tropic of Cancer. So if I could get that tension on the stage, that feeling of vulnerability? What an effective sea for the actors to swim in!

When I got back to Minneapolis, the company, the staff, everyone committed themselves generously to my salsa-flavored Shakespeare. A large undertaking was sped along by the positive spirits of my coworkers. The production that resulted was admired by a large part of the audience and some of the critics, who found the change of time and place "bold and original." There were others, however, far less enchanted. One wrote that "Shakespeare takes a back seat" and that "sensation, rather than ideas or emotion, dominates." I was disappointed, because the critics I respected were the nay-sayers. One of them was my favorite reviewer, Don Morrison, who let me have it with both barrels. It was the hack journalists from Grub Street who thought it "bold and original."

Whatever it was, it was big and showy and well-acted by a solid group of artists led by Robert Pastene (Caesar), Allen Hamilton (Brutus), Charles Keating (Mark Antony), John Ramsey (Cassius), and Patricia Conolly (Portia). It looked terrific, from the humblest Mayan native to the most splendiferous Creole grandee, thanks to an extraordinary costume designer, Carrie Robbins, a really exceptional artist at the beginning of her career. Dominating the world of the play from upstage was a single unit created by our set designer, Douglas Schmidt—a huge stone head of Caesar, twenty-five feet high, crowned with an extravagant Mayan headdress. A few years earlier, television had shown us the citizens of Budapest angrily hauling down the statues of Comrade Stalin and other Communist notables during the Hungarian Uprising. Caesar's effigy was made to suffer a similar fate in the rioting following his assassination.

Authenticity—that was the play's problem. (Says I, looking back from four decades later and re-assessing my excesses.) That's why the production didn't receive more plaudits. Though splendidly theatrical and (1 persist in believing) a valid transposition of the piece, it lacked authenticity. The audience couldn't believe that all those gringos were really citizens of a decadent Latin American tyranny circa 1840.

I had dropped the ball. I had this big idea, then didn't follow it up with the kind of work a repertory situation makes possible.

Instead of cursing the fact that I didn't have splendid Hispanic actors like Raúl Juliá or Edward Olmos to play the leading roles or authentic Latinos for the mob, I should have led the company on a journey of exploration and discovery. When theater artists are together for a long period of time, as happens in repertory, and when the philosophy that buttresses the enterprise rejects typecasting and insists on giving actors new and dangerous challenges, that is when the repertory system begins to show its advantages over one-shot, just-get-it-up theatrical production.

Long before rehearsals began, I should have stolen a few hours, gotten the company together and shown them some works like *Aguirre, the Wrath of God,* and others; I should have generated a library. I should have declared, "Let's get beyond *One Hundred Years of Solitude* and find translations of some of the hard-core revolutionaries of the nineteenth century. And get Pastene (cast as Caesar) reading about Simón Bolívar."

There would have been time to experiment: "Should we be thinking about accents for Brutus and the conspirators to set them apart from the oligarchs? But which accent? What does Quechua sound like anyway?" I could have encouraged specific actors to pursue specific ideas. For instance, Charles Keating had the requisite power for Marc Antony; he might have considered: "What if that power were expressed with a kind of torero physicality? That would be an interesting and authentic color: bullfighter macho."

But this hindsight is getting us nowhere.

Once rehearsals started, consumed by the demands of such a panoramic work, I found that in spite of myself I was putting together a conventional production of *Julius Caesar* and counting on my designers and Texas Dirt makeup to bail me out. It didn't happen.

As I write, this I am remembering my first visit to England's Royal National Theater. One night I watched Robert Stephens play, with great success, a frail, shy, ineffectual British twit in Noel Coward's play, *Hay Fever*. The following night, he:

- Took off most of his clothes.
- Painted his body brown.
- Exploded on stage and astounded us all with an utterly authentic, supercharged performance of great physical daring.

Stephens had found his way to the very soul of Atahualpa, last emperor of the Incas in the play *The Royal Hunt of the Sun*. And the rest of the company was not far behind. All these pallid Limeys had become authentic Spaniards or Incas of the sixteenth century. They were making great theater and, in the process, demonstrating the creative alchemy of repertory at its best.

In Minneapolis, with *Julius Caesar*, it was another story.

There are certain enterprises, extravagant in concept, rich in possibility, that turn out to be more exciting in their fabrication than in their realization. In other words, making the thing is far more exciting than the thing itself. Think of Fitzcarraldo (in Werner Herzog's film of that name) dragging that huge steamship over a mountain. That moment was more hold-your-breath exciting, certainly, than the grand opera it was supposed to make possible. Another example: Howard Hughes, with much fanfare, flogging that huge wooden airplane the Spruce Goose into the sky—a flight of piddling length with a maximum altitude of what? 50 feet? But coming in contact with the crazy passion that fueled those projects—*that* was the story.

And like them, there was *Julius Caesar* in Latin America—a universe away in renown from the above, but still a product of foolhardy daring that did manage to produce a good yarn or two.

One such is about how we inveigled the Minnesota Twins and over 25,000 baseball fans to become a Roman mob and help us create the sound effects for the production.

And another tells how set designer Doug Schmidt and our genius technical director Bob Scales devised the most sensational, cataclysmical, and thoroughly dumbfounding effect ever seen on the Guthrie stage! It was seen, but unfortunately only once and by a precious few, of whose number I was lucky enough to count myself.

Finally, there was the Night of the Burning Despot, when the huge iconic head of Caesar started to smoke in the midst of a performance. The show was stopped. The source was discovered to be a small blaze, that was soon being capably dealt with by a stage manager with a small fire extinguisher. The crisis had passed, the audience relaxed, the actors began returning to their places on stage. Then with no warning, as bewildered actors froze in their tracks, out of the tunnels charged a dozen helmeted firemen, axes aloft, ready, come hell or high water, to execute their chief's command. Posing heroically down right, the chief pointed to the towering head of Caesar and bellowed: "Take it to wood!"

———

Sadly, the time has come to recount the final days of the reign of the Pep Boys: Peter Zeisler, Mel Shapiro, and me. All these alarums and excursions took place many decades ago, mind you, and the Guthrie archives are strangely silent on this period, so the reader will have to trust to my imperfect memory. As I recall, it played out something like this:

Zeisler had always assured Shapiro and me that the Pep Boys were all equal—we shared the power. It was a fiction, of course. The Board had entrusted Zeisler with all the responsibility, and Shapiro and I were merely his hired hands. That was okay by me. I could concentrate on directing and didn't have to worry about dealing with a board of trustees. Zeisler did carry that weight, and apparently by the middle of 1969 things were not going well between them.

There were, I think, three major factors at work. First: No matter how strongly we felt the support of the community after the debacle in New York, it was the Board that had to deal with the balance sheet that those evil reviews had turned red. Second: Of the two seasons the Pep Boys had been responsible for, our first was the most successful in the theater's history; our second, which saw a steep decline in the number of subscribers and single-ticket sales, was the least. Finally, there was on Zeisler's part, I think, a sense of entitlement, deservedly, after eight years of obsessive labor in the cause. But he had a hard act to follow, and what the Tall Knight could get with a quip and a wave of the hand, would not be so easily granted to Zeisler. Truth to tell, that natural affinity between the manager and the board of directors that I wrote about previously was in jeopardy as soon as Zeisler was given artistic as well as managerial control.

After weeks of flying rumors, the bombshell dropped. Peter Zeisler, the last of the original troika, was leaving. Oh, there was some fiction to the effect that he might be back after taking a sabbatical, but nobody believed it. Until further notice, Zeisler's loyal assistant Don Schoenbaum would be running the theater.

Then Shapiro announced his departure. He'd be going back to New York to teach at N.Y.U. and work for Joe Papp.

Soon it would be time for Pamela and me to get the trunks out of our own basement. Our departure did not mean breaking a lot of ties, for many of them had already been broken. Dr. G had left and Tanya Moiseiwitsch with him. Zeisler was going, and though brother Campbell had been very generous and never excoriated me (as I'd expected) for my disloyalty in casting my lot with Zeisler, it would be decades before we got back on the old footing. At this point, fortunately, we were still seeing little of each other, as he was now busy with a touring enterprise he called Heartland Productions.

Though personal bonds were loosening, I still felt the strong undertow of loyalty to the theater that had so generously nourished my talents. Now, however, a new force propelled me outward, a sense of work to be done, of mission, if you will—almost what the religious folks call a vocation. I had come to believe deeply, not only in the kind of theater Dr. Guthrie made (classics-centered repertory) but also in the physical platform he made it on, that open stage.

Nowadays, when you hear theater people talk about the open stage, it is often in pejorative terms. A form that some of us still find exciting and galvanic seems to have become a sort of theatrical inconvenience.

> DIRECTOR. Please! I just can't be bothered with all those
> dreary people on the sides. If they want good seats,
> they'll just have to pay more money.
> ACTOR (COMIC). No one, but *no one*, can do a double
> take in three directions.
> ACTOR (TRAGIC). Am I supposed to say "To be or not
> to be" with a third of the house looking at my back?

The sight of the open stage does not fill most theater people with visions of new possibilities, or new challenges. Rather they are wont to sigh inwardly, convinced (mistakenly) that the three-sided nature of the audience will vitiate their creative endeavors.

Back in 1963, when I walked into 725 Vineland Place and saw the new stage, my reaction was mouth-agape wonder. From the Hephaestian forge of a great theater artist's imagination had come a shape never seen before. Set white-hot inside the big shed there, it sizzled quietly, daring us to venture onto its jagged, disorienting surface.

Led by the Worthy Knight, we dared. Thus began for some of us the most important adventure of our lives—years in which we learned more and lived more than at any time before or since.

A lot of the work we did in those early years was highly praised. I, for one, have always believed that a decent amount of that praise came less from what we did than where we did it—that the open stage itself gave a freshness and originality to the work that was done upon it.

I remember sitting in the Billy Rose Theater in New York (this at the start of our '68 tour) and watching *The House of Atreus*. In contrast to the wild experience in Minneapolis, everything seemed slightly distant, trapped and domesticated behind a proscenium arch. I saw stage pictures that looked familiar, not from what I'd seen in Minnesota, but from theater history books. *Oh, yes,* I thought, *I've seen something like that before in set renderings by Jo Mielziner, or was it Norman Bel Geddes?* Not so on the open stage in Minneapolis, where Guthrie had created a ritual from the very edge of civilization, an unearthly wonder that involved and enveloped its audience in an entirely original way.

Minnesota's own, Senator Hubert Humphrey, was wont to show up in the Guthrie Pleasure Palace from time to time with a fellow legislator in tow. After a tour of the premises, they would wind up in the theater and Senator Humphrey would go to work in that flat, insistent Midwestern voice of his, convincing his guest that an important part of his responsibility to his constituents was to see to it that they had "a nifty theater just like this one" in his home state. And truth to tell, we did begin to hear about open stages that might be built elsewhere. Was this the beginning of a national movement? The optimists among us began to think so. We saw ourselves riding on the crest of a wave that was about to sweep across the country.

As surely as the Modernists, in the early years of the twentieth century, had snatched painting from the hands of those who only focused on imitating reality and in the process found new and revolutionary modes of expression, so now did the theater, in the middle years of that century, oppressed as it was by the 400-year tyranny of the proscenium arch that separated the audience from the event, that resulted in tiered class-conscious auditoriums, that licked its chops when carloads of scenery arrived at its loading dock, all in service of making the poor boobs sitting in the dark believe that what they were about to see was real. All this was about to be undone, reversed, made obsolete, swept into the dustbin of history. A new form was about to revivify the theater. We optimists were too well-behaved to be noisy revolutionaries, shouting slogans and waving firebrands, but we carried within us a conviction, firmly held if seldom uttered, that the future of the American regional theater would take place on the open stage.

Michael Langham, in describing this new/old form which he used with such genius as Guthrie's heir at the Stratford Shakespeare Festival in Ontario, called it "one-room theater." That term contains an important insight. In this formulation, proscenium theater is two-room theater. Room A contains the audience, Room B, the event. There is a large hole in the wall between them, so the folks in Room A can watch what's going on in Room B.

The open stage, on the other hand, puts everyone in the same space, lets them breathe the same air and witness the same events. It's impossible to fool people in such a place that what they are seeing is real. How can you, when a large portion of the audience looks across the stage beyond the actors and sees—not lots of pretty scenery, but rather lots of other people watching the actors. Theater is cut loose from an imitation of reality and becomes a communal act of make-believe. It is free now to explore a different kind of aesthetic—one that is truly sculptural, based on three dimensions instead of two, where the nature of stagecraft and the scene designer's art, cut loose from the shackles of literalism, can be re-examined and redefined; where the actor, encompassed in a new way by his audience, will respond with a new expressiveness.

Now, after a long apprenticeship, I felt it was time to move on, time to carry the good news to the world at large. But not before a goodbye to the old Guthrie Pleasure Palace, my teacher and my friend, scene of my hard-won triumphs and equally hard-won defeats—my loving artistic home. She was floating listlessly with the tides—her paint was beginning to peel, and that mighty casement-rattling steam whistle gasped fitfully as she awaited a new commodore and a new itinerary. I said my sad goodbyes to the staff and then spent a few contemplative minutes alone in that stage-managerial pilot house where seven years earlier I had said "Go, Lights One" and out of the darkness came a helmeted soldier pacing the battlements of Elsinore.

Then I went down some stairs, through a long hall to the green room, and out the stage door for the last time.

———◆———

There was a whole new and quite different world out there waiting for me. So much in the theater had changed since 1963, all of it for the better.

In Seattle, the leftover facilities of the '62 World's Fair had become the home of the Seattle Repertory Company. In LA, a building in the splendid new Los Angeles Music Center, which originally had been designed for chamber music, was turned into an open stage under Gordon Davidson's adventurous leadership. Up the coast in San Francisco, Bill Ball's panache was keeping ACT at the top of its game. In DC, Zelda Fichandler, having permanently retired that careworn shoebox of subscriber data, had gotten Arena Stage a jazzy new playhouse and was shepherding a drama about prize-fighter Jack Johnson, called *The Great White Hope*, to Broadway and international renown. In Providence, Rhode Island, at Trinity Rep, Adrian Hall's masterly direction was creating superb theater, and a first-rate touring company that called itself APA (the Association of Producing Artists), led by Ellis Rabb, an up-to-date version of the Victorian actor/manager, was being acclaimed by critics all over the East. The newly-created Denver Center for the Performing Arts became my own new home in 1979, as artistic director. New theaters were lighting up the nights across the great American landmass. My hometown, our perpetually theater-deprived nation's capital had a grand new memorial—it was called the John F. Kennedy Center for the Performing Arts. Even Uncle Sam was getting into the act.

Truly, it was a good time for moving on, into a bustling, innovative new world of theater—and time, once again, for a verse or two from the Brooklyn sage:

> Have the elder races halted?
> Do they droop and end their lessons, wearied over there
>   beyond the seas?
> We take up the task eternal, and the burden and the lesson,
> Pioneers! O pioneers!
> All the past we leave behind,
> We debouch upon a newer mightier world, varied world,
> Fresh and strong the world we seize, world of labor and
>   the march,
> Pioneers! O pioneers!
> We detachments steady throwing,
> Down the edges, through the passes, up the mountains
>   steep.
> Conquering, holding, daring, venturing as we go the un-
>   known ways,
> Pioneers! O pioneers![14]

14   Walt Whitman, "Pioneers! O Pioneers!" *Leaves of Grass* (Philadelphia: David McKay, c1900).

Myself as artistic director of the Denver
Center Theatre Company, 1980.

THE PLAYERS ET CETERA

My stories include so many people, and organizations, and titles of plays, films, books… Here I've gathered them all in one place (often with the plays they were involved with when I mention them).

People from Those Years

George Abbott	American playwright (*Three Men on a Horse* with John Cecil Holm) (b. 1887, d. 1995)
Maude Adams	American stage actress (b. 1872, d. 1953)
Brian Aherne	British-American actor (b. 1902, d. 1986)
Edward Albee	American playwright (b. 1928, d. 2016)
Ivan Albright	American artist (b. 1897, d. 1983)
Erville Alderson	American actor (b. 1882, d. 1957)
Jean Anouilh	French playwright (*Ardèle*) (b. 1910, d. 1987)
Louis K. Anspacher	American poet and playwright (*Dagmar*) (b. 1878, d. 1947)
Joseph Anthony	American director (*The Homecoming, The Beauty Part*) (b. 1912, d. 1993)
Uncle Arc	best friend of my father
John Arden	British playwright (*Serjeant Musgrave's Dance*) (b. 1930, d. 2012)
Brooks Atkinson	drama critic at the *New York Times* (b. 1894, d. 1984)
René Auberjonois	American actor (*Endgame*) (b. 1940, d. 2019)
S. Leonard "Lennie" Auerbach	scenic and lighting designer (b. 1941)
Caroline Lexow Babcock	my aunt (b. 1882, d. 1980)

George Backman	British-American actor (*Twelfth Night* at Old Globe Theatre) (b. 1940)
William "Bill" Ball	American actor (b. 1931, d. 1991)
Paul Ballantyne	American actor (b. 1909, d. 1996)
Arthur Ballet	University of Minnesota professor of theatre and founder of its Office of Advanced Drama Research (b. 1925, d. 2012)
Pedro Calderón de la Barca	Spanish playwright (b. 1600, d. 1681)
Brigitte Bardot	French actress (b. 1934)
Clive Barnes	theater critic at the *New York Times* (b. 1927, d. 2008)
Eddy Barron	one of my classmates at University of Washington
Dave Barry	American humorist (b. 1947)
John Barrymore	American stage actor (b. 1882, d. 1942)
Samuel Beckett	Irish playwright (*Endgame*) (b. 1906, d. 1989)
Brendan Behan	Irish playwright, poet, and writer (b. 1923, d. 1964)
Norman Bel Geddes	theatrical and industrial designer (b. 1893, d. 1953)
Eric Bentley	American translator of Brecht's poetry (b. 1916, d. 2020)
Leonard Bernstein	American composer and conductor (b. 1918, d. 1990)
Frederic Bickel	American actor; later changed name to Fredric March (b. 1897, d. 1975)
Ray Bieri	American actor (at Stan Hywet Hall, ACT) (b. 1929, d. 2001)
George Caleb Bingham	American artist (b. 1811, d. 1879)
William Blake	British poet and painter (b. 1757, d. 1827)
Earl Boen	American actor (*The Caucasian Chalk Circle* at Guthrie Theatre) (b. 1941, d. 2023)
Simón Bolívar	South American military and political leader (b. 1783, d. 1830)
Bobby Bonaventura	ACT scheduling manager (b. 1944)

Mathew Brady	American photographer; father of photojournalism; photographer of Civil War (c. 1822–1896)
Bertolt Brecht	German playwright, director, and poet (b. 1898, d. 1956)
James Bridie	Scottish playwright (b. 1888, d. 1951)
Chamberlain Brown	Broadway agent (b. 1892, d. 1955)
Lewis "Lew" Brown	costume designer at Guthrie Theatre in first seasons (b. 1928, d. 2011)
Elizabeth Barrett Browning	British poet (b. 1806, d. 1861)
Robert Browning	British poet (b. 1812, d. 1889)
Pieter Bruegel the Elder	Flemish painter (c. 1525–1569)
Dr. Hans-Joachim Bunge	German dramaturge at Theatre am Schiffbauerdamm (b. 1919, d. 1990)
Billie Burke	American actress (b. 1884, d. 1970)
Richard Burton	Welsh actor (b. 1925, d. 1984)
Michael Cacoyannis	Greek theater producer and filmmaker (b. 1922, d. 2011)
Annie Payson Call	my great-aunt (b. 1853, d. 1940)
Donald Marshall Call	my father (b. 1892, d. 1984)
Donald Marshall Call Jr.	my eldest brother (b. 1921, d. 1962)
Edward Payson Call	my grandfather
Jack Call	my next brother (b. 1922)
Pamela Call	Actress, Ed's wife, today a psychiatrist in NY
Zoe Ada Caldwell	Australian repertory actress at Guthrie in first seasons (b. 1933, d. 2020)
Douglas Campbell	British-Canadian actor; associate artistic director at Guthrie in first seasons; spouse of Ann Campbell (b. 1922, d. 2009)
John Carradine Jr. (David)	American actor (at Stan Hywet Hall) (b. 1936, d. 2009)
Helen Carey	American actress (b. 1944)
Len Cariou	Canadian actor (b. 1939)
John Chapman	writer at the *Daily News* in New York City (b. 1901, d. 1972)

Richard Christiansen	theater critic at *Chicago Daily News* (b. 1932, d. 2022)
Tim Christie	actor at Guthrie Theatre in *The Caucasian Chalk Circle*
Clarence	neighbor on East Seventy-fourth Street in New York City
Harold Clurman	thater director and drama critic (b. 1901, d. 1980)
Lee J. Cobb	American actor (b. 1911, d. 1976)
Marc Connelly	American playwright (*Merton of the Movies* with G. S. Kaufman) (b. 1890, d. 1980)
Patricia Conolly	Australian actress (*Julius Caesar)* (b. 1933)
Nicolas Coster	American repertory actor at Guthrie Theatre in first seasons (b. 1933, d. 2023)
Christopher Craft	NASA's first Mission Control flight engineer (b. 1924, d. 2019)
John Cromwell	American director at Guthrie Theatre in first seasons; spouse of actress Ruth Nelson (b. 1886, d. 1979)
Hume Cronyn	Canadian-American repertory actor at Guthrie Theatre in first seasons (b. 1911, d. 2003)
Jackie Cooper	American actor (b. 1922, d. 2011)
Richard Daly	mayor of Chicago, Illinois, in 1968 (b. 1942, d. 1976)
Gordon Davidson	American theater director; artistic director at several major regional theaters (b. 1933, d. 2016)
Robertson Davies	Canadian novelist; attended original Guthrie Theatre opening night (b. 1913, d. 1995)
Charles Denner	French actor (b. 1926, d. 1995)
Colleen Dewhurst	American actress (b. 1924, d. 1991)
McIntyre Dixon	American comedic actor (b. 1931)
John Dos Passos	American author (b. 1896, d. 1970)
Mildred Dunnock	American actress (b. 1901, d. 1991)
Lyle Dye	producer at Equity Library Theatre (b. 1930, d. 2019)
Richard Dysart	American actor (*The Seagull* at ACT) (b. 1929, d. 2015)

Eleanor of Aquitane	queen of France and then England (b. 1122, d. 1204)
El Greco	Greek painter (b. 1541, d. 1614)
T. S. Eliot	ex-pat American poet and playwright (b. 1888, d. 1965)
Patricia Elliott	American actress (b. 1938, d. 2015)
Kate Emery	American actress at Guthrie Theatre in first seasons (b. 1906, d. 1980)
Euripides	ancient Greek playwright (*The Trojan Women*) (b.c. 480 BCE, d.c. 406 BCE)
Edith Evans	British actress (b. 1888, d. 1976)
Lawrence Eyre	British playwright (*Martinique*) (b. 1943)
Albert Finney	British actor (b. 1936, d. 2019)
Zelda Fichandler	American stage producer, director, and cofounder of Arena Stage in DC (b. 1924, d. 2016)
Pauline Flanagan	Irish actress at Antioch Shakespeare Festival (b. 1925, d. 2003)
Ed Flanders	American actor, in repertory at Guthrie Theatre in early seasons (b. 1934, d. 1995)
Allen Fletcher	American director (*Death of a Salesman* at ACT) (b. 1922, d. 2005)
Lynn Fontanne	American actress; spouse of Alfred Lunt (b. 1887, d. 1983)
Jean-Honoré Fragonard	French Rococo painter (b. 1732, d. 1806)
Shirli Frank	tech staff member at Guthrie Theatre in early seasons
Robert Frost	American poet (b. 1874, d. 1963)
Dolly G—	volunteer at Guthrie Theatre in first seasons
Fred Gaines	American playwright *(The Ghost Dancer)* (b. 1937, d. 2010)
Robin Gammell	Canadian actor *(Endgame, The House of Atreus)* (b. 1936)
Annette Garceau	British head of costume shop at Guthrie Theatre in first seasons (b. 1914, d. 2017)
Kelton Garwood	actor, friend (b. 1928, d. 1991)
Charles de Gaulle	French president (b. 1890, d. 1970)

Avery Hopwood	American playwright (*Fair and Warmer*) (b. 1882, d. 1928)
Edward Everett Horton	American actor (b. 1886, d. 1970)
Jean-Antoine Houdon	French neoclassical sculptor (b. 1741, d. 1828)
John Houseman	British-American actor and producer; founder of Mercury Theatre drama company in New York City with Orson Welles (b. 1902, d. 1988)
Howard Hughes	American business magnate (b. 1905, d. 1976)
Angelika Hurwicz	German actress (b. 1922, d. 1999)
Wildred Hyde-White	name of a fictitious British actor
Henrik Ibsen	Norwegian playwright (*Peer Gint, The Master Builder*) (b. 1828, d. 1906)
Eugène Ionesco	French-Romanian playwright in the French avante-garde theater (b. 1909, d. 1994)
Sally Irvine	patron of the arts in Minneapolis (b. 1910, d. 1979)
Ingushetians	a Sunni Muslim ethnic group of the North Caucasus Mountains
Stanley Jay	American actor (b. 1929)
John Jensen	set designer
Jack Johnson	prize-fighter; protagonist in *The Great White Hope* (b. 1878, d. 1946)
Margo Jones	founder of Theatre '47 (b. 1911, d. 1955)
Robert "Bobby" Jones	theatrical designer (sets, lighting, costumes) (b. 1887, d. 1954)
Raúl Juliá	Puerto Rican actor (b. 1940, d. 1994)
George S. Kaufman	American playwright (*Merton of the Movies* with Marc Connelly); *New York Times* theater critic (b. 1889, d. 1961)
Charles Keating	British actor at Guthrie in first seasons (b. 1941, d. 2014)
George Kelly	American playwright (*The Torchbearers*) (b. 1887, d. 1974)
Walter Kerr	*New York Times* theater critic (b. 1913, d. 1996)
Jerome Kilty	American director (*Man and Superman* at ACT) (b. 1922, d. 2012)

John Lahr	literary manager at Guthrie Theatre (1969) (b. 1941)
Rob Lancaster	director at Guthrie Theatre (*Twelfth Night*)
Michael Langham	British director and actor (b. 1919, d. 2011)
Dale Lash	basketball coach at Williston Academy
Tony Lavelli	one of my classmates at Williston Academy (b. 1926, d. 1998)
James J. "Jimmy" Lawless	American actor at Guthrie Theatre in first seasons (b. 1936, d. 2000)
John Lewin	American actor at ACT and playwright (*The House of Atreus*) (b. 1934, d. 2009)
Li Qianfu	fourteenth-century Chinese playwright
Jimmy Lineberger	American actor at Guthrie Theatre in first seasons
Arthur Lithgow	American actor, director, and producer (b. 1915, d. 2004)
John Lithgow	American actor (at Stan Hywet Hall) (b. 1945)
Gene Lockhart	Canadian-American actor (b. 1891, d. 1957)
Lydia Lopokova	Russian ballerina (b. 1892, d. 1981)
McNeil Lowry	arts patron at Ford Foundation; attended original Guthrie Theatre opening night (b. 1913, d. 1993)
Tony Lucetti	basketball player who was said to have invented the hook shot
Sidney Lumet	American film director (b. 1924, d. 2011)
Alfred Lunt	American actor and director; spouse of Lynn Fontanne (b. 1892, d. 1977)
Joe Maher	Irish actor (*Twelfth Night* at Old Globe Theatre) (b. 1933, d. 1998)
Ted Mann	Circle in the Square producer (b. 1924, d. 2012)
Gabriel García Márquez	Colombian author (*One Hundred Years of Solitude*) (b. 1927, d. 2014)
Billy Martin	Minnesota Twins ball player and scout (and later coach) (b. 1928, d. 1989)
Marx Brothers	American comedy act (active 1905–1949)
James Mason	British actor (b. 1909, d. 1984)
Edwin Justus Mayer	American screenwriter and playwright (*Children of Darkness*) (b. 1896, d. 1960)

Sandy McCallum	American actor (b. 1926, d. 2008)
Langdon McCormick	American playwright (b. 1873, d. 1954)
Terence McNally	American playwright (b. 1938, d. 2020)
Jo Mielziner	theatrical scenic and lighting designer (b. 1901, d. 1976)
Paul Milikin	Irish actor (d. 2014)
Arthur Miller	American playwright (b. 1915, d. 2005)
Robert (Bob) Milli	American actor (at Stan Hywet Hall, then Guthrie Theatre in first seasons) (b. 1933, d. 2019)
Philip Minor	American director (*The Beauty Part* at Guthrie Theatre)
Donald Moffat	British actor (at Stan Hywet Hall) (b. 1930, d. 2018)
Anna Moffo	American opera singer (b. 1932, d. 2006)
Benno Moisiewitsch	Russian-British concert pianist, father of Tanya (b. 1890, d. 1963)
Tanya Moiseiwitsch	British theater designer at Guthrie Theatre in first seasons (b. 1914, d. 2003)
Monty Python	British comedy troupe (intermittent 1969–2014)
Michael Moriarty	American-Canadian actor (b. 1941)
Brad Morison	head of the Guthrie Theatre public relations department in first seasons (b. 1924, d. 2008)
Don Morrison	American writer at the *Minneapolis Tribune* and the *Minneapolis Star* in Minnesota (b. 1922, d. 1983)
Zero Mostel	American actor (b. 1915, d. 1977)
Rose Muckley	one of the original Guthrie Theatre opening night attendees (b. 1884, d. 1969)
Arthur Naftalin	mayor of Minneapolis (spouse of Frances Healy Naftalin); attended original Guthrie Theatre opening night (b. 1917, d. 2005)
Condé Nast	publisher of *Vogue* and *House and Garden* (b. 1873, d. 1942)
Alla Nazimova	first of the great Moscow Art Theater actresses to perform in New York City (b. 1879, d. 1945)

Ruth Nelson	American actress at Guthrie in first seasons; spouse of John Cromwell (b. 1905, d. 1992)
Vladimir Nemirovich-Danchenko	Rusian-Soviet theater director and producer (b. 1858, d. 1943)
Mike Nichols	American film and theater director (b. 1931, d. 2014)
Evy Nordley	patron of the arts in Minneapolis (b. 1925, d. 1997)
Sir Laurence "Larry" Olivier	British actor (b. 1907, d. 1989)
Clifford Odets	American playwright (b. 1906, d. 1963)
Edward Olmos	American actor (b. 1947)
Oliver Olsen	costume designer (at Stan Hywet Hall)
Eugene O'Neill	American playwright (b. 1888, d. 1953)
Ossetians	an Iranian ethnic group of the Caucasus Mountains
Michael O'Sullivan	American actor (*Dear Liar* at ACT) (b. 1934, d. 1971)
Mrs. James Otis	attended original Guthrie Theatre opening night (b. 1919, d. 2013)
Peter O'Toole	British actor (b. 1932, d. 2013)
Frank Ottiwell	Alexander Technique trainer (b. 1929, d. 2015)
Rochelle Owens	American playwright and poet (b. 1936)
Geraldine Page	American actress (b. 1924, d. 1987)
Rex Partington	production stage manager at Guthrie Theatre in first seasons (b. 1924, d. 2006)
Robert Pasolli	writer at the *Village Voice* in 1968
Robert "Bob" Pastene	American repertory actor at Guthrie Theatre in first seasons (b. 1918, d. 1991)
Angela Paton	American actress (*The Seagull* at ACT) (b. 1930, d. 2016)
Matt and Dori Pelto	my neighbors on East Seventy-fourth Street in NYC (Matt b. 1924, d. 2004)
Austin Pendleton	American actor (*The Seagull* at ACT) (b. 1940)
S. J. Perelman	American playwright and author (*The Beauty Part*) (b. 1904, d. 1979)

Mary Perez	American Sioux actress (*The Caucasian Chalk Circle* at Guthrie Theatre)
John J. Pershing	General in WW I (b. 1860, d. 1948)
Franklin Peters	an extra at Guthrie Theatre in first seasons
Lauri Peters	American repertory actress at Guthrie Theatre in early seasons (b. 1943)
Luigi Pirandello	Italian playwright (b. 1867, d. 1936)
Herb Pilhofer	German music director at Guthrie Theatre in first seasons (b. 1931)
Harold Pinter	British playwright (*The Homecoming*) (b. 1930, d. 2008)
Zazu Pitts	American actress (b. 1894, d. 1963)
Bill Pogue	American repertory actor at Guthrie Theatre in first seasons (b. 1930, d. 2014)
Addison Powell	American actor (Circle in the Square) (b. 1921, d. 2010)
Robert Preston	American actor and singer (b. 1918, d. 1987)
Tom Prideaux	theater critic and senior editor of *Life* magazine; attended original Guthrie Theatre opening night (b. 1908, d. 1993)
José Quintero	Panamanian director and producer (b. 1924, d. 1999)
Ellis Rabb	American actor; founding director of the Association of Producing Artists theatre company in New York City (b. 1930, d. 1998)
Basil Rathbone	British actor (b. 1982, d. 1967)
Oliver Rea	New York-based theater producer (b. 1924, d. 1995)
Karl Redcoff	actor (*Peer Gint*) (b. 1924, d. 1991)
Pierre-Auguste Renoir	French painter (b. 1841, d. 1919)
Lee Richardson	American repertory actor at Guthrie Theatre in first seasons (b. 1951, d. 2020)
Sir Ralph Richardson	British actor (b. 1902, d. 1983)
Joseph F. Rinn	American playwright (*Zeno*) (b. 1868, d. 1952)
Jason Robards Jr.	American actor (b. 1922, d. 2000)
Carrie Robbins	costume designer at Guthrie Theatre in 1969 season (b. 1943)

Pernell Roberts	American actor (b. 1928, d. 2010)
Johnston Forbes-Robertson	British actor and theater manager (b. 1853, d. 1937)
Ann Roth	costume designer (*The Seagull* at ACT) (b. 1931)
Ken Ruta	American repertory actor at Guthrie Theatre in first seasons (b. 1933, d. 2022)
Carl Sandburg	American poet (b. 1878, d. 1967)
Vincent Sardi	New York City restaurateur (b. 1915, d. 2007)
Bob Scales	technical director at Guthrie Theatre in 1969 season (b. 1935, d. 2019)
Ekkehard Schall	German actor (b. 1930, d. 2005)
Douglas Schmidt	set designer at Guthrie Theatre in 1969 season (b. 1942)
Don Schoenbaum	assistant to Peter Zeisler (b. 1926, d. 2012)
George C. Scott	American actor (b. 1927, d. 1999)
F. A. Seiberling	cofounder of Goodyear Tire & Rubber Company (b. 1859, d. 1995)
Arch Selwyn	Canadian-American theater and film producer with his brother (b. 1877, d. 1959)
Edgar Selwyn	Canadian-American theater and film producer with his brother (b. 1875, d. 1944)
Peter Shaffer	British playwright (*The Royal Hunt of the Sun*) (b. 1926, d. 2016)
George Bernard Shaw	British playwright (b. 1856, d. 1950)
Sam Shepard	American playwright (b. 1943, d. 2017)
Edvard Shevardnadze	leader of Georgia, 1972-1985 (b. 1928, d. 2003)
Pat Slingsby	an extra at Guthrie Theatre in first days (b. 1935, d. 1963)
Gordon Smith	one of the assistant stage managers at Guthrie Theatre in first seasons
Konstantine Stanislavski	Russian director, actor, and teacher (b. 1863, d. 1938)
August Strindberg	Swedish playwright (b. 1849, d. 1912)
Dan Sullivan	drama critic at the *Los Angeles Times* (b. 1935, d. 2022)
George Tabori	Hungarian writer and theater director (*The Resistible Rise of Arturo Ui*) (b. 1914, d. 2007)

Tamburlaine the Great	fictionalized name of Timur the Lame, a fourteenth-century Asian ruler (b. 1336, d. 1405)
Jessica Tandy	American actress at Guthrie in first seasons; spouse of Hume Cronyn (b. 1909, d. 1994)
Booth Tarkington	American playwright (b. 1869, d. 1946)
Dylan Thomas	Welsh poet and writer (b. 1914, d. 1953)
Sada Thompson	American actress (*Tartuffe* at SCT) (b. 1927, d. 2011)
Ernest Truex	American actor (b. 1889, d. 1973)
Pamela Ullman	tech staff member at Guthrie Theatre in early seasons; my second wife
Mrs. Van Horne	my first landlady in Minneapolis
Nina Vance	founder of the Alley Theater in Houston, Texas (b. 1914, d. 1980)
Miss Waddey	my fifth-grade teacher, in DC
Chuck Wallen	house electrician at Guthrie Theatre in first seasons
Mr. and Mrs. Watkins	hypothetical Midwestern theater devotees
Jean-Antoine Watteau	French painter (b. 1684, d. 1721)
Richard Watts	American drama critic at the *New York Post* (1968) (b. 1898, d. 1981)
Carl "Charlie" Weber	German theater director; Brecht's protégé; head of the drama department at Stanford University, 1985-2013 (b. 1925, d. 2016)
Robert Weede	American singer and singing teacher (b. 1903, d. 1972)
Rita Weinberg	my first wife
Orson Welles	American actor, filmmaker, and founder of Mercury Theatre drama company in New York City with John Houseman (b. 1915, d. 1985)
Bob Werner	one of my roommates at Williston Academy
Don West	American actor (*The Caucasian Chalk Circle* at Guthrie Theatre, *Twelfth Night* at Old Globe Theater)
Sophie White	American Sioux actress in *The Caucasian Chalk Circle* at Guthrie Theatre
Frank "Doc" Whiting	head of University of Minnesota theater department in 1962 (b. 1907, d. 1996)

Walt Whitman	American poet (b. 1819, d. 1892)
Richard Wilbur	American poet, translator of *Tartuffe* (b. 1921, d. 2017)
Thornton Wilder	American playwright (b. 1897, d. 1975)
Tennessee Williams	American playwright (b. 1911, d. 1983)
Georges Wilson	French actor (b. 1921, d. 2010)
Stuart Wurtzel	American set designer (*The Seagull* at ACT) (b. 1940)
William Butler Yeats	British poet (b. 1865, d. 1939)
Peter Zeisler	Broadway stage manager (b. 1924, d. 2005)
Don Zimmer	MLB baseball player (and later coach) (b. 1931, d. 2014)
Anthony Zerbe	American actor (b. 1936)

Theaters, Companies, and Other Organizations in Those Years

Actors' Equity Association	labor union representing people who work in live theater
Actors Studio	professional membership organization for theater people, in New York City
Akron Shakespeare Festival	the brief re-emergence of Arthur Lithgow's Antioch Shakespeare Festival, in Akron, Ohio (1959 at Stan Hywet Hall; 1960 at Ohio Theatre in Cuyahoga Falls)
Alley Theatre	in Houston, Texas
Ahmanson Theatre	one theater within the Los Angeles Music Center
American Academy of Dramatic Arts	school started by Franklin Sargent, in New York City
American Conservatory Theater (ACT)	began in Pittsburgh, Pennsylvania; moved to San Francisco, California
American National Theatre and Academy (ANTA)	official United States nonprofit national theatre designed to train producers and sponsor plays beyond New York City

Antioch Shakespeare Festival	held 1951–1957 at Antioch College, in Yellow Springs, Ohio; alternate name Shakespeare Under the Stars
Arena Stage	in Washington, DC
Association of Producing Artists (APA)	theater company in New York City (1959–1969)
Barter Theatre	longest-running U.S. Equity theater, in Abingdon, Virginia
Berkshire Playhouse	in Stockbridge, Massachusetts; now the Berkshire Theatre Festival
Berliner Ensemble	German theater company started by Brecht and spouse Helene Weigel in 1949
Bill Rose Theatre	in New York City; now the Nederlander Theatre
Carnegie Institute of Technology	one of the first universities to offer theater training; now Carnegie Mellon University
Carter Barron Amphitheater	in Washington, DC
Circle in the Square Theatre	in New York City, currently at West Fiftieth Street; the 1960s building was at 159 Bleeker Street; original building was at 5 Sheridan Square
Cleveland Play House	in Cleveland, Ohio
Crawford Livingston Theater	500-seat additional venue for Guthrie Theater, in St. Paul, Minnesota
Don Martini Studios	dance studio in DC in the 1940s
Eltinge 42nd Street Theatre	in New York City (1912–1954)
Equity Library Theatre	in New York City (1943–1989)
Ford Foundation	
Group Theatre	in New York City (1931–1941)
Guthrie Theater Company	Current name, in Minneapolis. Related names: Minnesota Theatre Company (early history), Tyrone Guthrie Theatre (early history), Tyrone Guthrie Theater Foundation
Henry Jewett Players	stock company in Boston, Massachusetts (c.1910s–1930s)
Hilltop Theater	movie house in Baltimore, Maryland (1947–1952)
Jan Hus Playhouse	at Jan Hus Presbyterian Church in New York City

Los Angeles Music Center	in California; contains the Mark Taper Forum
Kansas City Repertory Theatre	in Kansas City, Missouri
Marines Memorial Theatre	theater building in San Francisco, used by ACT
Mark Taper Forum	a theater within the Los Angeles Music Center
McCarter Theatre	in Princeton, New Jersey
Mercury Theatre	drama company in New York City created by John Houseman and Orson Welles (1937–1946)
Milwaukee Repertory Theater	in Milwaukee, Wisconsin
Minnesota Theater Company	original name of Guthrie Theater Company
Moscow Art Theatre	in Moscow, Russia (1898–1987)
Old Globe Theater	in San Diego, California
Old Vic	in London, England
The Other Place	200-seat additional venue for Guthrie Theater, in Minneapolis (1968–1971)
Pasadena Playhouse	in Pasadena, California
Minnesota Centennial Showboat	sternwheeler with theater aboard (1958–2016)
Scott Hall	the University of Minnesota campus playhouse
Seattle Repertory Company	in Seattle, Washington
Shakespeare Under the Stars	alternate name for Antioch Shakespeare Festival, in Akron, Ohio
Stagecoach Theatre	in Shakopee, Minnesota (closed 1998)
Stanford Repertory Theater	in Stanford, California
Stratford Shakespeare Festival	in Ontario, Canada; now the Stratford Festival
Sullivan Street Playhouse	off-Broadway theatre in Greenwich Village, New York City (closed 2002)
Theater am Schiffbauerdamm	in West Berlin, Germany; home of Brecht's Berliner Ensemble
Theatre '47	in Dallas, Texas; the number in its name updated each year (closed 1959)
Theatre Guild	theatrical society in New York City (1918–1996)
Théâtre National Populaire	in Paris, France

Trinity Repertory Company	in Providence, Rhode Island
Tyrone Guthrie Theater	an early name of Guthrie Theater Company
Walker Art Center	in Minneapolis

Titles from Those Years

Plays, Both Legitimate and Musical

A Funny Thing Happened on the Way to the Forum	musical with music and lyrics by Stephen Sondheim and book by Burt Shevelove and Larry Gelbart (premiered 1962)
Ah, Wilderness	by Eugene O'Neill (premiered 1933)
All My Sons	by Arthur Miller (premiered 1947)
The Ancient Test of the Chalk Circle	play within the play *The Caucasian Chalk Circle*
And Things That Go Bump in the Night	by Terence McNally (premiered 1964)
Antony and Cleopatra	by William Shakespeare (premiered 1607)
Ardèle	by Jean Anouilh (premiered 1948)
Arms and the Man	by George Bernard Shaw (premiered 1894)
Arsenic and Old Lace	by Joseph Kesselring (premiered 1941)
As You Like It	play by William Shakespeare (published 1623)
The Beauty Part	by S. J. Perelman (premiered 1962)
Beggar's Opera	ballad opera by John Gay with music arranged by Johann Christoph Pepusch (premiered 1728)
Beyond the Fringe	British comedy stage revue (premiered 1960)
Candida	by George Bernard Shaw (premiered 1894)
Candide	operetta adapted from the play by François-Marie Voltaire (published 1759) by librettist Lillian Hellman and composer Leonard Bernstein (premiered 1956)
The Caucasian Chalk Circle	by Bertolt Brecht; German name *Der Kaukasische Kreidekreis* (premiered 1948)
Charley's Aunt	by Brandon Thomas (premiered 1892)
The Cherry Orchard	by Anton Chekhov (published 1904)
Children of Darkness	by Edwin Justus Mayer (premiered 1929)

The Cocktail Party	by T. S. Eliot (premiered 1949)
The Confidential Clerk	by T. S. Eliot (premiered 1953)
Cymbeline	by William Shakespeare (premiered 1611)
Cyrano de Bergerac	by Edmond Eugène Alexis Rostand (published 1897)
Dagmar	by Louis K. Anspacher (published 1923)
The Dance of Death	by August Strindberg (published 1900)
Dear Brutus	by J. M. Barrie (published 1917)
Dear Liar	by Jerome Kilty (published 1957)
Death of a Salesman	by Arthur Miller (published 1949)
The Doctor's Dilemma	by George Bernard Shaw (published 1906)
Don't Be Afraid	by Avery Hopwood (undated)
Endgame	by Samuel Beckett (published 1957)
Fair and Warmer	by Avery Hopwood (published 1915)
The Famous History of the Life of King Henry VIII	by William Shakespeare and John Fletcher (published 1623)
The Fantasticks	musical with music by Harvey Schmidt and lyrics by Tom Jones (premiered 1960)
The First Part of Henry IV	by William Shakespeare (published c. 1597)
Florida Aflame	historical musical pageant by John Caldwell (published 0000)
Futz	by Rochelle Owens (published 1961)
The Ghost Dancer	by Fred Gaines (premiered 1969)
The Glass Menagerie	by Tennessee Williams (premiered 1944)
The Great White Hope	by Howard Sackler (premiered 1967)
Guys and Dolls	musical with music and lyrics by Frank Loesser and book by Jo Swerling and Abe Burrows (premiered 1950)
Hamlet	by William Shakespeare (published c. 1600)
Hay Fever	by Noel Coward (premiered 1925)
Henry VI	trilogy of plays by William Shakespeare (published 1591)
The Homecoming	by Harold Pinter (published 1964)
The House of Atreus	play adapted from *The Oresteia* by Aeschylus (premiered c. 458 BCE) by John Lewin (published 1966)

The Iceman Cometh	by Eugene O'Neill (premiered 1946)
Irene	musical (revival), book adapted by Hugh Wheeler and Joseph Stein, lyrics by Joseph McCarthy, and music by Harry Tierney (premiered 1973)
Julius Caesar	by William Shakespeare (published c. 1599)
Just Herself	by Ethel Watts Mumford (premiered 1914)
The Life and Death of King John	by William Shakespeare (published c. 1623)
The Life and Death of King Richard II	by William Shakespeare (published c. 1595)
The Life of Henry V	by William Shakespeare (published c. 1599)
Life of Galileo	by Bertolt Brecht (premiered 1943)
Long Day's Journey into Night	by Eugene O'Neill (premiered 1956)
Macbeth	by William Shakespeare (published 1623)
Martinique	by Lawrence Eyre (premiered 1923)
Masque of Reason	by Robert Frost (published 1945)
The Master Builder	by Henrik Ibsen (premiered 1893)
The Matchmaker	by Thornton Wilder (premiered 1954)
The Measures Taken	by Bertolt Brecht (premiered 1930)
Merchant of Venice	by William Shakespeare (published c. 1597)
The Merry Wives of Windsor	by William Shakespeare (premiered c. 1598)
Merton of the Movies	play adapted from the novel by Harry Leon Wilson (published 1922) by George S. Kaufman and Marc Connelly (Guthrie Theatre revival premiered 1974)
Miracle in Minnesota	Guthrie Theatre promotional short film (premiered 1964)
The Miser	by Jean-Baptiste Molière (premiered 1668)
Mother Courage and Her Children	by Bertolt Brecht (published 1939)
Mourning Becomes Electra	by Eugene O'Neill (premiered 1931)
Much Ado About Nothing	by William Shakespeare (published c. 1598)
Murder in the Cathedral	by T. S. Eliot (premiered 1935)

My Fair Lady	musical adaptation of the play *Pygmalion* by George Bernard Shaw (premiered 1913), with book and lyrics by Alan Jay Lerner and music by Frederick Loewe (premiered 1956)
On Borrowed Time	by Paul Osborn (premiered 1938)
The Oresteia	trilogy by Aeschylus (premiered c. 458 BCE)
Our Town	by Thornton Wilder (premiered 1938)
Peer Gint	by Henrik Ibsen (published 1867)
Peter Pan; or, The Boy Who Wouldn't Grow Up	by J. M. Barrie (premiered 1904)
Mr Puntila and His Man Matti	by Bertolt Brecht (premiered 1948)
The Quare Fellow	by Brendan Behan (premiered 1954)
The Resistable Rise of Arturo Ui	by Bertolt Brecht (published 1941)
The Resistable Rise of Arturo Ui: A Gangster Spectacle	adapted by George Tabori (premiered 1972)
The Royal Hunt of the Sun	by Peter Shaffer Atahualpa (premiered 1964)
The Seagull	by Anton Chekhov (premiered 1896)
The Second Part of Henry IV	by William Shakespeare (written c. 1599)
Serjeant Musgrave's Dance	by John Arden (premiered 1959)
Six Characters in Search of an Author	by Luigi Pirandello (premiered 1921)
The Skin of Our Teeth	by Thornton Wilder (premiered 1942)
SS Glencairn	collection of four one-act plays by Eugene O'Neill (written 1914–1918)
A Streetcar Named Desire	by Tennessee Williams (premiered 1947)
Summer and Smoke	by Tennessee Williams (premiered 1948)
Tango	by Sławomir Mrożek (published 1965)
Tartuffe	by Jean-Baptiste Molière (premiered 1664)
The Tempest	by William Shakespeare (written c. 1611)
Three Men on a Horse	by George Abbott and John Cecil Holm (premiered 1935)
Three Sisters	by Anton Chekhov (premiered 1901)
Tiny Alice	by Edward Albee (premiered 1964)
The Torchbearers	by George Kelly (premiered 1922)

The Tragedy of King Richard III	by William Shakespeare (written c. 1594)
Troilus and Cressida	by William Shakespeare (written c. 1602)
The Trojan Women	by Euripides (written 415 BCE)
Trouble In Tahiti	one-act opera by Leonard Bernstein (premiered 1952)
Twelfth Night	by William Shakespeare (written c. 1602)
Uncle Vanya	by Anton Chekhov (published 1898)
Under Milk Wood	radio play by Dylan Thomas (premiered 1954)
The Waltz of the Toreadors	by Jean Anouilh (premiered 1951)
The Way of the World	by William Congreve (premiered 1700)
Who's Afraid of Virginia Woolf?	by Edward Albee (premiered 1962)
Zeno	by Joseph F. Rinn (premiered 1923)
The Zoo Story	by Edward Albee (premiered 1959)

Books

A Life in the Theatre	by Tyrone Guthrie (published 1959)
The Best of Thurber	by James Thurber (published 1977)
Brecht on Theatre: The Development of an Aesthetic	edited and translated by John Willett (published 1949)
The Fighting Littles	by Booth Tarkington (published 1941)
Gone with the Wind	by Margaret Mitchell (published 1936)
Guinness Book of World Records	(published annually)
The Hour-Glass	poem in prose and verse by William Butler Yeats (published 1922)
The Iliad	epic poem attributed to Homer, written c. eighth century BCE
Leaves of Grass	by Walt Whitman (published c. 1900)
A Life in the Theatre	autobiography by Tyrone Guthrie (published 1959)
Lincoln and Other Poems	by Edwin Markham (published 1901)

The Modern Theatre Volume 6	edited by Eric Bentley, chapter by Bertolt Brecht: "The Measures Taken (Die Maßnahme)" (published 1960)
One Hundred Years of Solitude	novel by Gabriel García Márquez (published 1967)
Parables for the Theatre	by Bertolt Brecht (published 1948)
The Poems of W. B. Yeats: A New Edition	edited by Richard J. Finneran (published 1933)
Salt-water Poems and Ballads	by John Masefield (published 1916)
Three Sisters: An Authoritative Text Edition	by Anton Chekhov, translation by Tyrone Guthrie and Leonid Kipnis (published 1965)
U.S.A. Trilogy	trilogy of novels by John Dos Passos (published 1930–1936)
The Waste Land	poem by T. S. Eliot (published 1922)

Newspapers, Magazines, and Journals

Boston Herald	daily newspaper in Massachusetts
Chicago Daily News	daily newspaper in Illinois
Collier's	American magazine (1888–1957)
Daily News (New York)	daily newspaper in New York
Los Angeles Times	daily newspaper in California
Minneapolis Tribune	daily newspaper in Minnesota
New York Post	daily newspaper in New York
New York Times	national newspaper
New York Times Magazine	section of the *New York Times*
Safety Harbor Beacon	a local Florida newspaper
St. Paul Dispatch	daily newspaper in Minnesota
San Francisco Examiner	daily newspaper in California
Saturday Review	national weekly magazine
Time	national weekly magazine
Variety	New York City-based weekly entertainment news magazine
Village Voice	New York City-based weekly newspaper
Women's Wear Daily	national daily fashion-industry news journal

Films

Aguirre, the Wrath of God	directed by Werner Herzog (premiered 1972)
Lifeboat	directed by Alfred Hitchcock (premiered 1944)
A Night at The Opera	directed by Sam Wood, starring the Marx Brothers (premiered 1935)
Our Gang	series of shorts by various directors; also known as *The Little Rascals* (1922–1944)
The Postman Always Rings Twice	directed by Tay Garnett (premiered 1946)
Pride of the Yankees	directed by Sam Wood (premiered 1942)

ACKNOWLEDGEMENTS

Thank you to Pm Weizenbaum for her thorough and sensitive editing. To Mark Jenkins who kept the flame alive.

To his Caregivers who gave Ed a safe and loving last few years, THANK YOU.! Rebekah Talevich, Annie Hauge, Marcia Carter, and Melissa Woods.

Peter Davis
Edcall090@gmail.com

Milton Keynes UK
Ingram Content Group UK Ltd.
UKHW051144241123
432909UK00016B/398